Stopford Augustus Brooke

English literature from the Beginning to the Norman Conquest

Stopford Augustus Brooke

English literature from the Beginning to the Norman Conquest

ISBN/EAN: 9783337815615

Printed in Europe, USA, Canada, Australia, Japan

Cover: Foto ©Andreas Hilbeck / pixelio.de

More available books at **www.hansebooks.com**

ENGLISH LITERATURE

FROM THE

BEGINNING TO THE NORMAN CONQUEST

ENGLISH LITERATURE

FROM THE BEGINNING
TO THE NORMAN CONQUEST

BY

STOPFORD A. BROOKE

[Augustus]

London
MACMILLAN AND CO., Limited
NEW YORK: THE MACMILLAN COMPANY
1899

Copyrighted in the United States
First Edition 1898. Reprinted 1859

PREFACE

THIS book is necessarily, as far as the chapter on King Ælfred, a recast of my previous book on *Early English Literature up to the Days of Alfred*. That book, in two volumes, was too expensive and too long for students in schools. I chose to write it at that length, and I am glad I did so. I was enabled to introduce a great deal of correlative matters which I thought were needed to bring the literature into touch with the history of the country; and in order to give life, colour, and reality to a time so far away, and in which so little interest is taken by the English public. But having tried to do this, I have now left out these correlative matters; shortened the whole of the history up to Ælfred; rewritten it, and rearranged it. Of course, some of the older book remains mixed up with the new;—those parts of it especially which give an account of the poems. The translations, though carefully revised, are the same; but many of them have been omitted. I have written about King Ælfred at a length somewhat out of proportion with the rest of the book, but the freshly awakened interest of the public in his life and character induced me to give a full account of all that was personal in his literary work. The chapters from "Ælfred" to the end of the book carry the history of Anglo-Saxon or Old English Literature up to the Conquest. A concluding chapter sketches the tale of Old English as far as the beginning of the thirteenth century. The Appendix consists of translations of some remarkable Anglo-Saxon poems; and I have to thank Miss Kate Warren for her excellent translation in full of the "Battle of Maldon," as well as for the Index and the Bibliography, which, to my pleasure, she undertook. My gratitude is also due to Professor John Rhys and to Professor Ker for their kind answers to a number of questions.

STOPFORD A. BROOKE.

SCHAFFHAUSEN,
23rd August 1898.

CONTENTS

CHAPTER I
PAGE
THE RELATION OF EARLY BRITAIN TO ENGLISH LITERATURE   1

CHAPTER II
OLD ENGLISH HEATHEN POETRY 36

CHAPTER III
BEOWULF 58

CHAPTER IV
BEOWULF—THE POEM 68

CHAPTER V
SEMI-HEATHEN POETRY 84

CHAPTER VI
THE COMING OF CHRISTIANITY 98

CHAPTER VII

LATIN LITERATURE—FROM THE COMING OF AUGUSTINE TO THE ACCESSION OF ÆLFRED . . . 106

CHAPTER VIII

CÆDMON [650-680] . . . 126

CHAPTER IX

POEMS OF THE SCHOOL OF CÆDMON . 134

CHAPTER X

THE ELEGIES AND THE RIDDLES . . 152

CHAPTER XI

THE SIGNED POEMS OF CYNEWULF . . . 163

CHAPTER XII

POEMS ATTRIBUTED TO CYNEWULF OR HIS SCHOOL . 180

CHAPTER XIII

OTHER POETRY BEFORE ÆLFRED 203

CHAPTER XIV

ÆLFRED 212

CHAPTER XV

THE OLD ENGLISH POETRY IN AND AFTER ÆLFRED'S TIME   PAGE
242

CHAPTER XVI

SECULAR POETRY AFTER ÆLFRED TO THE CONQUEST . 253

CHAPTER XVII

ENGLISH PROSE FROM ÆLFRED TO THE CONQUEST . 269

CHAPTER XVIII

THE PASSING OF OLD ENGLISH . . 300

APPENDIX 309
BIBLIOGRAPHY 326
INDEX 337

ENGLISH LITERATURE

FROM THE

BEGINNING TO THE NORMAN CONQUEST

CHAPTER I

THE RELATION OF EARLY BRITAIN TO ENGLISH LITERATURE

THE land in which English literature has grown into the mighty tree which now spreads its branches over so many peoples was for many centuries unconscious of any English footfall. Its first indwellers, at a time when it formed part of a continent stretching far into the Northern and Western seas, lived in caves or in trees or in rude huts made of boughs, and saw the great glaciers of the quaternary age push from the mountains into the plains, retreat, advance again, and pass away. Their climate was cold and wet. A short warm summer was succeeded by a long winter. Heavy and constant mist hung over the stagnant fens and woods and the icy gorges of the hills, but the men enjoyed the hunting and fishing by which they lived. They learned at last to smite the flints and chert into axe, spear and arrow-heads; they invented the bow; they made their knives of flakes of flint, and as time went on fitted these weapons into rude handles of horn and bone. Skins, roughly sewn together with sinews, clothed them; they could make the fire by which they cooked the beasts they slew, but they had no domestic animals. Nor were they, after some centuries had gone by, without pleasure in the work of their hands. They drew, incising the handles of bone and horn, the figures of the beasts they hunted—the stag, the reindeer, the hairy mammoth, and the bison. These were the *Palæolithic* tribes of prehistoric Britain, and they were contemporary at their beginning with the cave lion and hyæna, with a sabre-toothed tiger, with the brown and the grizzly bear, with a woolly rhinoceros and three kinds of elephant, with the great urus, the elk, and the bison, and with other animals existing at the present day.

No one can tell how long this people lasted, nor what space of time separates them from the *Neolithic* tribes whose remains we find in caves, in tombs, and in the lake-dwellings which, as their civilisation grew, they learnt how to build. It is possible that the people we call Neolithic were the direct and developed descendants of the Palæolithic folk. The glaciers had now gone; the land had risen and was divided from the continent by the Channel. The more ancient and the more savage animals had disappeared. The urus, the brown bear, the great stags, the reindeer remained among the mountain valleys and the northern moors; and the wild boar, the wolf, the fox, the wild cat, and a host of the beasts of flood and field haunted in vast numbers the thick, dark, monstrous woods. The climate was warmer and more damp. The lowlands were half water,—out-spreading fens, and swamps, and chains of lakes. The estuaries, like that of the Thames, opened out into leagues of morass and sand. The ice-carved mountains were bare and inaccessible, but all along the coast where the fens did not encroach, in the hidden creeks and reedy isles, on the edges of the lakes, on the knolls in the fens, by the river-channels, and on the low dry downs and rocky plateaux, lived and hunted a short, black-haired, dark-skinned, dark-eyed race, with an oval face and a long and narrow skull, who had with them domesticated animals. Their weapons were of bone and flint, chert and greenstone, polished and carefully wrought, not rough like those of their predecessors. They were hunters, but they mingled the mere hunting life of the savage with pastoral employments. Living at first in caves, they finally settled into hamlets or into lake-dwellings built on piles. They kept sheep and cattle, wove a rude cloth for garments, and made pottery and ornaments. Sometimes they buried their dead in caves, but they came to bury them in large-chambered tombs, under long barrows and mounds of earth, lined with stones; and the greater number of "standing stones," "stone circles," and the rude burial huts built of great blocks of rock,[1] which are the denuded remnants of these tombs, attest their reverence for the dead, and their activity. These barrows occur over our land from Dorset to the Yorkshire Wolds, and from the Wolds to Caithness, and they prove that this people occupied the whole country. They also lived over the length and breadth of Ireland. Some think that they came from North Africa across Spain, and the Basque people are certainly their descendants; others think that some of them came from Spain to Ireland, and thence made their way to Britain, but it is also maintained that they came across the north of Europe. They were not an Aryan race, but they are of a very enduring type. Even now, we meet their descendants in the west of Ireland, and traces of their nature-myths, their religion, and their customs, enter into the Irish mythology—sombre and grim traditions, as of those who had come out of the "night-country." Their Irish tribal names, so far as we have been able to isolate them, have to do with gloom and mist, as dark as their eyes and hair. In Wales, the main body of the Silures, small men, dark, and of a courageous nature, belonged, as well as other scattered folk in North Wales, to this Neolithic people. Men have also traced strange out-crops of this swarthy race in the midland and south-western counties of England, even in the present day. Beyond the English and Scottish border, and on it, they were less got rid of by the Celtic invaders and more mingled with them. A separate body of them, after much admixture, isolated themselves

---

[1] In French archæology these are called *menhirs*, *cromlechs*, and *dolmens*; but in England we call the pile of three or four upstanding stones with a flat rock resting on them, a *cromlech*, not a *dolmen*.

in Galloway. On the west coast and islands of Scotland, they lasted, and kept up their tribal life alongside of the Scots from Ireland, the Brythons, and afterwards the English. But the larger number of them settled in the Northern Highlands; and the description which Scott gives in the *Legend of Montrose* of the "Children of the Mist" may serve to paint what this fine and steady-hearted race would become when, left to its wild instinct for liberty, it was hunted like a beast of the field. The Celtic races owed much to these predecessors, more perhaps than we imagine, and through the Celt the English may have assimilated some of the elements of the nature of the Neolithic race. There are certain weird, primæval, unaccountable, dark, sometimes monstrous conceptions in our nature-poetry which may have their far-off roots in the dim world the Neolithic people made for their imagination.

The next race which invaded our island, and who, it is supposed, established settlements from Sweden to Spain, were tall men, round-faced, with short round skulls, stoutly built, light-haired, with probably gray eyes. It is still debated whether they were or not an Aryan race. Some scholars call them Celtic—the earliest band of the Celtic migrations. Others consider them to be of a Finnish or Ugrian type. They were warriors and hunters, and their weapons of battle and chase were at first of stone, shaped with great skill and highly polished. But when they came to our land they had learnt how to make bronze weapons, and are the first men of the bronze age in this country. But they were much more than warriors and hunters. They established some kind of commerce with the continent, and they kept flocks and herds. Their stone querns prove that they had some knowledge of agriculture. Their persons were decorated with gold and silver ornaments, with amber, jet and glass beads and necklaces. They beat gold wire into their swords, wore a woven cloth, and made good pottery,—vases, cups, food-dishes, and incense-burners. They dwelt in communities and continued, like the Neolithic folk, the building of large, underground, chambered tombs. They set up temples, perhaps like Stonehenge, to their gods. But their barrows, which are crowded round Salisbury Plain, are not long but round and shaped like a bowl. Lastly they mixed with, rather than conquered the Neolithic people. This type may also be distinguished, it is said, in various parts of England to the present day.[1]

History, save in the description by Latin writers of the rude tribes in the interior of Britain, is silent of these two races, the second of which, until more evidence is brought to prove it to be Celtic, we may believe to be as pre-Celtic and non-Aryan as the first. Though history is silent concerning them, they have left traces behind them of their occupation of the country in the myth and legend of the Celtic races which succeeded them, and mingled with them. Old words, not Celtic, in the Celtic tongue, some place-names, some personal names of Celtic heroes, some sculptured stones with unknown designs and unknown alphabetical signs, some strange customs, chiefly of inheritance, are found among the Celts and derive from their predecessors.

How long these races lived undisturbed from without cannot be known, but they were at last broken into by the first great Celtic migration, which, coming along the southern shores of the Baltic between the forest and the sea, passed down the Rhine and the Moselle, and a part of which crossed the narrow seas to our land. This people established itself during some centuries over

---

[1] It has been sought to mark out, with greater definition, these pre-Celtic peoples. M. de Jubainville, speaking of France, arranges them in this manner. (1) The quaternary man. (2) A people who lived in caves, had no knowledge of the metals, and hunted the reindeer. (3) A more civilised folk who knew something of the metals, who could make drawings on horn and bone, who built megalithic monuments, who buried their dead in *cabanes funéraires* (*dolmens* = our *cromlechs*). (4) A still more civilised folk who burned their dead, put the ashes into urns, and hid them under tumuli. (5) The Celts or Gauls, an aristocratic race, who enslaved the conquered; with long iron swords and war chariots, who buried but did not burn their dead. For a Celt to burn his dead was to do them dishonour. (6) The Roman period. (7) The Frank. Such a division might do for Britain also, if we divide the Celts into two related races, the Goidels and the Brythons (Gauls), and read *the English* for *the Frank*.

the habitable parts of England, Ireland, and Scotland, driving the Neolithic folk before them to the remoter lands, but also absorbing them in their progress. It may be that a number of them landed first in Ireland, and afterwards crossed the Irish Channel into Wales. Such Irish immigration has taken place in historic times. It is probable it also took place in prehistoric times. These are the Gaelic or *Goidelic* tribes. Their occupation of the country lasted for some centuries. Meanwhile a new migration of the Celtic hordes had begun. This Second Wandering, as it poured down towards Western Europe, took a more southward direction than the first. When it reached the Alps, some of the folk descended into Italy or went eastward by the Danube; but others, crossing the mountains, made their way into the regions we call Gaul and Spain. Those of them who finally settled on the northern coasts of Gaul, either pushed from behind, or eager for adventure and land, or lured by the shimmer of the white cliffs in the morning sun and by the mysterious legends of a land of the happy dead, which, in the elder days, gathered round our islands, made their way over the straits, perhaps as early as 300 B.C., and fell upon the Goidels of the south-eastern shores. We call this second people of the Celts *Brythons*. Like the English afterwards, they first settled themselves in Kent and round the mouths of the Thames. Like the English also, their immigration was gradual. They came, one relay after another, and the Goidels were only slowly driven back before them. The last who arrived, about 100 B.C., if not earlier, were the Belgæ. When the Romans came first, 55 B.C., these tribes certainly held all the south-eastern districts, and those along the east coast as far as the Wash; but they probably held also the land east of the Trent, the Avon, the Parret and the Stour of Dorsetshire —that is, nearly half of our England. During the ninety years between the invasion of Julius Cæsar and the fresh conquests under Claudius, 43 A.D., the Brythons pushed steadily on, and the whole country, with a few exceptions, fell under their power. These exceptions were the counties of Devon and Cornwall, all

South Wales, west of the Severn and south of the Teme and the Wyre, North Wales and Anglesea from the river Mawddach to the Dee, Cumberland and Westmoreland and part of Lancashire. In these lands the Goidels remained, mixed more or less with the Neolithic races which preceded them. But even this remnant of the Goidels became, as time went on, Brythonic in language, manners, and customs, so that we may say that at last no tribes existed in England and Wales speaking the Goidelic tongue.

North of the Solway and the Tweed the country was less exclusively Brythonic. The Goidels in Scotland were even more mixed with the Neolithic tribes than in Wales; and into this admixture the Brythons drove their way, penetrating from the East in wedges into the Goidels northwards and westwards, either subduing them or intermingling with them, or living in alliance with them. So it came to pass that the three races—the Neolithic folk (who may be said to represent the Picts of history), the Goidels, and the Brythons—ran in and out of one another over the southern half of Scotland, like the changing patterns in a kaleidoscope made by three differently coloured pieces of glass. The Brythons were thickest in the east. The Neolithic people concentrated themselves in Galloway and the western isles, but the Goidels were so dominant among them that their speech and traditions became in time Goidelic. In the northern isles and Highlands the Neolithic people were most numerous, but they also, partly influenced by the invading Scots from Ireland, adopted, as the centuries went on, the customs and speech of the Goidels. At last Scotland broke into two main divisions. The Highlands became Goidelicised. The Lowlands, with the exception of Galloway, were rapidly becoming Brythonised, when the victory which made Kenneth MacAlpin (844-860) King of the Picts introduced again the Goidel elements, and by the time of the Norman Conquest the Lowlands were probably Goidelicised again. But this was after the time of which we speak. At present, we may sum up the whole by saying that those who spoke Goidel, and became at one with the Goidel strain, existed in the north of Scotland, in Galloway, in the Isle of Man, and in Ireland. The rest of England, Scotland, and Wales spoke the Brythonic tongue, and, though largely mixed with Goidels and Neolithic folk, had all become or were becoming Brythons in name and manners.

Into this heterogeneous mass of three or perhaps four races, two pre-Celtic, two Celtic, and the last two infiltrated by the Roman law, language, and custom, the English in the fifth century began to push their plough. During the first hundred years of their conquest their main policy was destruction,[1] and they almost blotted out the Roman and Brythonic civilisation from Kent to Devonshire; from the eastern counties to an east-curving line drawn from Chester to Bristol; from the Humber to the Forth, and thence westward over more than half of Northern England and the Lowlands to the borders of the kingdom of Strathclyde. Their policy of destruction was then followed by a policy of amalgamation, whenever they took any new portions of the Brythonic lands into their power. At last the pure Brythons were isolated into three places—into Cornwall, into our Wales, and into Cumbria—and the name adopted by the Brythons of Wales and Cumbria was Cymry, that is, "fellow-countrymen."

This general sketch of the localisation in Great Britain and Ireland of the various races which occupied the country, and of their intermingling, is of more use to a history of English literature than one would at first imagine.

Questions of race are often questions of literature. They cannot, it is true, provide us with certainties, only with conjectures; but good conjectures, subject to strict experiment, may lead to certainties; and problems—such as the fuller growth of early English poetry in the North rather than in Wessex or Mercia; the remarkable development of the ballad poetry of the sixteenth,

---

[1] The Brythons were by no means all destroyed. From the first years of the Conquest, and for more than a century after, a large proportion of them emigrated to Armorica. Moreover, as the Brythonic women were kept for slaves, the English blood was from the beginning mixed with a Celtic strain. The admixture increased to the west and north.

seventeenth, and eighteenth centuries, chiefly in the wild marchland of the Border; why the English lyric poetry began, with few exceptions, near the Welsh border; how it happened that the later poetry of natural description had a more original and earlier beginning in Scotland than in England, and yet was only brought to its finest form in England; and many other problems belonging to the introduction of fresh elements into our poetry, are, not completely, but partly solved by the distribution of races in this country, and by our knowledge of the characteristics of these races.

Four other subjects, on each of which a little book might be written, remain to be briefly treated in this introduction. (1) The first of these is the early condition of the country, and how far it bore on literature. History, before the time of Cæsar, is almost silent with regard to Britain. We know, however, that Timæus, the Sicilian historian, who flourished 350-326 B.C., was aware of the British tin trade; and Pytheas, his contemporary, whose *Travels* were set forth shortly after 330 B.C., eight years after the death of Aristotle, speaks, in the fragments which alone remain of his book, of the Cornish miners bringing their tin eastward along the coast, storing it in an island,[1] and exchanging it for goods with the Gauls of the continent. This intrepid voyager of Marseilles, who seems to have sailed as far as the Northern seas until he touched the ice, landed twice on the south-eastern coasts of our island, and found the inhabitants fairly civilised by their trading.

Posidonius, who voyaged to Britain about 90 B.C., visited Cornwall; and Diodorus Siculus, probably quoting Posidonius, gives an account of the tin trade between Britain and Gaul, in which the tin brought from Belerion (Cornwall) was carried to an island called Ictis (Vectis?), and from thence to Gaul and the mouth of the Rhone. The inhabitants, he says, are fond of strangers; and, from their intercourse with foreign merchants, are civilised in their manner of life. The nature of the other trades we learn from Strabo, who wrote about 1-19 A.D. The Britons

[1] Some suppose this island to be Thanet, and others, more probably, that it was the Isle of Wight. I daresay both islands were used.

exported corn, cattle, gold, silver, iron, skins, slaves, and dogs. They imported, among other things, "ivory bracelets and necklaces, red amber beads, vessels of glass, and such-like trumpery." Cæsar mentions the tin of the interior, and speaks of copper as one of the British imports.

South-eastern and south-western Britain had thus reached a somewhat civilised manner of life when Cæsar came to Britain. In fact, whatever civilisation the Gauls had gained in contact with the Greek and the Roman they carried with them into Britain, and we hear even of a rude luxury and splendour in the dress and manners of the Brythons. Inland, however, where the Goidels yet roamed and fought, the men had not passed beyond the pastoral stage. They were as wild as the Highlandmen of the seventeenth century; and lived in much the same way. They grew no corn, were clad in skins, and painted themselves for love and war. The farther men were from the coasts the less was civilisation possible, not only from the absence of trade-influences, but also from the condition of the country.

Before the Romans came, far the greater portion of Britain was uninhabitable, a desolation of vast woods full of sleepy swamps into which the choked-up rivers spread; huge tracts of bleak moorland covered with low scrub and heather and dry grass; and in every hollow deep and treacherous bogs, while rugged and pathless labyrinths of rocks led up to the higher mountains. The interior was wholly unexplored. Over it the wolves ranged in packs and ran down the stags; the wild swine fed in thousands on the acorns and mast of the oak and beech forests; the white-maned urus ran through the glades among the tangled undergrowth of yew and holly and wild briars, and the wild, small black cattle, short-horned and with close-curled manes, herded on the hills. The bear still lingered in the deepest recesses of the forests, and in the caves of the northern mountains. The reindeer was still to be found in Scotland. The beavers built their dams across the rivers; hosts of the smaller wild beasts, the fox, the weasel tribe, the badger, the otter, the wild cat, devoured one another; and enormous flocks of land- and water-birds hunted their prey in the woods and over the widespread marshes. The forests in many places approached the coast, and left only a narrow strip of land fit for the dwelling of man. Elsewhere, the tides carried the sea, especially on the eastern shores, far into the land, making waste leagues of reedy fen over which the cold or clammy mists rose and fell in the sunless summers, and where the winters settled down as grim as death. Men lived only on the outskirts of these ragged solitudes of forest and fen, on the fringe of coast, along the .rivers, in sparse glades of the woods, on the hills and downs, and on the ridges and moors of chalk, granite, limestone and sandstone that rose above the levels of the steaming forest land.

The Romans, under Agricola and after his time, wrought a great change on this condition. Where they settled, the rivers were embanked, the morasses bridged, the fens drained; the trees felled along the roads, the woods cleared back from the river-valleys, the valleys made fit for tillage and pasture. Agriculture increased, great corn-fleets carried the produce of Britain to the provinces on the continent, the deep grass of the river-valleys nourished vast herds of cattle, the hills were covered with thousands of sheep, the export of wool was immense. Gold, silver, and iron were sent out of the country, and the tall powerful hunting dogs of Britain were imported by the wealthy Romans. Yet scarcely a sixth of the land was redeemed. When the English came, the forest-land opposed their advance continually. The fen-lands of the east and the wide marshes of Somerset remained desolate. The great woods of Andred, of Arden, of Dean, and of many others, were still huge wastes where only the outlaw lived. Wales was one enormous woodland. Even in Elizabeth's time a third of England was waste land.

The constant presence of this wild country has had a remarkable influence on literature. That influence is strongest where the Celtic element is strongest in our folk, and it appears among such folk as a love of wild nature. The early English poetry of

Northumbria is full of the sentiment of the savage weather and storm-lashed cliffs of the sea-coasts, and of the passion of the furious sea. The poem of Layamon, written on the Welsh border, is alive with the natural description of the wild scenery which the poet loved. The work of the Lancashire poet who wrote *Sir Gawayne and the Grene Knight* is equally full of the love of the rocks and hills and woodland of that Celtic country. When the description of nature in the reigns of Henry VII. and VIII. is conventional in England, it is passionate and done directly from nature in Scottish poetry. Spenser's special pleasure in uninhabited forests and lonely streams, swift rivers and rugged mountains, came partly of his stay in Lancashire and of his life in Ireland. Nor is it without significance that the love of nature for its own sake in modern English poetry began in the eighteenth century from Scotland, and that the great nature-poetry of the nineteenth century was born and grew into strength in the heart of a Cumbrian poet.

The wild country acted differently on the German side of the English race. It was felt, not as a thing to be loved, but to be feared. The solitary moors, the cruel woods, the fens where the wild birds cried like demons, the black morass, are alive in early English literature with the evil-bringing powers of nature. Monsters like Grendel haunted the misty moors and the black seapots where the waves boiled; the dragon lurked in the fen or in the caves of the rocks; hateful phantoms rode on the storm-clouds or lay in wait for the traveller when he crossed the swollen stream or passed the gray stones on the heath. A whole world of fearful imagination was born which has never left our literature.

Out of both, out of the Celtic love and the German fear of wild nature, has grown at last the modern poetry of nature, a mingled web of love and awe. And between both, and also influencing modern poetry, was all the romance of the wildwood which collected itself in story and ballad round the life of the bold outlaw in the forests, and was mingled with the gaiety of the fairy crew that danced by moonlight in the pleasant glades.

(2) The second subject of which a sketch is here to be given is the Roman occupation, and how far it influenced our literature. On such a land as I have described the Romans came for the first time with Julius Cæsar in 55 B.C., and then again the year after; and the noble defence of south-eastern England made against them by Cassivelaunos in his stronghold of Verulam is not unremembered in literature. Nor has Caratâcos missed in letters the tribute due to his courage and his patriotism. He, leading the Silures, of a sturdier temper than the Celtic tribes, defended the northern and midland parts of Britain against the legions of the Emperor Claudius, when, ninety years after Cæsar's landing, the Romans made the south-east of the island into a province of the empire. In Nero's reign, Suetonius Paulinus took and sacked the island of Mona, slew the Druid bands and cut down their sacred groves. But he had left the east of Britain unprotected, and Boadicca (Boudicca), Queen of the Iceni, raised the country to avenge her bitter wrongs, and destroyed with terrible slaughter London, Verulam, and Camalodunon, but was at last defeated and died of poison. These two events have often been celebrated by English poetry. Cowper sang, with his own melodious grace, the British Queen in her wrath and sorrow. One of Tennyson's daring experiments in metre sang of the Druids, the Brythonic gods, the yellow-haired queen, the bloody vengeance which she took, and invented her prophecy of the fall of Rome and the glory of England.

The better government of Agricola, under Vespasian, redeemed the cruelties of Paulinus and drew all the British chieftains below the Forth and the Clyde into the Roman peace. The line of forts he set up between Glasgow and Edinburgh was made into a wall by Antoninus in 140 A.D.; and Hadrian, twenty years before, had built another wall, whose ruins now stretch between Newcastle and Carlisle. These huge walls with their forts and towers, the fortifications with which the Romans encompassed their towns, their white stone buildings, the temples, theatres, and public baths, the rich country-houses and the magnificent roads with which they quartered the land, were marvels to the Britons. They were still more wonderful to the English. Early English poetry is full of allusions to these "works of giants"; and one of its finest Elegies describes the wondrous walls, the gates, the crumbling towers, the heap of shattered houses, the pillars and pinnacles, the marketplace and the marble baths of Bath—or perhaps of Caerleon on Usk, built by the second Augusta legion—a noble town which, in literature, is "towered Camelot." In this way the Romans left some trace on the letters of England.

It was the Romans, also, who brought Christianity into Britain, and British Christianity has faintly entered into English literature. It seems possible that some of the soldiers of the legion which had served at Jerusalem, and which was sent to Britain in the first century, may have been Christians, and have spread their faith among the British folk; and Wülker conjectures that it is owing to this that the Eastern elements were so strong in the British Church. When Christianity came, it grew steadily. Tertullian speaks of the British Christians at the end of the second century; and at the end of the third and beginning of the fourth century Britain had three martyrs of the faith—Alban of Verulam, and two citizens of Caerleon, Aaron and Julius. After 386 A.D. the Church of Christ was fully established.

It is in the legends of saints, as, for example, of Alban of Verulam, handed down from the days of the Roman occupation, that we find traces of the influence on English literature of the Christianity Britain owed to Rome. The chief story is that of Helena and her "Invention of the true Cross." Constantine, who was proclaimed emperor at York, was the son of Helena, the daughter of a Dacian innkeeper, whom legend made into a British princess. One of Cynewulf's noblest poems celebrates the dream and victory of Constantine, the voyage of Helena to Jerusalem, and her discovery of the Rood; nor is the story unrepresented in the later literature of England.

But, on the whole, the influence of British Christianity on English literature is all but imperceptible. The slaughter the

English heathen made of the British, and the destruction of their shrines in the first hot years of the Conquest, left only a few traces of the Roman civilisation and Christianity. Canterbury may have retained a remnant of Christian churches and schools. Roman civilisation and Christianity remained alive in Wales, but where the English heathen passed, ruin was on their right hand and their left. When England became Christian, the memory of those cruel days kept the British Church apart in hatred from the English; and when in the later conquests the Britons were absorbed into the English, they became children of the Latin not of the British Church. There was one place, however, where British Christianity and its traditions were handed on without a break into English Christianity, and whence the Celtic devotion and imagination flowed into English literature. That place was Glastonbury. When Cenwealh, in 658, passing over the great marshes, captured Glastonbury Tor, he found there the British Church and monastery, which, since the overthrow of Ambresbury, had been the centre of British Christianity. Unlike Ambresbury, it was not destroyed by the English, for Cenwealh, lately made a Christian and founder of the bishopric of Winchester, saw brethren, not enemies, in the monks of Glastonbury. When Ine, some thirty years after, came to the throne of Wessex, he too honoured the ancient site, added to the ancient Church another of his own, and enriched the monastery. Hence Glastonbury was the only place in southern England where British Christianity continued into English, where the religion, the traditions, the legends of saints, and a church of the Brythons mingled in a happy marriage with those of the English. The Celtic Christian legends, which carried the story of Glastonbury back to Joseph of Arimathea, to the Apostles, even to the Last Supper and the Cross, though they took their literary form much later, had lived at Glastonbury in embryonic Celtic forms, some of them heathen in origin. The story of the Holy Grail, springing out of early Irish roots, grew, like a myth, by accretion, in Glastonbury, and taking at last a literary form, not only brought the central doctrine of the Roman Church into those imaginative affections of the common people which story-telling nourishes, but also went from England all over Europe. But its origins were in the Celtic Christianity which passed through Glastonbury into the English Church.

It was not only Brythonic Christianity which had a centre of dispersion at Glastonbury. The place had close connections with Goidelic, with Irish Christianity. It is supposed that a second Patrick refuged there. Columb and Bridget are both brought to Avalon. We know that many pilgrims came yearly from Ireland to worship at Glastonbury, and that many Irish scholars studied in the monastery, added to its library, and brought to its folk the legends of their saints, perhaps the stories of their heroes. Irish influence thus came into England, not only from the north through Iona, but from the south through Glastonbury. In fact Goidelic, Brythonic, and English Christianity met and mingled their powers in this ancient seat of learning. The spirit of all these powers, though they had grievously dwindled when he was young, concentrated itself in Dunstan, who, brought up as a child in the sight of the monastery and taught by its Irish pilgrims, became its abbot in manhood, and made it the source from which the revival of monastic life and learning spread over England. The literature which blossomed in Æthelwold, and bore such copious fruitage in Ælfric, was sown in the great school of Glastonbury, and by the hand of Dunstan. And Dunstan was perhaps as much the child of Celtic as of English Christianity.

To return from this necessary episode, not much now remains to say of Roman Britain. Severus, in 210, drove back the tribes beyond the walls with great slaughter. Seventy years afterwards two other foes added to the troubles of the provincials. The Scots from the north of Ireland began in 286 their constant raids on the north and west of the island. The Saxons, as the Britons called them, ravaged the eastern and south-eastern coasts for the first time in 290 A.D., and so incessant was their piracy that the whole coast from Southampton to the Wash was called by the

Romans the "Saxon shore." By the middle of the fourth century these greedy enemies of Britain leaped from every side upon her flanks. They were beaten back by Theodosius; and returning, were again routed by Maximus in 384. In 396 and 400 the north and the south were again attacked, and Stilicho rescued the provinces for the last time. "Me perishing by my neighbour's hands," sang Britannia in Claudian's poem, "Stilicho defended, when the Scot excited all Ierne to arms, and the ocean was white, beaten by the oars of the invaders." But Rome was now defending her heart against the German sword, and the invasion of the Vandals drew the Romans away from Britain. Constantine, a private soldier, made emperor of the west by the army, sent for the Roman legions from Britain in 407. One of his generals, Gerontius, a Brython, conceiving himself injured by Constantine, invited the Germans to join him in a conquest of Britain. The "cities of Britain" rallied to their own defence, repulsed the invaders, and declared their independence of Rome. The Emperor Honorius agreed to that which he was powerless to prevent, and bid the cities take care of themselves. They replied by banishing all the Roman officials, and setting up governments of their own. Britain now, in 410, stood alone, but she was not able to support her freedom. Her various governments had no bond of union; they fought with one another; famine and pestilence followed on civil war; and then her three enemies, Picts, Irish, and Saxons, closed in upon her. She fought with great courage for more than thirty years against desperate odds, but she was at last worn out. In 446 or 447 it is said that a piteous letter of appeal was addressed by the Britons to Aetius. "We are driven by the savages into the sea, and by the sea we are thrown among the savages—we are either butchered or drowned." It is not likely that this appeal, if it ever was written, was ever presented. At any rate, no help came from Rome; and in an evil hour for the Britons, Gwerthigern (Vortigern), their most powerful king, called on the English marauders for their help; and Hengist and Horsa, whose names also belong to Saga, landed in Thanet. They

c

quarrelled with Vortigern; the land pleased them better than their Jutish flats; they sent with fraternal pleasure for more of their bands; and in 451 A.D. their conquest of Kent began the conquest of Britain by the English.

It may well be asked how it was that the civilised rule of Rome for so long a period had no influence whatever on English law and literature, and left so few traces on the British. With regard to the British, the hatred between them and the Romans was deep. The relation between them had grown into the relation between cruel oppressors and their victims. The arrival of the tax-gatherers in a British town was like the arrival of a band of plundering and torturing Pindarees in an Indian village. The Britons and their tyrants were two nations in one country. When the Romans left, it was almost as if they had never come. Even the Latin language only existed for a short time. It had been spoken largely in the towns and their suburban country; thousands of Britons served in the Roman legions, and of course spoke the tongue of Rome, but it did not get far into the interior of Britain. It has been conjectured that a Romance language arose. This is excessively improbable. As in Wales and Ireland when conquered by the English, so in Britain conquered by the Romans, two languages were spoken; and when the Romans left, Latin, as a popular tongue, except among the priests and upper classes, died away. The tribes also went back at once, each to his own individuality,—to that jealous separate existence which is so dear to all races in the earlier stages of their history, and which Rome strove to destroy. It was suppressed in Britain but not destroyed. The Roman unity had never taught the British tribes to live, govern, or war as one people. Nor did the denationalising Roman law and order penetrate into the British nature, any more than English law and order has penetrated into the nature of the Irish people. Britain hated the Romans and their laws because they strove to turn the Britons into Romans, to destroy their nationality. Ireland and Wales have hated the English and their laws whenever they strove to turn them into English; and it is no wonder. The account which Gildas gives of the condition of the British kingdoms, however exaggerated by personal feeling, shows how ineffective the Roman order and obedience had been to root out each tribe's desire of self-government. Rome left the land, and the land forgot her with joy. What happened is what would happen now in India if the English Raj were withdrawn. In a few generations an invader would scarcely be aware, save by their public works, that the English people had ever been in the provinces of India.

So when the English invaded Britain, they found, save among the remnant who fought at the siege of Mount Badon, little of the Roman government or power, and the little that was left they destroyed. Nothing, save the roads and the ruins, was left of British-Roman civilisation from Canterbury to Bristol and from London to York. This destruction seemed to educated men of the time, like Gildas, to be an irreparable evil. All civilisation, they said, was blotted out; God Himself has forsaken mankind; the most cruel heathenism has destroyed Christianity in one of its most sacred homes.

But these cultured people are the most often mistaken. It was of first-rate importance for the progress of the world that the steadfast and powerful individuality of the English people should be unhampered by the decayed civilisation of Rome, or by the reckless nature of the Celtic Gauls; that England, when she came to exist, should develop her Christianity in her own fashion, and weave her literature out of the threads of her own nature. The English tongue, the English spirit, and the English law were secured to mankind by the merciless carnage of the early years of the Conquest. The true influence of Rome came back again with the Roman Christianity, and brought with it Rome's amalgamating and uniting power, not in the political, but in the spiritual realm; and a mighty influence it had on the development of a national literature. But by that time the special language, character, customs, ways of thought and feeling of the English people had so established themselves, that they remained, in spite of the large Celtic admixture, in spite of Rome, in spite of the Danish invasions, in spite of all the French influences which bore upon them, the foundation power, the most enduring note in our literature from the songs of Cædmon to the poems of Tennyson, from the prose of Ælfred to the prose of to-day. And this has been more the case with England than with any other nation which came under the influence of the Roman Church.

(3) The third question to ask is—What indirect influence, if any, the Goidels had on the early literature of England. We have seen that the Goidels only existed, as a race apart, in Ireland, in Man, and in the western and northern parts of Scotland, where they were largely mixed with a previous Neolithic people. They seemed from their remoteness to be very unlikely to touch us with their spirit. The Brythons, on the other hand, were not remote from the English. They lay, side by side with them, along the border of Devon and Cornwall, along the March in Mercia, and along the edge of Cumbria, in the land of mountain and moor which extended from the Ribble to the Clyde. Both these Celtic races had each a literature of tales and songs, but owing to strange circumstance it was the Goidels, the more distant of the two, which first influenced England. Ireland in the sixth century had a plentiful literature in her own tongue, and a great school of learning; and the learning and the literature were brought to the west coast of Scotland by Columba in 563. There he founded the monastery of Iona, and for twenty years evangelised the mainland from his lonely island. He died in the very year, 597, in which Augustine landed at Thanet. He was himself an Irish poet, and we still possess some lyrics of his, of warm devotion and of passionate regret for his exile from Erin. His friend, Dallan Forgaill, who wrote his *Praises*, was chief of the multitudinous Irish bards. From his monastery, where Irish poetry was loved and honoured, Northumbria, after Paullinus's flight, was evangelised by Irish-speaking, Irish-hearted monks; and all the elements of religion and devotion which move and pierce the soul

most deeply, and which through the soul develop the imagination, came to the northern English, and indeed into a great part of Mercia and Anglia, through the Irish spirit. It is scarcely possible to deny that this had some effect, and perhaps not a small one, on the growth in Northumbria, where the Irish influence was greatest, of a larger imagination and of a love of natural description, such as we do not find elsewhere in early English poetry. There is no direct connection between Irish and Northumbrian poetry; it is always plainly English poetry on which we look, but it is English poetry with a difference, and we may justly claim that difference as due to the Celtic spirit. And this claim is supported by historical facts. There was evidently, even before Aidan crossed the border, an educational relation between Iona and the court of Northumbria. Oswald, with twelve princely companions, six of whom were sons of Æthelfrith, was trained at Iona. He came to that monastic school when he was thirteen years of age, about 616. He lived at Iona for seventeen years. He and the rest of the Æthelings learned Irish and spoke it fluently. He must have known the Irish poetry that Columba knew, and the Irish monks had no religious objections to their own sagas of war and love and sorrow. When he and his princes returned to Northumbria (and he came to the throne in 633) they brought back with them the Irish learning charged with the Irish spirit. He summoned Iona monks to Christianise his kingdom, and when Aidan brought to Northumbria "the milk of the Gospel," Oswald travelled with him, interpreting his preaching to the nobles and the people, until Aidan had learned English. Oswin in Deira, and Oswiu when he made Northumbria into one kingdom, were both attached to Aidan and carried still further the Irish influence. Oswiu had been baptized and educated at Iona; and after the battle of Winwæd, when Northumbria was freed from the terror and paganism of Penda, the country was pervaded by monasteries set up on the Irish model, and directed by monks who had learnt all their religion and the spirit of their devotion from Irish teachers. As Oswald had set up Lindisfarne and its subject monasteries, so Oswiu now set up Whitby on the same Irish pattern. And Whitby became the educational centre of more than half of Northumbria, and sent forth from its loins a number of related monasteries, of bishops and missionaries to the midland and south of England. The monasteries were founded on the Irish model, the men had received an Irish training, and knew at least some of the Irish literature. Later on, even after the Synod of Whitby, 664, when the Roman Church established its ascendancy over the Celtic, the Irish influence, though lessened as an ecclesiastical, remained as an intellectual and literary power. Shoals of Irish scholars came over to Northumbria, and numbers of English went to Ireland to drink the wine of knowledge, to read and love the Irish tales and songs. King Aldfrith also, who died in 705, almost as fond of literature as Ælfred, was educated in Ireland and Iona, as well as at Canterbury, and was recognised as a scholar by Ealdhelm. It was only when Bæda had raised the school of Jarrow into pre-eminence, and when, after his death, the school of York became the centre of European learning, that the Latin influence entirely prevailed over the Celtic in Northumbria. This was the Goidelic invasion of England.

Its first indirect influence—I have said that its direct influence was very small—has been already alluded to. It was the infiltration into the northern English character of a more emotional atmosphere of feeling, of a more imaginative way of looking at man and nature, of a more intense sense of life in all things, than the German tribes possessed. It was the creation in the English soul of a direct love of nature for her own sake which the German people did not at this time possess at all. To this we owe Cynewulf's passion for the sea, for the changes of the sky, for the storms and the wild scenery of the eastern coast. To this we owe the vivid personification and description of natural objects in the *Riddles* of Cynewulf, the extraordinary fire of his religious hymns, and the singular self-consciousness of his poetry. We owe to this the fulness with which he conceives the varied and rejoicing life of heaven, and the mythical elements with which he has suffused his picture in the *Phœnix* of the land of eternal youth. I believe that we also owe to it the delightsome elements in the *History* Bæda wrote, its profound pleasure in mystic and romantic legends, the charm of its story-telling, and the grace of its tenderness. It is certainly at these points that Bæda differs as a writer from Ælfred or Ælfric. Lastly, it is not improbable that the eagerness of the Irish feeling for sagas had something to do with the preservation of *Beowulf* in the North, and with the poetising of the saga stories of the Old Testament in the early *Genesis*, in *Exodus*, and in *Judith*, all of which, as I think, took form in Northumbria.

The second influence the Goidelic invasion had on English literature was also indirect, and the assertion of it is open to dispute. I believe that the steady tendency in Northumbria towards the making of religious poetry in the vernacular rather than in Latin, was owing to the Irish influence, which, carrying with it the Irish passion for the use of the national tongue, bore upon the English poets. The Irish, always using their native language for war-tales, used it also for religious tales and songs; and a people Christianised by the Irish would tend to do the same. It would not even occur to a Northumbrian poet trained by Aidan or his followers to write sacred poetry in Latin verse. It is the first thing which would occur to a poet trained in the Latin schools of Theodore, of Ealdhelm, of Bæda, of Egcberht of York. Bæda, it is true, loved English verse, and wrote it; but his chief verse was in Latin, and his practice illustrates what would have happened in Northumbria had all the monasteries been, like Jarrow, linked to Rome. Ealdhelm, also a writer of English songs, wrote on all serious subjects in Latin. His English verses were probably popular lays. Some say they were hymns, but the only one which lasted to William of Malmesbury's time was a *carmen triviale*. But the Northumbrian poets, with the Irish tradition behind them, wrote on the great subjects of the Old Testament, on the mysteries of redemption, on the lives of apostles and martyrs, in their own tongue. When Cædmon began to sing in English, the heads of the monastery received his English verse with joy, and urged him to go on writing on sacred subjects in English. This would not have been the case at Canterbury under Theodore, or at Malmesbury under Ealdhelm. And that it was the case in the North was largely due to the Irish influence.

These were the good things which the Goidelic branch of the Celts did for English literature and learning. Its influence, however, soon lessened, and its direct force perished in the Danish invasion. I believe, however, that it continued in Scotland when it had faded in England, and that we owe to it not only the remarkable love of nature for its own sake which we find in Dunbar, Douglas, and even Lyndsay, but also the rough, satirical, rollicking humour of these and other Scottish poets. The "flytings" of Dunbar may be said to be the direct descendants of the satirical poems of the Irish bards. And Fergusson and Burns, both in their love of nature and their satire, share in the Irish spirit. But the full Celtic spirit did not reassert itself until the prose poems published under the name of *Ossian* by Macpherson in the last century drew again the heroic imagination of Europe around the adventures of the Feinne and the gests and sorrows of Cucullainn. Macpherson found the skeletons of his tales in the Highlands, and he filled them up with such literary flesh and blood as it was given him to create. It was a pity he claimed them as true translations. For their value lay in their not being translations, but original transformations of old legends. Their power was derived partly from their origin and partly from Macpherson's own Celtic genius, and they carried with them a great deal of the ancient passion of the legends. They have been unduly depreciated, and we must not forget that they were one of the most stirring and kindling elements in the movement which reawakened romance and the love of nature in the poetry not only of England but of Europe. But having done this, the Gaelic witch fell asleep again. She had been clothed in false garments, and though her beauty shone through them, she put them away and retired to hidden hills and woods. Her influence is felt, but her direct voice is not heard in the poetry of Wordsworth, Byron, Scott, Shelley, Keats, Browning or Tennyson. But of late she has again awakened, and clothed by scholars in her own garments, has once more unfolded, for the pleasure and pricking of poets, the sagas and the songs of the first Celtic immigrants into Great Britain and Ireland.

(4) The Brythonic Celts whose influence on our literature we have now to indicate began almost immediately after the first English conquests a movement which had in the end a good deal to do with English literature. They also produced about the same time one writer, whose Latin book, *De Excidio*, and his *Epistola*, have come down to us. The movement was the emigration of many of the Britons to Armorica : the writer was Gildas.

Gildas was the first national historian of the Britons, a man whose learning was recognised in Ireland, in Britain, and in Brittany; a saint, of whom two ancient lives exist, one of which is based on the traditions and documents of the Abbaye de Ruis, an Abbey of which he was the founder. He was born in 493 (the *Annales Cambriae* make the date 516), and died in 570? He gives an account of the landing of the Jutes in their "three keels." The passage in which he describes the dreadful slaughter and cruel destruction of the British towns is the vivid record of an eye-witness of the ruin, and the language in which he denounces the English "whelps of the barbarian lioness" is worthy of a priest. It is strange to think that two hundred years after he wrote of the hopeless overthrow of all culture and religion by these heathen butchers they were to become the instructors of all Europe in learning and the most active supporters of Christianity at home and abroad.

His *Epistola* addressed to the kings and priests of the Britons, and written within and without with lamentation and mourning and woe, is a bitter denunciation of the iniquities of the kings and a still more bitter attack on the false and immoral priesthood. Its denunciations are those natural to a man who lived apart from the stress of life in a cloister, and we gather from their violence that the Britons were bad, but not so bad as he represents. He uses, to express his wrath, long strings of texts taken in order from all the prophets and from the New Testament, and this unrelenting accumulation of prophetic angers has a weight and menace in it which at last affects the reader like the darkness and flashing of a thunder-storm. But violent words in those days brought no trouble to a priest, and he seems to have lived an honoured and a safe life. He had many relations with the Irish, especially with S. Brigit and S. Finnian of Clonard. When he was weary of the troubles in Britain he fled to Gaul, built his Abbey, and died in peace. British-Roman culture says its last word in this writer.

As to the movement now begun, it was the emigration of the Britons to a new home in Armorica, and Gildas notices it in a single sentence. It began after the battles of Aylesford and Crayford, 455, 457. The English slew all the Britons they caught, but a good number escaped over the Channel. For we find that the first band of hunted Britons, the source of the Breton people, were numerous enough in 461 to have a church and a bishop of their own. Mansuetus, Bishop of the Bretons, Metropolitan of Armorica, represented them at the Council of Tours in 461. We hear from Sidonius Apollinaris that in 468 there were Bretons above the Loire (*Britannos super Ligerinum sitos*), that is, north of the Loire, in Armorica. This was the beginning of an emigration which so steadily continued, as the English pushed their conquests farther to the west, that, in the middle of the sixth century, Armorica is altogether Brittany—name, language, manners entirely changed. Cornwall and Devon sent their emigrants over between 509 and 577, and the emigration did not lessen till the beginning of the seventh century. It was "not an infiltration, but an inundation." Nevertheless, it was slowly done, and without violence. The people of Armorica were not slaughtered, they settled down with the emigrants, and the isolated and successive British bands that came over for a century and a half found plenty of land and room for all their wants.

Here then, in a much more unmixed way than in England,

the old traditions, legends, myths, customs, and the imaginative spirit of the Brythonic Celt, both in poetry and in tale-telling, were supported and developed: and even Wales was less purely Brythonic than Brittany. Of course, a certain amount of Goidel blood and tradition went from Devon, Cornwall, and South Wales into Brittany, but it was not a large amount, and the Brythonic spirit dominated it. That spirit passed with the wandering Breton bards into Normandy, and having mingled with French romance was brought back by the Normans into England, and added its power afterwards to the literature of England. The best illustration of this is the Arthur story. As a story it was not indigenous to Brittany. It had not developed in the seventh century. But when it came to Brittany from Wales it was rapidly assimilated: pure Brythonic-Breton myths were added to it; it was freshly developed and locally expanded; and falling then into the hands of the neighbouring Normans, was thrown out of scattered legends into clearer form and so brought back to England, where it first received its fuller development as a great tale at the hands of Geoffrey of Monmouth. The emigration of the Briton to Brittany was of high import to English literature.

This seems the best place to say a word about the *Historia Britonum* which goes under the name of Nennius, and which is a phantom-companion of the book of Gildas. Gildas has weight as an historical authority. But we know nothing of Nennius, and the book which goes under his name is a compilation from various sources. Critical investigation has selected two pieces out of the eight which compose this history as the kernel of the book—the *Historia Britonum* and the *Civitates Britanniae*. The first of these is judged from internal evidence to have been written about the year 822, and both are the only pieces which occur in all the manuscripts. The compiler, says Guest,[1] "used fragments of earlier works which are of great interest and value." But the most interesting part to an historian of literature is that which treats of the struggle of the Britons against the English under the

[1] *Origines Celticae*, vol. ii. p. 157.

leadership of Arthur. It contains and secures for us the first and most ancient record of those popular legends of Britain which gave birth afterwards to the romances of the Brut, of Merlin, of Arthur, and of the cycle of romance which goes under his name. They are not the inventions of the writer; they are the genuine record of popular stories, stories afterwards used by Geoffrey of Monmouth, and added to by him from Welsh and Breton legends and from his own imagination.

After Gildas there is silence, save for the cries of the conquered. The emigration went on, but the Brythons who had remained at home had, in the last quarter of the sixth century, been driven back by the English to Devon and Cornwall and the south of Somersetshire, and to the lands on the west from the Severn to the Clyde. In 577 Ceawlin, by the battle of Deorham, divided the Brythons of the south-west from those who dwelt in our Wales, and the influence of these south-western tribes on our literature is scarcely appreciable. It is well, however, to reassert in this place three considerations: first, that Glastonbury in the unconquered part of Somerset held till 658 the Brythonic as well as Goidelic traditions and legends, and handed them on unbroken to the English, so that they stole into English thought; secondly, that when Devonshire was conquered, the Brythons were not destroyed, but being amalgamated with the English carried their thought and feeling into the life of their conquerors; thirdly, that the Brythons who, mixed with the Goidels, had emigrated from West Wales into Brittany, took with them their heroic tales and their imaginative spirit, and in after-times sent both back to England through the additions which the Norman versifiers made to the Breton versions of the Arthurian legends.

The influence of the Cymry was much more important. They were the Brythons who dwelt from the Severn to the Dee in Cambria as Wales came to be called, and in Cumbria from the Dee to the Clyde. Cambria and Cumbria are two forms of the ame word—the land of the Cymry. At what date these Bryonic tribes took the common name of *Cymry* is not known, but as it means "fellow-countrymen" it points to a time when all the tribes recognised their unity as against a common enemy. Some great misfortune probably drove them into this unity of feeling, and no greater misfortune befell the Cymry than the fatal battle of Chester in 613 when Æthelfrith cut into two parts the Cymric kingdoms, seized on the tract of land between the Dee and the Derwent, and isolated the northern Cymry from the Cymry of Wales.

It is possible that at this time the name of Cymry passed into common out of casual use. At any rate, it was now that a desperate struggle began on the part of all the Brythonic tribes to recover the continuity of the country which had been lost; and it seems that they were helped by their Celtic brethren in other lands. The Brythons of Damnonia and Armorica, the Goidels of Dublin and of Scotland, allied themselves with the Cymry against the English, and the struggle carried on by Cadwallon and that of his son Cadwaladr, in alliance with Penda of Mercia, against the Northumbrians, and during the reigns of Eadwine and Oswald, only ended when Oswiu overthrew the Cymry and Penda at the battle of Winwæd in 655. That is the date of the final overthrow of the Cymry State as it was of old, when it stretched unbroken from the Severn to the Solway, and from the Solway to the Clyde.

During the whole of this time, from the middle of the sixth to the middle of the seventh century, the Cymry, who were a singing people, sang the fortunes of the strife, its battles and defeats, its sieges and feasts. Four great bards are said to have flourished among them towards the end of the sixth century, and some of their work continued into the seventh. They were Aneurin, Taliessin, Llywarch Hen, and Merddin. We cannot quite tell whether the names represent real men. Merddin, who became the Merlin of the Arthur tales, and Taliessin, seem to grow before our eyes into mythical personages, but at least we have the poems attributed to these names. They exist in manuscripts which date from the twelfth to the fourteenth century. They have been modernised, added to and mishandled, but the ancient body of them is allowed to be historical and contemporary with the events of which they sing. Though the poems have no direct influence on English literature, yet they are the earliest records we possess of English war. Poems attributed to Taliessin and to Llywarch Hen record the wars of Urien, Rhydderch Hen, Gwallawg and Morcant against the Angles of Bernicia under Hussa, King of Bernicia, 567-574. A well known Taliessin poem, the "Battle of Argoed-Llwynfain," sings the struggle, 580-587, of Urien and his son Owain against Deodric the Flamebearer, the son of Ida of Bamborough. It is probable, as Dr. Guest believes, that the old Marwnad or Elegy on the death of Kyndylan, contained in the *Red Book of Hergest* and said to have been written by Llywarch Hen in his old age, is an account of the sacking of the town of Uriconium, the "White Town in the Valley," by Ceawlin, King of Wessex, in 584, when the English eagles, "eager for the flesh of Kyndylan," came down from Shrewsbury and Eli, burnt the town and slew the chieftain. *Y. Gododin*, part of which seems to be by Aneurin, tells of the fight at Cattraeth and Gododin, two districts near one another and the sea, and probably in the north of Lothian. There the Britons and the Scots fought about 596 with the Pagan English and the Pagan Picts. For many years afterwards, until the death of Cadwallon in 659, the poets chanted the great patriotic struggle of Cadwallon and Cadwaladr against the Angles in poems, some of which remain in modernised versions to the present day. The poems then, if we follow Mr. Skene, arose among the northern Cymry, and at first drifted loosely from mouth to mouth, but were thrown into some ordered form in the seventh century. After the battle of Winwæd, the northern Cymry remained under English rule, till Ecgfrith fell on the fatal day of Nechtansmere. The Cymry north of the Solway were then independent till 946, when the Scots' kingdom, established at Alclyde, was subdued by Eadmund, who bestowed all Cumbria from the Derwent to the Clyde on Malcolm the Scottish king.

Meanwhile a great migration of the northern Cymry took place to Wales, and the heroic history of Cumbria was transferred to Cambria. This is Mr. Skene's explanation, and I give in what follows his theory of what now took place.[1] He holds that the bards of the migration carried with them the north-Cymric poems (the *first* period poems) to the dwellings which the migratory tribes were given in South Wales, and, as time went on devouring the memories of the past, "the recollection of the kingdom they had left passed away from them," but the poems remained. These "poems, obscurely reflecting the history of the North," were now applied to the present in which they lived. The names, battles, and exploits of old Cumbrian warriors were fitted to the history of North and South Wales, and to the new land the northern Cymry now inhabited. This transference was chiefly made in and about the time of Howel the Good, who reigned over the whole of Wales from 940 to 948, and its poetry makes the *second* period of old Cymric poetry. About the same time the older Mabinogi took their finished form.

Not long afterwards a *third* "school of Welsh poetry, which speedily assumed large dimensions and exercised a powerful influence, arose in North Wales; while the literary spirit of South Wales manifested itself more in prose composition," that is, in the creation of new mythical and romantic tales.

Still later, and growing gradually, a *fourth* school of poetry grew up in South Wales. It imitated the old poetry of the North, and wrote in the names of Taliessin, of Llywarch Hen and the rest of the ancients, striving with varying success to reproduce the spirit and the style of the men it imitated. This "spurious poetry" belongs, for the most part, to the time of Rhys ap Tewdwr, who was slain in 1090. At his death the Normans occupied Glamorganshire, and the kingdom of South Wales came to an end. But the production of this imitative poetry, under forged names, continued through the Norman-Welsh rule, until, in the time of Henry II.,

[1] See for a full account of this theory, Skene's *Four Ancient Books of Wales*, pp. 244, etc.

some of the ancient poems were first transcribed in a manuscript of the twelfth century—the *Black Book of Carmarthen*. Three other books, containing the old and the spurious-old poetry, appeared in the following centuries—the *Book of Aneurin*, the *Book of Taliessin*, and the *Red Book of Hergest;* the last is a manuscript of the fourteenth century.

Of the poems contained in these books I have only alluded to those which bear on English history. The rest of them, and they are many, ranging from the sixth to the twelfth century, are employed only on subjects belonging to the Cymry, on their early traditions, their cities, legendary heroes, sieges, battles, defeats, and on the personal feelings of the bards who sang these fates of men. Along with these war-poems there is a crowd of miscellaneous poems on religion, on the lives of the writers, on philosophic subjects, on the natural scenery and animal life of the seasons of the year; and some of these last appear to have had an influence on the rise of the lyric poetry of England. Such an influence was certainly exercised by the Welsh poetry of a *fifth* period, which, growing more copious after the twelfth century, unfolded itself into impassioned lyrics of love and of nature; lovelier but weaker than the older work, and exceedingly personal both in love and in sorrow. As time went on this poetry grew more feeble and, at last, merely sentimental. This further development, however, lies outside of the limits of this book.

Looking back, then, over the six centuries on which we write, we find that a great mass of poetry and legendary tales, differing from that of the English, and full of a different spirit, existed among the Cymry, and were sung and told along the marches of the Cymry and the English. These two people came to act frequently together in war, and to communicate in peace. In such border relations a bilingual community grows up, and the songs and stories of each people become common property, and mix together their imaginative elements.

The legends, tales, and poems of the Brythons, and the manner in which they felt about man and nature, could not fail to have some influence on their English conquerors. And for this there was plenty of opportunity. We hear so much of the annihilating slaughter done on the Brythons, that we forget how closely, in after-times, they were bound up with the English. Even in the first fifty years of the Conquest a number of the non-fighting Brythonic population must have been kept by the English as slaves and concubines. The Britons of West Wales, of Devon, Cornwall, and part of Somerset, and perhaps of certain parts of Wiltshire, were received into the English peace in the seventh century, and Ealdhelm, to take one example, was in courteous communication with the King of Damnonia. After the Conquest we find, from *Domesday Book*, that almost all the landed proprietors of Cornwall have English names—farmers who lived, harmoniously enough, among a population which was Brythonic in language and manner.

The intercourse which thus prevailed between the dwellers in West Wales and the English existed also on the borders between the English and the Cymry of Cambria and Cumbria; but after the migration of the Cumbrians to South Wales, it was greatest on the borders of Cambria. In the seventh century, to begin with an early example, Penda was in full alliance with Cadwallon, the King of the Cymry, and helped him for a whole year in his mortal attack upon Northumbria. Mercians and Cymry fought together, camped and sang together. When Offa pushed forwards the border of Mercia, the land he took in had more Brythonic than English indwellers, and the two races intermingled all along the new strip from Chester to Bristol. The border inhabitants of north-west Yorkshire, Durham, and Northumberland were in constant touch with the Cymry of Lancashire, Westmoreland, and Cumberland, with Dumfries, Roxburgh, and Berwick; and, when Westmoreland and Cumberland were conquered by the Danes and afterwards taken into England, the Cymry infused their spirit into their Danish and English conquerors. In Ælfred's time Wessex was in full relation with Wales. The story of Asser and Ælfred shows how close and frequent was this inter-communication. Many of the Welsh kings took Ælfred for their overlord. Many charters of Æthelstan are signed by chieftains (reguli) of Wales; and there are traces in the Welsh legends of English names and English stories. The genius of the Celt, and perhaps as much of the Goidel as of the Brython, stole in with more or less influence across the northern and western borders of England, from Berwick to Carlisle, from Carlisle to Chester, from Chester to Bristol, and from Bristol to Glastonbury and Exeter.

After the Conquest, this mingling of the English and Cymric spirit along the border went on with greater speed, but a third element, the Norman element, was now added to it. The French, the English, and the Welsh spirit were woven together in the doings of poetry and of story-telling all over Hereford, Montgomery, Radnor, and Monmouth. "In Powys, at the end of the eleventh century, the English element was considerable. Bleddyn, King of Powys, at the battle of Mechain in 1068, had under his orders a large body of English troops. From the end of the eleventh century, when the Normans took possession of a good part of South Wales, the relations between them and the Welsh chieftains are continuous; and at the end of the twelfth century the two aristocracies are entirely mingled together."[1] In like manner the Norman and Welsh mingled and interchanged their literature of tales and poetry. We can trace in the Arthurian stories of Wales elements which have come over from Normandy, and, in the Norman stories, elements from Wales.

It remains only to mention the rise of that great Brythonic subject which passed from the Brythons, whether in Wales or Brittany, into England and into Europe. This is the subject of Arthur, who has been so mighty a king in English literature, from the days of Henry II. to the days of Victoria. I might trace in the close of this chapter the upgrowth of the myth of Arthur, from the time when the Brythons were still on the Continent to the time when the Normans crossed the channel, but it will be better

[1] J. Loth, "Les Romans Arthuriens," *Revue Celtique*, vol. xiii.

to keep the whole story together, and to tell it in a history of Middle English. It appears first in English in the *Brut* of Layamon. In that poem, English poetry having been, like Arthur, almost wounded to the death by foes; having, like him, lain hid in Avalon watched by weeping queens; returned again, as was prophesied of Arthur, to life and war, to singing and to love. It returned hand-in-hand with Arthur; and, as the centuries moved on, bound into one fair unity of story-telling the imagination of the Celt, the romance of France, and the strength of England.

CHAPTER II

OLD ENGLISH HEATHEN POETRY

THE Teutonic tribes who came to our island, and from their name of Engle called it England, dwelt in the peninsula of Denmark and around the mouths of the Elbe. The most northern of these tribes lived in South Sweden and the upper part of Denmark, and the men of it were called the Jutes. Their southern boundary was the river Sley near Schleswig. Below them were the Angles, in a little country "about as large as Middlesex," and its capital town was named, said Ethelweard in his *Chronicle*, "in Saxon Sleswic, but in Danish Haithaby." The same town is mentioned in Ohthere's account to King Ælfred of his second voyage down the west of Norway to Sciringesheal, and thence to Haithaby. "Two days before he came to Haithaby," wrote the king, "he had on the right Jutland and Zealand and many islands. In these lands dwelt the English before they came into this land." Below the Angles, on the neck of the peninsula and probably in the existing islands of Harde, Eiderstedt, and Nordstrand were the settlements of the Saxons; but these islands were at this time not islands, but spaces of higher ground in a tract of marshy land which is now a great lagoon. This was the homeland of the Saxons, but they were continually extending themselves along the coast and inland, and Old Saxony finally stretched westward from the mouth of the Elbe across the Low Countries and into the lands of the Chauci and the Frisians.

The Angles also were not confined to the small piece of land between the Jutes and the Saxons. *Widsith*, the *Traveller's Song*, tells of Offa of Ongle "that he won the greatest of realms with his single sword; he advanced his boundaries towards the Myrgings by Fifeldor, and the Angles and the Sueves henceforth stayed on in the land as Offa had won it." Fifeldor, or the Monster's Gate, probably means the mouth of the Eyder. The island of Angeln was one of their colonies. We hear from Tacitus and Ptolemy that Angles had settled along the Elbe, "between the river and the forest," somewhere in the north of Hanover; and Tacitus makes them one of the tribes who had a right to worship "Mother Earth" in the awful forest of the Holy Isle. As their original country, like that of the Saxons, was chiefly marsh, and their life a continual battle with the encroaching sea, we are not surprised when we hear from Bæda that the whole population left it for Britain, and that, in his time, it remained a lonely waste.

The land of the Jutes as it rose towards the north, and the eastern coasts and islands of the peninsula, seem to have been the most fitted for habitation. Hundreds of small settlements were crowded together on the eastern side, where the sea did not, as on the west, ceaselessly eat away the land. But on the west, where rivers had laid down wide morasses, and the land lay level or even lower than the sea, the dwellers—Jutes, Angles, and Saxons—from the northern point of Jutland to the Rhine, had to fight daily a fierce contest with the waves. When a high tide, driven by a storm, ran landwards, it overwhelmed their dwellings, and it is told of them that when this took place, the warriors seized their arms and, as they fled, shook sword and spear in wrath against the gods of the sea who dared to disturb them. Full of bold defiance, they returned and built their houses in the same places when the sea retreated, "fearing," as was said of them, "neither flood nor earthquake." Pytheas describes those who lived about the Elbe in the middle of the third century before Christ. They dwelt in a great fen-land, over which the tide flowed and ebbed twice a day, traversed by a number of channels which the river made for itself through the delta. Some of these, near the lands of the Chauci and Frisians, Pytheas calls the Ostians. Their dwellings were also in the fens. "In their huts on the banks they looked like sailors aboard ship when the tide was in, and like shipwrecked men at the ebb. They hunted the fish round their hovels as they tried to escape with the tide; they had no cattle, made fishing-nets out of tangle and rushes, and were stiffened with the cold." These, if they were Saxons, were the more miserable folk, and though likely to make bold sailors under bold leaders, would not be the owners of those pirate boats who made life so difficult to the Gauls and the Roman provincials of the "Saxon shore." The pirate bands lived probably higher up the rivers in clusters of villages, or on the northern and eastern coasts of Denmark among the fiords or in its archipelago of islands; building their hall and town, as Heorot is built in *Beowulf*, on the fringe of land between the sea and those inland wastes of moor which had no indwellers but the wild beasts and the black elves. It is said that Heligoland was the favourite assembling place of these sea-rovers. Taught to build ships and sail them, perhaps by Carausius about 287, they soon excelled their teachers and became the terror of all the neighbouring coasts, "terrible for courage and activity, vehemence and valour, strength and warlike fortitude," equally famed for merciless cruelty and destructiveness, sudden as lightning in attack and in retreat, of an incredible greed for plunder, laughing and joyous in danger. They chose the tempest in which to sail, that they might find their enemies unprepared, and wherever the wind and waves drove them, there they ravaged. "Every oarsman among them is a leader; they all command, all obey, all teach and learn the art of pillage. Fiercer than any other enemy, if you be unguarded they attack; if ready for them they slip away. Those who resist them they despise; those who are off their guard they destroy; when they pursue they overtake; when they retreat they escape. Shipwrecks do not frighten, but discipline them: they not only know, but are familiar with the perils of the sea." These were the dwellings, and this the character of the three tribes whom the Britons called Saxons, but who called themselves by the common name of English.

They were, like other nations of the time, like even the savage hordes of the Huns, a singing folk. Every chieftain had his bard, his Scôp, attached to his hall, who sang in the evening at the feast the war-deeds of the day or the sagas of the past. Often the chieftain, like Hrothgar in *Beowulf*, was himself a singer. The store of lays contained, and was, the history and the literature of the tribe. The warrior went into the fight chanting as he smote with the sword; the pirate captain stood on his vessel's prow in the tempest and sang defiance to the winds and waves; the dying hero versed his glory in war and his farewells to his people. When the feast was over and the drinking began, the wandering guest told his story to the harp and claimed hospitality. Lays were sung in the chambers of the women. Ælfred heard the ballads of his people when he was a boy. At the feasts of the commoner folk it was the same as in the nobles' hall. Freedmen, peasants, even the serfs, sent round the harp to each in turn. A man was ashamed who could not sing his tale, as Cædmon was ashamed at the feast at Whitby.

Christians as well as heathen sang. Preachers like Ealdhelm chanted old ballads to lure the people into the church. Dunstan carried his harp with him from house to house and sang the legends of Glastonbury, the stories of the hamlets near his birthplace, or the battles of Ælfred. A legend makes Ælfred himself a singer. We know from the *Chronicle* that great victories were handed down to fame in verse. The very weapons when their lord bore them into battle were thought to break into music. The spear yells, the shield hums, the bow screams, the sword shouts, the chariot wheels roar in the battle, and above the fight the Shield Maidens sang aloud the joys of a warrior's death. The raven, the wolf, the gray-winged eagle, lifted their "dreadful song, hoping for the carrion."

The art itself, thus widely spread, was greatly honoured. It came from the gods. Saga was Odin's daughter among the northmen. There was a god of song, and when men sang well it was by his inspiration. And the Christian singers did not change the thought, though they changed the inspirer. Every one at Whitby said that Cædmon's gift was from God Himself. "God unlocked my heart," said Cynewulf, "and gave me the power of song." The gift itself was a "gift of joy." Glee, delight, and rapture are synonymous with music and singing. The lay in *Beowulf* is the "ravishment of the hall." The harp is the "wood of delight." Playing and singing are the "awaking of glee," and all the listeners "sit by in silence, thinking of the past," stirred to joy or sorrow, as Ulysses was in the hall of Alcinous, when they hear the poet sing.

But we must not mix up the Christian poet with the Scôp. When Cædmon began to write, he changed the position of the poet. The Scôp, that is, the shaper, had a fixed position. He received lands and rights from his lord. He was the equal of the noble, often himself a noble. The Christian singer might be of a lower class, a dependent of a monastery, as Cædmon was, a monk as he chose to be; a layman under monastic guidance, as Cynewulf in all probability became. But he was no less noble in men's eyes. His Master was Christ, and under that Master all were great who served well. Sometimes the Scôp who had sung in youth at the chieftain's board changed into the poet who sang at evening in the refectory, and this double career seems to have been Cynewulf's. But whatever change was wrought in the lives of the poets, whether they were Christian or not, they honoured their own art. The Christian singer praised it no less than the heathen bard, and lived for it with the same eagerness. Nor did he ever forget the poetry out of which his own poetry sprang. He transferred its usages, its phrases, its motives to his own work, especially when he sang of the great subjects of his predecessors, of battle and of ships at sea. The Christian poets transfused their own matter with the spirit of the ancient song.

As far as we can go back with certainty we find the Teutonic tribes harpists and singers. "A fair-haired folk," says Tacitus, "blue-eyed, strongly built, who celebrate in ancient lays Tuisco, their earth-born god, and Mannus his son"; ... "who have songs in honour of Arminius and others which they sing at their feasts and in their bivouacs." Religion, then, and war, were the fullest sources of their poetry, and both flowed together when they went into the fight, for, of all ceremonies, going into battle was the most religious. At one special point, however, their religion and their war (and this is common to all nations) were combined into song— in the mingling of the great myths with the lives of the tribal heroes. The English, like the other Teutonic nations, worshipped originally the Heaven and the Earth, the Father and Mother of all things, and their son, the glorious Summer, who fought with the Winter and the Frost Giants, with the cloud monsters who made the blight and the fog and drove the destroying hail on the works of the farmer. And the doings of the light and darkness, of the heat and cold, were made into mythical stories which gathered around a few and afterwards round many gods whom the personating passion of mankind fitted to the various doings of Nature. These stories grew into lays and sagas of the gods. They became a part of worship. But the myths thus existing took a fresh life in the war stories. When a great hero arose, did famous deeds and died, his history also grew into a saga, and in a few generations he became almost divine in the minds of men. Then, because wonder must belong to him, the Nature-myths stole also into his story, and the tales of winter and summer, of the gentle doings of the light and of the battle of light with darkness, were modified and varied into the hero's real adventures, till at last we can scarcely distinguish between the hero and the divine being, between, for example, Beowulf and Beowa, in all those matters which from day to day represent the struggle between winter and summer, light and darkness. The religious myth becomes inextricably mixed up with the heroic tale of war. Thus both the fruitful sources of poetry, worship and battle, give passion and dignity to the character and deeds of the hero.

This was the origin of the early unhistoric sagas, like that of *Beowulf*, and such a saga was the highest form of the oral literature of the German tribes. It was not, however, thrown into a complete form, like that which we possess in *Beowulf*, till long after its origin. It existed at first in short ballads, each celebrating some separate act of the hero. Such short lays, and other lays celebrating the battles of the day; marriage songs, funeral dirges, and religious hymns, were the daily literature which went unwritten from mouth to mouth. Of all this heathen poetry we have scarcely any remains in England. It was not likely to be written down by the monks, and it perished before the disapproval of Christianity. There exist, however, the remnants of the original lays which are embedded in *Beowulf;* a fragment of a saga concerning Finn, *The Battle of Finnsburg;* another fragment of the story of Walther of Acquitaine, *Waldhere;* a poem made in praise of his art by a wandering bard, *Widsith;* another by a bard whose lord had abandoned him to poverty, *The Complaint of Deor;* and a few scattered verses in the *Charms* which the peasant sang when he ploughed, when he swarmed his bees, when he went on a voyage, or when he suffered from cramp and fever.

The *Charms*, in which we find the oldest heathen remnants, were kept in the mouths of the people, and their paganism was afterwards overlaid by Christianity. They are like an ill-rubbed palimpsest. The old writing continually appears under the new; the new is blurred by the old, the old by the new. The heathen superstitions have Christian clothing, and the Christian heathen. The monks could not destroy them, but they changed the gods. Jesus, the Holy Ward of Heaven, replaces Father Heaven; and the prayer to Mother Earth is made into a prayer to the Virgin Mary. In one of the *Charms*, that *for bewitched land*, we have some lines of poetry which are quite heathen; and other lines in which heathen and Christian work are intermingled. The first is the prayer to the Earth :—

> Erce, Erce, Erce ! O Earth, our Mother !
> May the All-Wielder, Ever-Lord, grant thee
> Acres a-waxing, upwards a-growing,
> Pregnant with corn and plenteous in strength ;
> Hosts of grain-shafts and of glittering plants !
> Of broad barley the blossoms,
> And of white wheat ears waxing,
> Of the whole land the harvest.

This is part of an ancient lay sung by the ploughers in the old Germanic lands long before the English tribes came to Britain. The only Christian touch is the "Ever-Lord," for the "All-Wielder" may well stand for the Father of gods and men. The song breathes the pleasure and worship of the tillers of the soil in the pregnancy and labour of Mother Earth and in the plenteous children of her womb. It has grown, it seems, out of the breast of Earth herself into the gratitude of men. A few lines after, in the same *Charm*, we come upon another fragment, gray with antiquity, and sung when the plougher had cut the first furrow, in which we hear of Father Heaven embracing his spouse the Earth, and filling her with fruitfulness :—

> Hale be thou Earth, Mother of men !
> Fruitful be thou in the arms of the god.
> Be filled with thy fruit for the fare-need of man !

I daresay these verses were sung by the first dwellers on the North Sea when the Teutonic folk were born and cradled. They may be the oldest stave in any modern language. A little farther on, when the farmer had taken each kind of meal and kneaded them into a loaf with milk and laid it under the first furrow, he sang again :—

> Acre, full-fed, bring forth fodder for men !
> Blossoming brightly, blessed become !
> And the god who wrought with Earth [1] grant us gift of growing
> That each of all the corns may come into our need !

And when the farmer had so sung, the rite was done and he drove the plough straight through his acre.

[1] "These grounds" or "fields."

In the first verses of the same *Charm* we have a heathen lay to Heaven and Earth overworked by some Christian monk of the eighth or ninth century very curiously. The farmer, having said nine times " Wax and increase and fill this land" over turfs taken from four parts of the field and hallowed, said as often the Pater Noster, and bowed himself nine times very humbly, and sang :—

> To the East I stand, and for help I bid me !
> To the Mighty One I pray, to the Mickle Lord,
> To the Holy One I pray, to the Ward of Heaven's realm ;
> And to Earth I pray, and to Heaven on high,
> And to Mary, ever holy, and for ever true,
> To the Might of Heaven and to his high-built hall,
> That I may this evil spell utterly dissolve away
> By these words I sing, and by thoughts of power,
> To waken up the swelling crops for the needs of men.

This is half heathen, half Christian, and the ceremony which precedes it is a heathen ceremony with Christian rites and names imposed upon it. The turfs which here are taken to the Church and their green side turned to the altar, the names of the evangelists written on the crosses of bast, and the repeating of the Lord's Prayer, are the old sacrificial rites of the ploughing, when the turfs were taken to the shrine of the god, and their green side turned to his symbol, and divine names were written on strips of bast, and the song of dedication and prayer was sung to Earth and Heaven in times when the cornfield, as Professor Rhys says, was the battlefield where the powers favourable to a man made war on those that wished to blast the fruits of his labour.

In two other *Charms* we may meet with the Valkyrie or with the Fate-Maidens. In the first of these, a charm for swarming bees, the spell-master, taking some earth and throwing it with his right hand under his right foot, sings :—

> Lo, this Earth be strong 'gainst all wights whatever,

then, throwing gravel over the bees, cried this verse of the old time :—

> Sit ye, Victory-women, sink ye to the earth !
> Never to the wood fly ye wildly more !

The next brings us closer to the Valkyrie, for the "Victory-women" addressed to the bees is more like a term of endearment than an allusion to the wild maidens of Woden. But in this new *Charm*, they come riding over the hill, whirling their spears, as Wagner has drawn them in music. The charm is against a stitch or cramp made by the spear of a witch-maiden. The charm-doctor stands over the sick man with his shield outstretched against the dart, and anoints him with a salve, and sings this rattling heathen song:—

> Loud were they, lo! loud, as over the land they rode;
> Fierce of heart were they, as over the hill they rode!
> Shield thee now thyself, from their spite thou may'st escape thee.
>   Out, little spear, if herein thou be!
> Underneath the linden stand I, underneath the shining shield,
> For the mighty maidens have mustered up their strength,
> And have sent their spear, screaming through the air!
> Back again to them will I send another,
> Arrow forth a flying from the front against them!
>   Out, little spear, if herein thou be!

In the *Nine Herbs Charm*, a most curious piece, we come on full heathendom in four lines about Woden:—

> These nine herbs did work nine poisons against.
> A snake crept on sneaking and with teeth tore the man!
> Then Woden in hand took the nine wonder-twigs,
> And with these he smote the adder that it flew in pieces nine.

But these verses, since the mythical Heaven and Earth, the nature deities, are here succeeded by the far more personal Woden of the third century, are later in time than those which preceded them. For the first worship of the English, as we see by these fragments, was a nature-worship of Father Heaven and Mother Earth, and of their benignant children, of whom Thor was one; and to these we may add some kind of war-god, whose name was Tiw. Below these deities there were semi-divine ancestors of the folk, and each family had probably their own household spirits. The rites of these worships were conducted partly in the households and partly in temples belonging to the tribe, or in places like the Holy Isle held in wide and profound veneration. After these great personages, a lower worship, founded on fear, was given to the dark and destroying powers of nature, embodied as giants, elves, and monsters, and also to the elements, places, and things in which the gods, the ancestors, and the meaner beings were supposed to dwell—the icy cliffs and lands, the fire, the ocean caves, the dark hill-lake, the howes and burial barrows, the islands in the river, the open spaces in the woods, the great trees, the wells, the ancient pillars of stone they found on the hill-tops and the plain. But the root-thoughts of their religion, as we see from these songs of the earth, were homely and noble, reverent and simple. There were dark and dreadful elements as well, even in the worship of the high gods; but these, as in certain mystic rites to the earth, appear but seldom, and did not touch the daily life of men.

These fragments in the *Charms* date back to the old England before the conquest of Britain. Of the other heathen poems there is one—the *Widsith* lay—the personal part of which belongs also to this early date. When the singer of *Widsith*, the far-voyager or voyage, describes the Angles as still on the Eyder, the Bards and the later Longobards as on the lower Elbe, the East-Goths as on the Vistula and eastward of it, he describes conditions which only existed before the conquest of Britain by the English. Moreover he speaks, though this is no proof of his living at this early date, of his being contemporary with the earliest chiefs whose names are well-known in the Teutonic saga-cycle. That cycle did not begin before the time when the folk-wanderings began—that is, in 375; and its main heroes were Theodoric (475-526), the East-Goth, Gunther the Burgundian, and Hagen. The poet of *Widsith* writes of Gifica (Gibich) the father of Gunther, of Guthhere (Gunther), and of Hagena (Hagen). He declares that he knew Eormanric (Ermanaric), King of the East-Goths, who died in 375, and was alive in the time of Ætla (Attila), who was king in 433. We cannot say for certain that he lived between these dates, but it is extremely probable. If so, he lived to listen to the first songs of the saga of Ermanaric, and before the great saga of Theodoric had begun to form itself.

This is a romantic thought, but it is still more romantic to think that the poet heard, fully formed, the lays of a saga-series earlier even than those of Ermanaric, for he speaks of Finn the Frisian, of Hnæf, of Ongentheow, of Hrothgar, concerning whom lays are sung by the bards in *Beowulf*. He speaks, as if that chief were near his own time, of the Offa who ruled over the ancient Engleland. These names belong to the earliest part of the *Widsith*; but its later editors, to display their learning, have introduced into the poet's list of the kings and places he visited other names which carry us backwards and forwards from the middle of the fifth century. We hear of Alexander the Great, of Cæsar, of Alboin who was king in Italy in 568; and, along with the German folk, of the Syrians and Medes, the Egyptians, the Persians, and the Hebrews. These are plainly later interpolations, perhaps of the eleventh century, to which date our manuscript of the poem belongs.

As to the poem itself, the personal part is the oldest and the most interesting. It begins with, "Widsith told his tale, unlocked his word-hoard, he who most of men saw many kindreds and nations, and often received for his singing fair gifts in hall. Of the tribe of the Myrgings,[1] he went as Scôp with Ealdhild, the weaver of peace, to visit Eormanric, King of the Hrethen, who lived east from Ongle. Then Ætla ruled the Huns, Eormanric the Goths, Becca the Banings, and Gifica the Burgundians." This prefaces the long list of kings and places which continues to the 87th line, when the personal matter again begins:—

> For a longish time lived I with Eormanric !
> There the King of Gotens with his gifts was good to me ;
> He, the Prince of burg-indwellers, gave to me an armlet :
> This I gave to Eadgils, to my lord who guarded me,
> For my master's meed, Lord of Myrgings he !
> And another gift Ealdhild gave to me,

---

[1] They dwelt between the Elbe and the Eyder.

> Folk-queen of the doughty race, daughter of Eadwine!
> Over many lands I prolonged her praise;
> Scilling oft, and with him I, in a voicing clear,
> Lifted up the lay to our lord victorious;
> Loudly at the harping lilting high our voice,
> That our hearers many, haughty in their heart,
> They that couth it well, clearly cried their praise—
> That a better lay never had they listened.

This pleasant picture of his friend Scilling and himself singing in hall to the applause of the warriors, comes to us from the old fatherland beyond the seas, and paints the Scôp in his prosperity. Nor was he unworthy to sing of war; for, if we may trust the verses, he had shared in the battles the Gothic chiefs had fought with the Huns in the dark woods of the Vistula. "Fierce often was the fight when the Hreth-Goths warded with swords their fatherland all about the Wistla Wood, when Wudga and Hama sent the spear yelling through the air amid the grim-faced folk."

Of these things he sang, and he closes his poem by glorifying his art. "I have fared," he said, "through many strange lands; good and evil have I known; but the wandering gleemen are always welcomed and have joy in their art." Wherever they go, they

> Say in song their need, speak aloud their thankword,
> Always South or North some one they encounter
> Who, if he be learned in lays, lavish in his giving,
> Would, before his men of might, magnify his sway,
> Be of earlship worthy. For, till all shall flit away—
> Life and light together—laud who winneth thus,
> Under Heaven hath high-established power.

In another heathen poem, *The Complaint of Deor;* or, *The Singer's Consolation*, we meet with a Scôp who has borne as much adversity as Widsith had prosperity. Deor is no rover like Widsith; but, like Widsith, he has had a lavish lord who enriched him with gold and lands. But all has been taken from him by his rival Heorrenda, and he writes this poem to console his heart. We see from it that the saga of Weland was known to the earlier

English, as it was known to Ælfred, and to the carver of the ivory casket in the British Museum.[1]

The poem also alludes to the sagas of Theodoric and of Gudrun, for Heorrenda is the Horant of the Gudrun saga. It is plain that the English kept touch with their brethren abroad, and received from them, as the fragment of *Waldhere* also proves, the great Germanic stories. And *Deor's Complaint*, though its manuscript dates from the eleventh century, and though it contains a Christian interpolation, is plainly of the old heathen time. None of its examples are Christian; all are from the heroic sagas. Its form also is remarkable. It has a "refrain," elsewhere unknown in Anglo-Saxon verse. And it is a true lyric, with one constant, dominant motive, varied from verse to verse unto the close. I give the first two verses which have to do with the Weland story, and the last.

> Weland, for a woman, knew too well exile;
> Strong of soul that Earl, sorrow sharp he bore;
> To companionship he had weary care and longing,
> Winter-frozen wretchedness! His was Woe again, again,
> After that Nithad in a Need had tied him,
> Severing his sinews! Sorrow-smitten man!
>   That he over-went, this also may I.
>
> Not to Beadohild was her brother's death
> On her soul so sore, as was her self-sorrow,
> When that she was sure, with a surety far too great,
> That with child she was! Never could she think,
> With a clear remembrance how that came to be.
>   That she over-went, this also may I.
>
> Of the Heodenings, I was hight of old the Scôp;
> Dear unto my Lord, Deor was my name.
> Well my service was to me, many winters through;
> Loving was my Lord, till at last Heorrenda—
> (Skilled in song the man)—seized upon my land-right,
> Which the Guard of earls granted erst to me.
>   That he over-went; this also may I.

---

[1] There is a full account of this casket in my book on *Early English Literature*, vol. i. p. 60.

Another fragment of an Old English poem, written on two vellum pages which had been used for the binding of a book, was found by Professor Werlauff in the National Library at Copenhagen. The two sheets were not continuous, but different portions of the same poem—a poem belonging to the saga of Walther of Acquitaine. This saga, then, which was one of the Theodoric cycle, was domesticated in England; and if one story out of the cycle, and that one of the least important, is found in a southern English dialect, it is of the highest probability that the Old English possessed the rest of the Theodoric stories. The manuscript, Stephens thought, was of the ninth century, but the Old English poem may be much older, as old perhaps as the seventh century.

There are three forms, independent of our fragments, in which the story has come down to us—in a German form only known to us by a translation into Latin hexameters written by Ekkehard of St. Gall in the tenth century; in a Frankish form, and in a Polish form. Our English poem is derived from the original German form, not from its Latin translation. It has characteristics not found in the later forms. The Anglo-Saxon Hildeguthe (Hildegund), with whom Waldhere has fled from the Huns, does not cry out when Guthere and Hagena come riding in pursuit—"Slay me, lest I belong to the Huns, and not to thee; flee, flee!"—as she cries in the Latin version of the poem, but kindles Waldhere to the fight like an ancient Teuton maid, though he is one against twelve pursuers. "Honour me in honouring thyself. Be, as always, Ætla's foremost fighter." "This points," says Wülker, "to a high antiquity," and indeed the lines I quote have all the ring of the earliest warrior times. Not a Christian thought intrudes. We are with Weland and his sword Mimming (Mimungr), the most famous sword of the northern world; with Widia, his son, the kinsman of Nithad who delivered Theodoric from grievous straits; that is, we are placed among the earliest lays of the Theodoric saga. Here is Hildeguthe's cry to Waldhere, couraging him greatly :—

> Truly of Weland the work ne'er deceiveth
> Any of men who Mimming can wield,
> Hoary of edges ! Oft fail in the war
> Man after man, blood-marbled, sword-wounded,
> But thou, who art Ætla's forefighter, O, let not thy force
> Fail downward to-day, O droop not thy lordship !
>   Now is the hour,
> That thou shalt have one thing, or else another,
> Or lose thy life, or long-lived dominion,
> Make thine among men—Ælfhere's Son !
> At no time, my Chief, do I chide thee with words ;
> For never I saw thee, at the sword-playing—
> Through wretched fear of whatever warrior—
> Flee out of the fight, or in flight at the slaughter ;
> Or care for thy corse, though a crowd of the foe
> On thy breast-byrny with bills were a-hewing ;
> But fighting forward was for ever thy seeking.
>   Now honour thyself
> By thy great doings, while good is thy fortune.

And this good fortune is to stand in the battle, one against twelve. It is not the thought of the woman of the ninth, but of a much earlier century, of that seventh century when a multitude of lays were produced among the Lombards. There are, for example, in the record of Paul the Deacon, two close paraphrases of Ælfwine lays, and Ælfwine is Alboin, King of the Lombards, who died in 572. The original German *Waldhere* belonged to this seventh century, and our English fragments seem to be of the same date.

To an older realm of saga than that of Theodoric belongs the fragment we possess of the saga of Finn, in the *Battle of Finnsburg;* and its story is either preceded or continued by another portion of the same saga in the poem of *Beowulf*, and which is sung by the Scôp at the feast in Heorot. The arrangement of these two fragments of the same tale is differently made by different critics. Which is true, does not so much matter. What I give here is Grein's, but that of Wülker [1] seems equally probable.

---

[1] Grein makes the fragment in Beowulf *follow* the fragment of *Finnsburg;* Wülker makes the *Beowulf* fragment *precede* the fragment of *Finnsburg*, so that this latter comes in between the lines 1145 and 1146 in *Beowulf*.

What is important to us is the poetry. Finn, King of the North Frisians, was married, to heal a feud, to Hildeburh, daughter of Hoc the Dane and sister of Hnæf. Finn invited Hnæf, much as Ætla invites the Niblungs, to stay with him, desiring to slay him. Hnæf, with his comrade Hengest and sixty men, are lodged in a great hall, and at night Finn and his men encompass them with fire and sword. At this point our fragment (which was discovered by Dr. Hickes on the cover of a manuscript of homilies in Lambeth Palace) begins with the alarm of Hnæf,[1] who has leaped to his feet, young and war-like, and shouts to his men :—

> This no eastward dawning is, nor is here a dragon flying,
> Nor of this high hall are the horns a-burning;
> But the foe is rushing here! Now the ravens sing;
> Growling is the gray wolf; grim the war-wood rattles;
> Shield to shaft is answering! Shining is the moon,
> Full below the welkin.
> Now awaken, rouse ye, men of war of mine,
> Ready have your hands, think on hero-deeds,
> In the front be fighting, be of fiery mood.
>   Then did many a thegn
> Spring to feet, begemmed with gold, girt him with his sword;
> And two lordly warriors went to guard the doors,
> Sigeferth and Eaha, and their swords they drew.
> . . . .
> At the other doors up-stood Ordlaf and Guthlaf;
> And Hengest himself—he strode upon their track!

Then a fierce hero cried from without—Who holds the gate? and Sigeferth answered—

> Sigeferth's my name, quoth he. I'm the Secgas' lord
> Widely known a wanderer! Many woes I've borne,
> Battles hard to bear.

And now there rose the wail of deadly battle, and the shields and helms were shattered, and the house-floor rang, till Garulf fell, and many with him. The raven, swart and sallow-brown, flew round and round, and the sword flashed so that all Finn's

---

[1] According to Wülker, Hnæf has already fallen, and it is his war-comrade Hengest who cries out that the redness is not the dawn.

Burg seemed aflame. Never did sixty swains of war better pay their due to Hnæf for gifts and mead than these his fighting men. Five days they fought and held the doors. Then Hnæf was slain —and here the fragment ends, and that in *Beowulf* begins. There we hear that Hengest fought on until nearly all Finn's men were slain, and among them Finn's sons by Hildeburh. So, Hildeburh had lost her brother Hnæf by her husband's hands, and she has lost her sons by her brother's hands. Peace is made, but the things done hold so much of brooding in them, that the peace cannot last. All the passion of the situation is in Hildeburh's burial of her sons, which is sung in *Beowulf*. Beside the pyre of Hnæf Hildeburh bade—

> Lay her well-beloved son, all along the low of flame;
> So to burn his bonechest, on the bale to set him!
> Wretched was the woman, wept upon his shoulder,
> Sang her sorrow-dirges! Now the war-death-smoke arose;
> Curling to the clouds, flamed the greatest of corpse-fires,
> O'er the howe it hissed, till the heads were molten,
> And the gates of wounds were gaping, and outgushed the blood,
> From the foes' bite on the body. Then the blaze devoured all,
> Of all ghosts the greediest.

But Hengest, staying with Finn and Hildeburh in Friesland, kept wrath in his heart, and when the waves were unlocked from ice, thought still more of vengeance; and as he brooded, Finn knew of his thought and had him slain. Then Guthlaf and Oslaf took up the feud, attacked Finn in his hall and brought sword-bale to him, and bore back Hildeburh to her own people. So they avenged the death of Hnæf and Hengest. The events are passionate, and it is to our sorrow that we have not the whole of this saga which, arising on the North Sea, spread itself among the Franks and Frisians.

Beowulf contains in its episodes fragments of, or allusions to sagas older or later than the time of the historic Beowulf, and these are heathen sagas. The myth of Scyld begins the poem, a thing hoary with antiquity. The rivalry of Breca and Beowulf in swimming through the sea lashed by the northern wind may be a part of the ancient myth of the summer and the winter, but it also contains the common story of the young men of the North fighting in youthful rivalry with the great water-beasts of the sea. The story of Heremod was in vogue when *Beowulf* grew into a poem— the story of the bad chieftain who was false to the heathen standard of generosity, of honour, and of gentleness to his comrades. The story of Thrytho, the wicked woman, is part of the ancient saga of Offa of Engle, son of Wermund, a saga sung long before the English came to Britain. The story of Hrothgar's daughter Freaware, and of Ingeld the son of Froda, tells us of another saga, a portion of which has slipped into *Beowulf*. In a battle between Hrothgar and Froda, Froda is slain, and Hrothgar, to heal the feud, gives Freaware his daughter to be wife to Ingeld, Froda's son. When Freaware comes into Ingeld's hall, one of her seven brothers (of whom seven sagas were written) carries the sword of Froda by his side, and a gray-haired warrior knows the jewelled hilt and turns to Ingeld: "Know'st thou not the sword? Dear was that blade when the Danes murdered Froda; thyself of right should'st have it," and Ingeld, stirred to revenge, had his wife's brother slain, and the feud burst forth again. We know the conclusion of the matter, not from the poem of *Beowulf* but from that of *Widsith*. There we hear that Ingeld led a fleet into the fiord, stormed over the hills and attacked Hrothgar in Heorot; but "Hrothwulf and Hrothgar hewed down at Heorot the host of the Heatho-beardnas. There they bowed the point of the sword of Ingeld."

In *Beowulf* also we touch for a moment on a yet older saga than the saga of Finn or Offa or Ingeld—on the oldest perhaps of all the pure sagas, certainly on the most famous. The singer at Hrothgar's court, thinking as he walked the meadows in the dawn of what he will sing at night, recalls the story of Sigmund the Wælsing, which afterwards grew into the Volsunga-Saga and into the Nibelungen Lied. It is interesting that we have here in English the very oldest form of this great Teutonic story. The slayer of the dragon here is not Sigfrid, the son of Sigmund, but Sigmund himself. Sigfrid does not yet exist. Nor is the dragon called Fafnir, nor is the story at all connected either with Woden or the Dwarfs, or with the Burgundian story of Gunther and Hagen, or with any women. The singer sings only "of Sigmund's noble deed, of his battles, of the feuds and the crime, of his far journeys of which men knew nothing certainly, save Fitela (Sinfiotli) who was with him, for ever they were true comrades in fighting and many of the race of the Eotens they had slain with swords. But fulness of fame came to Sigmund after his death, for he had slain the Worm, the Watcher of the hoard. He alone, the Ætheling-born, dared the dreadful deed, going into the cave under the gray rocks, and Fitela was not with him. Yet his sword drave through the wondrous worm, till the good steel clashed against the rock-wall, and there the Drake lay dead. So had he, painfully fighting, wrought with his strength till he could have the hoard of rings at his own will. And he called his sea-boat; and the offspring of Wæls bore the gleaming gems and gold into the womb of the ship. But the worm melted away. Of all rovers he was the most famous for strong deeds, a shelter of warriors, and for that in old time he had great honour."

This is all *Beowulf* knows of the famous story, and its interest lies in its simplicity. We catch the first sketch of that tale which was developed into a national epic in Iceland and in Germany, which has in so many centuries engaged the arts, and at last, in the hands of Wagner, the art of music.

One other piece may be, I think, isolated from the poem of *Beowulf*, not as a fragment of a saga, but as a separate lay of the heathen time. Like the Sigmund story, it is an example of the short ballads in which sagas began. Introduced into *Beowulf* to usher in the story of the dragon's hoard and concerning things which happened three hundred years before the historic Beowulf, it is of great age and singular charm. A prince, three hundred years ago, dwelt in the land of Hygelac, where Beowulf now is king. A deadly life-bane swept away his folk and he alone was left. And he wandered to and fro mourning, yet wishing delay of death that he might still look on the leavings of a high-born race —the heaped-up rings and gold cups, jewels, helms, swords and byrnies, a golden banner, great dishes of gold, and old work of the Eotens. At last, as death drew near, he hid them in a high mound, in the dip of a headland, in sound of the moving waves, and sang over them this lament, which has some likeness to the poem of the *Ruined Burg*:—

> "Hold thou here, O Earth, since the heroes could not,
> Hold the wealth of Earls! On thee long ago
> Warriors good had gotten it. Ghastly was the life-bane,
> And the battle-death that bore every bairn of man away,
> All my men, mine own, who made yielding of this life!
> They have had their joy in hall . . .
>   None is left the sword to bear,
> Or the cup to carry, chased with flakes of gold;
> Costly was that cup for drinking, but the Chiefs have gone elsewhere!
> Now the hard-forged helm, high-adorned with gold,
> Of its platings shall be plundered; sleeping are its polishers,
> Those once bound to brighten battle-masks for war!
> So alike the battle-sark that abode on stricken field
> O'er the brattling of the boards biting of the swords,
> Crumbles, now the chiefs are dead! . . .
>   Silent is the joy of harp,
> Gone the glee-wood's mirth; nevermore the goodly hawk
> Hovers through the hall; the swift horse no more
> Beats with hoof the Burg-stead. Bale of battle ruinous
> Many souls of men sent away afar."
> So in spirit sad, in his sorrow he lamented,
> All alone when all were gone—Thus unhappy did he weep,
> In the day and in the night, till the surge of Death
> On his heart laid hold.

Moreover, in the midst of an account given in *Beowulf* of the Tales of the Sons of Hrethel, which might be called the Saga of Hrethel the Geät, and of Ongentheow the Sweon, there is a lay which voices the grief of Hrethel for his eldest son. It has the quality of a lyric; and it seems to me as if the poet knew of this mournful song and used it for this place. Picturesqueness, simplicity, passion, and a sweet movement characterise it.

> Sorrow-laden does he look, on the Bower of his son,
> On the wasted wine-hall, on the wind-swept resting places,
> Now bereft of happy noise. . . .
>   For the Riders sleep;
> In their howe the heroes lie. Clang of harp is there no more,
> In the dwellings no delight, as in days of old.

There are other lays in *Beowulf*, but they belong to the very body of the poem—the last and the longest of those Old English songs which arose on the continent, which have come down to us from heathen time, but which were afterwards overlaid by Christian editing.

CHAPTER III

BEOWULF

THE poem of *Beowulf*, consisting of 3183 lines, records in two parts two great deeds of the hero Beowulf—his fight with the beast-man Grendel, and with his dam, and his fight with the dragon. The first has two divisions—the death of Grendel and a later addition, the death of Grendel's mother. More than fifty years elapse between the overthrow of the monsters and the last fight of Beowulf with the dragon. Several episodes are introduced, one of which gives the history of these fifty years, and others are taken from sagas of an earlier origin than the story of Beowulf.

The poem is an example of that mingling of myth and heroic story of which we have spoken, of the clothing of an historical personage with mythical garments. There was an historical Beowulf, a Geät who was a nephew of Hygelac. Hygelac is the Chochilaicus whom Gregory of Tours in his history of the Franks (Bk. iii. ch. iii.) tells us made a raid on the Attuarii of the Frisian shore—the Hetware of the poem—sometime between 510 and 520. He swept away many slaves and spoil, but Theodoric, then King of the Franks, sent his son with an army of Franks and Frisians to the rescue. The ships were already laden when Hygelac was overtaken. He fell in battle and all the booty was recovered. Beowulf was with Hygelac, and avenged his lord's death on his slayer, and he tells the story before he goes to fight the dragon. This puts the historical part of the poem into the sixth century. Hygelac died in 520; Beowulf reigned for fifty years after the death of Hygelac's son. The lays, then, about the historic Beowulf were fully sung in the beginning of the seventh century, about the time of Æthelfrith in England, before Northumbria had become Christian.

But these historic lays are of scarcely any consequence in the poem. They only exist as episodes, and they are chiefly found in the account Beowulf gives in his death-song of his early years, and in Wiglaf's tale of the feud between the Geäts and the Sweons. The main story of the poem lies in the transference to the historical Beowulf of the mythical deeds of Beowa, who is here the god of the sun and of the summer. The lays which told this story were sung in South Sweden and Denmark, in the Isles, and about the Elbe, long before the historic Hygelac and Beowulf were born. They probably came to England with the Angles, who possessed them before they left their country. These lays told how Beowa, bringing with him summer, attacked and slew the winter-powers on the sea-coast; not only the demoniac welter and destroying strength of the icy and stormy sea, but also the deadly fogs, hail and rain of the winter-moorland which brought disease to men and agriculture. These winter-powers are represented by the monsters, Grendel and his mother. Ettmüller's derivation of Grendel, if Grendel be German,—from *grindan*, "to grind to pieces, to utterly destroy,"—agrees with the myth. Grendel is the tearer, the devourer of men; the crushing ice-laden sea that grinds the rocks, breaks the ships and rends the seamen. This Beowa myth is transferred to Beowulf and becomes his adventure with the dreadful creatures which harry Heorot, the hall of Hrothgar; and the fight with Grendel's mother is a later and an additional form of the fight with Grendel and of the same myth.

The second part of the poem is the fight between Beowa and the dragon; the representatives of the ancient myth of the light and the darkness, of the sun overcoming the night and dying in the contest in order to live again. This, the oldest myth in the world, was extended, and especially in the North, to the battle between the winter and summer, between the frost-giants and the beneficent beings who brought life to men and fruitfulness to their labour. Then it was further specialised to represent different phases of the contest, and its scenery was modified by the peculiar features of the climate and aspects of the place in which these special developments arose. The scenery in which the contests with Grendel and the dragon are placed is characteristic of the coasts about Denmark and Sweden and of their climate, but the special features of the fight of Beowulf and the dragon represent (it is thought by the mythologists) that phase of the winter and summer myth in which the sun, here Beowa, fighting his last fight with the winter-dragon, rescues from him in late autumn the treasures of the earth, the golden corn and ruddy fruits, but, having given them back to men, dies himself of the winter's breath, to rise again, in the next summer, and renew the ever-recurring battle. Whether we can specialise as closely as this the myth into the poem is a matter open to much dispute. Those who are devoted to the nature-myths specialise even further the poem of *Beowulf*. There is an episode in it of Beowulf and a rival of his, Breca, who have a swimming adventure together on the stormy sea and slay a number of nickers. The mythologists declare that Breca is either the stormy wind of spring—the Breaker—who rivals Beowa, the sun, in breaking up the ice; or that Beowa is a wind-hero—the cloud-sweeper—and that Breca who rules over the Brondings, that is, the sons of the flaming brand, is the child of Beanstan, the sun, and then this episode means that the wind and the sun with rival powers fight the winter. But this is one of the instances, it seems, where the nature-myth is driven too hard. All we have here to say is that lays which told of Beowa, conceived of as the summer god contending with the winter-monsters in early summer and then contending with the winter-dragon in late autumn, were transferred to the historic Beowulf, and made, with local colouring, into adventures of his own. How, where and when this transference was made, after the year 600, we cannot tell, but it was probably made in the lands where the story of Beowulf took place

—in South Sweden and Jutland; and the tale, thus developed, was brought to Northumbria by belated Angles, who, as they came from the peninsula where a great part of its scene was laid, had a special national interest in it. It would be gladly received by the dwellers in Bernicia, Deira, and Mercia, and probably reached its half-epic proportions before 650 in England. Poets who lived in different parts of England would add to it lays and episodes of their own; and in this way perhaps, to take two instances, the story of Scyld was placed at its beginning, and the fight with Grendel's dam added to the original Grendel story. Then in the eighth century a poet—who I think was a Northumbrian, but others a Mercian—drew the main story and its additions together, gave it unity, and filled it with his own personality. He is thought to have added to it the Christian elements we find therein, but if so, he did this with so sparing a hand that we owe him gratitude. It may even be the case that these Christian elements were added, not in the eighth century, but by the translator who much later put the whole poem into the West-Saxon dialect, and from whom we have the existing manuscript in the Cottonian Library.

The story of Beowulf, before the business of the poem, that is, before his mythical adventure begins, is to be gathered from various parts of the poem; but his character, which is the English and North Germanic ideal of a hero, is to be inferred from the whole of the poem, and is the creation of the single poet who took the old lays and wrought them into a united poem. The character is historical even in the mythical portions, that is, it is built up out of the ideals of the time in which the poem was written. So also the manners and customs are historical. They are those of our forefathers in the continental lands of the English, and there is no other record of them, save a few hints derived from the ancient Teutonic laws. We see the works of war and peace, the chief's hall, the settled town with its houses and gardens and the moorland beyond the cliffs and stormy sea, the harbour and the coast-guard, the ships sailing and at anchor, the hunt, the feast, the warriors gathered to hear the bard declaim his sagas, the chief and his friends, and his way of governing. We understand the ideal of a king, his relations to his war-comrades and people, the etiquette of the court, the character and position of women, the sort of life the young men lived who went a-sea-roving, the conduct of ceremonial receptions, the burial of great personages. We have the doings of one whole day from morning to night related in detail. Behind the wars and contentions of the great we watch in this poem the continuous home-life, the passions and thoughts of our fathers who lived for one another, fought and loved, from the sixth to the eighth century. This is the historical value of *Beowulf*, and the record is one of surpassing interest.

It collects around the character of the hero, and this lives for us apart from the mythical framework. He was the son of Ecgtheow, of the family of the Wægmundings, a wise warrior who served Hrethel King of the Geäts, and to whom Hrethel gave his daughter to wife. Of these two came Beowulf, and to him Hrethel left a coat of mail which Weland himself had smithied. Hrethel had three sons, of whom only one, Hygelac, is alive when the action of the poem opens, and he is uncle of Beowulf and his lord. At the end of the poem, Hygelac and all his kindred are dead. Thus on his mother's side all Beowulf's relations are gone. On his father's side also, no one is left alive but Wiglaf, his supporter against the dragon, and Beowulf himself is childless. This loneliness is one of the pathetic points of the hero's character. He speaks of it again and again. It is his last thought when dying. This, as well as his immense strength, isolates him, and the inward pathos of it gave him, it may be, the gentleness for which among a violent race he is renowned in the saga.

Then, Ecgtheow is known for his wisdom—"All the wise men far and wide remembered him." This wisdom descends to his son. We hear of Beowulf's good counsel as much as of his strength. Wealtheow, the queen of Hrothgar, begs him to be of

good advice to her sons. Hrothgar says that he holds his fame
with patience, and his might with prudence; that he is a comfort
to his people and a help to heroes. When Beowulf is dying, he
thinks more of his wisdom as a ruler than of his great deeds in war.
Even in his youth he speaks to Hrothgar, who might be his
father, with the steady gravity of an experienced man. "Sorrow
not over-much for your friend; rather avenge him! Wait the
close of life; win honour; that is everything; and be patient of
your woes." Along with this went an iron resoluteness. He had
the gentleness of Nelson, and his firmness in battle. "Firm-
minded Prince" is one of his names. Fear, as also in Nelson, is
wholly unknown to him, and he has inspired his comrades with
his own courage. They all lie down and go to sleep in the hall
which Grendel haunts. It is a trait worthy of the captains at
Trafalgar. But his gentleness does not destroy the North Sea
elements in him. His defence against those who attack him is
fierce, full of scorn, of savage retort. But when Unferth, who
mocks him, repents, he forgets the wrong with a swift generosity.
This also is in Nelson's character. But the boastfulness of
Beowulf did not belong to Nelson. He is as boastful of his deeds
as all the Northern heroes are. It is their fashion; part almost of
their duty. Nor is he less prompt in the blood-feud than in
speech, but his vengeance was not hasty or private. He "shared
in no blood-brawls," it is said of him, "he did not kill his drunken
companions, nor was his mind cruel." So also his sense of
honour of which he was so jealous, was not in a nice readiness to
take personal offence, but in faithfulness to his word, to his duty,
to his war-comrades. "I swore no false oaths," he said when
dying. "On foot, alone, in front, I was ever my lord's defence."
When the kingdom was offered him, he refused, for Heardred,
Hygelac's son, was alive. It is true he was but a boy, but
Beowulf was faithful to the family of his lord. He trained the
child to war and learning, "guarded him kindly with honour,"
served him and avenged his death. His generosity and courtesy
were part of his honour. He gave away the gifts he received;

women loved his gentleness as much as his audacity. But, above all, he had the honour of undaunted courage. The two great duties of an English chieftain's life were to govern men in peace so as to make them wise and happy; and to win fame in war out of the jaws of death. Beowulf never fails in battle, and he dies, at the end, for the love and welfare of his people. "Let us have fame or death," he cries; "gain praise that shall never end, and care nothing for life." "Beloved Beowulf," said Wiglaf to him, when the dragon's breath poured flame around him— "bear thyself well. Thou wert wont in youth to say that thou would'st never let Honour go."

Before he went to Hrothgar he had borne himself bravely in wars and troubles. In the long life that followed he was set to do many heroic things and to bear the weight of government. So, even when he was young, life seemed to him grim, needing fortitude more than joy. And when he was old, and though he thought his work well done, it had been done with bitter care. Nevertheless his soul had conquered fate. This double aspect of life was deepened in colour by his belief in Wyrd, the Fate Goddess of the North. She was the mistress of man, and none could avoid her doom. But on a strong and noble character, like that of Beowulf, the weight of unavoidable fate acts with distinction, and so it is represented in the poem. "Wyrd will do as she choose," he says, as he goes forth to fight Grendel and to slay the dragon, but the goddess "may save a man if his courage keep his fighting power at full stretch." Yet, the doom is settled, and the mingling of unbreakable courage and of grave sadness which arose from Beowulf's conception of the Wyrd gives him that noble aspect which made Wulfgar say of him, when first he saw him, "Never saw I a greater Earl, nor one of a more matchless air."

This is the hero's character; the English ideal of a prince and warrior of the seventh century. It is well hewn out in the poem, the best piece of art in it. And it is the type of all the great sea-captains of our race; and more, of the just governors who are called by the peoples they have ruled, as Beowulf was called, "the good king, the folk-king, the beloved king, the war-guard of the land, mildest and kindest to his comrades, gentlest to his people, keenest of all for fame"; who having won treasure in death for his folk, thinks of those also who sail the sea; and making his barrow a beacon for seamen, is burned amid the tears and praise of all.

Many tragedies and wars took place when he was young, and in all these he bore his part. At last, times of peace came on, and Hygelac is established on the throne. Then Beowulf looks for adventure, as was the manner of young men. He hears of how Grendel torments Hrothgar, King of the Danes; and he resolves to go and slay the monster. And so the poem begins. Beowulf becomes Beowa. The Summer goes to slay the Winter.

I have adopted in this chapter the explanation given by mythologists of the legends in *Beowulf*—of the Grendel story and of the fight with the dragon. It is the common explanation, and is doubtless part of the truth. The stories came to mean the battle of the summer god with the winter giants, and the variations of that combat. But in a large and general way, not in detail. The detail for the most part was the creation of the poet's imagination, and was modified by the climate and natural scenery of the place where he lived, and by the character, manners, and customs of its indwellers. Matters which the mythologists have explained as nature myths—such as the story of the swimming-match between Beowulf and Breca, which seems to be nothing more than a great feat of rivalry between young men on a seal-hunt—are common events made heroic by the poet for the sake of exalting the hero. Moreover, a good many things in the story of Grendel go back to a time when the nature-myth business—that is, the poetic personification of the forces of nature—had not come at all into the minds of men, when their minds were not far enough advanced for such conceptions, and when actual savage men and women existed in the dark woods and moors, among the cliffs and caves, beyond the strip of cultivated land along the sea-shore.

The original germ of Grendel, and of a host of other cognate stories among many peoples, was sown at a time when the primeval indwellers of the sea-coast were driven back by the first invaders into the wild moors and rocks of the inland, where the miserable remnant of them took refuge. There, deprived of the fruit of the sea, they were starved, and some became cannibals, if they were not so before. There they gradually died down into a very few who made raids at night on their conquerors. The mystery which surrounded them made them a terror; their hideous violence, hunger-born, their tiger-desire for revenge, made them seem more than human, and mingled them with the brute. The darkness of the night and the pale mists of the moors magnified their size into monstrous proportions, and their life and its madness gave them the strength of a wild beast.

This is at the root of the Grendel story and of stories of the same kind, of ogres, trolls, and of their kindred forms, which we find all over the world. It is a piece of common history, enshrining the last struggle between the earliest savages and their first half-civilised conquerors, perhaps between Palæolithic and Neolithic man. Having this basis in actual experience, it became a folk-tale; incessantly, in every settlement, changing its form, and modified by the individual fancy of every teller of the tale. Later on, when men did begin to personify the forces of nature, the folk-tale was taken up into the myth and woven into it; and when a poet took up the story and wound it round a hero, he used both the folk-tale and the myth unconsciously, and gave them his own meaning; moralising them into a character, such a character as the poet drew in Beowulf. Naturally, then, many odd, old, savage things derived from the folk-tale of the eldest times remained; curious reversions to the original type—the claws on Grendel's hands, the pouch, the baleful eyes flaming in the night, the mist that follows him, the terrific strength, the beast-delight in blood, the rending of the bodies of his victims, the cannibalism, the poison in the pool on the moor, the corrupted blood in the welter of the sea-pot, none of which seem justly or naturally to belong to a nature-myth. The story of Grendel and Beowulf is thus a mixture of the folk-tale, the nature-myth, the heroic legend, and the poet's imagination of a noble character.

CHAPTER IV

BEOWULF—THE POEM

THE poem opens with an account of the forefathers of Hrothgar, the King of the Danes, and this opening may have been a preface added after the body of the poem was composed. It is probably a fragment out of a mythical saga concerning Scef (who is here called Scyld), the first Culture-hero of the North, and it is only in our England that the myth has been preserved. Four English chroniclers, Æthelweard, William of Malmesbury, Simeon of Durham, and Matthew of Westminster, as well as *Beowulf* record it. Their stories, which differ somewhat, as if from different sources, have their common origin in one heathen myth. They describe a boat drawing out of the deep to the Scanian land, and a boy asleep in it, his head resting on a sheaf of corn. Around him are treasures and tools, swords and coats of mail. The boat, richly adorned, moves without sail and oar. The people draw it to land, take up the child with joy, make him their king, and call him Scef or Sceaf, because he came to them with a sheaf of grain.

This is the same story as that in the beginning of *Beowulf*, but it is told in the poem of Scyld the son of Scef. Though the myth is only found as a whole in England, yet the names of Scyld and Scef are scattered under various forms in the sagas which belong to the tribes round the mouth of the Elbe, to Denmark and South Sweden, that is, to the countries of the English. It is the legend-myth of the man who first taught them agriculture—the father of the sheaf. The lines in *Beowulf* continue the sketch of him as the Culture-hero, who, having taught agriculture, teaches law and government when he grows to man's estate. "Then he subdued the scattered tribes around him, and wrought them into one nation. All the folk around him gave him service."

This is the history, under the myth, of the first civilisation in Scania. Of him was born Beowa, "the son of Scyld in Scedeland," the personage whose myth is transferred to the Beowulf of the poem. Then Scyld died and was buried, and the ancient lay of his burial ends the preface of the poem. When the day came his comrades bore him down to the flowing of the sea to bury him, as Haki is buried in the Ynglinga saga; as Sigmund buries Sinfiotli, as the gods themselves bury Balder. Haki, sore wounded, has his ship laden with dead men and weapons, and a pyre made in the midst of it. He is laid on the pyre, the sail is hoisted, the wind blows from shore, the pyre is kindled. Sigmund bears Sinfiotli to the beach, and Odin, mantled in gray, receives the young warrior in his boat and sails away. Balder, lying on a great pyre in the womb of the ship, is pushed from the land into the deep. The pyre is lit, the flame soars high, the wind arises, and the ship rushes out to sea, blazing till all the headlands shine. But Scyld is not set on fire; he sails away as he came, and none ever knew who received him.

> There at haven stood, hung with rings the ship;
> Ice-bright, for the out-path eager; craft of Æthelings it was!
> Then their lord, the loved one, all at length they laid
> In the bosom of the bark; him the bracelet-giver;
> By the mast the mighty King. Many gifts were there,
> Fretted things of fairness brought from far-off ways!
> Never heard I of a keel hung more comelily about
> With the weeds of war, with the weapons of the battle,
> With the bills and byrnies. On his breast there lay
> Jewels great and heaped, that should go with him
> Far to fare away in the Flood's possession.

. . . . . .

> Then they set a standard, all of shining gold,
> High above his head. And they let the heaving ocean
> Bear him; to the sea they gave him. Sad their soul was then,
> Mourning was their mood. None of men can say,
> None of heroes under heaven, nor in hall the rulers,
> For a truthful truth, who took up that lading.

It is a fair and noble tale. As the hero came from the sea alone, so at death he passes alone into the silence of the deep, with the wind in his golden banner. It is also the burial of a great sea-king, and the earliest of all such records. Moreover it strikes the sea-note of the whole poem. We are never in *Beowulf* without the presence of the ocean. Beowulf is in his youth a sea-rover, a fighter with sea-monsters, a mighty swimmer of the sea. All the action is laid on the sea-coast. Grendel and his dam are as much sea-demons as demons of the moor. The king and the dragon fight in hearing of the waves. Beowulf's barrow, heaped high on the edge of Hronesnæs, the cliff whence men watched the tumbling of the whales, is a beacon for those who sail through the mists of sea. The background of this story of the fates of men is that ocean life and ocean mystery which here begins the English poetry, and whose foam and roar and salt winds have in this century, after long and curious neglect, entered again with an equal fulness into its singing.

The first thing told of Beowulf sounds again that note of the sea which is struck in the preface. He hears at Hygelac's court of the monster Grendel who haunts Heorot, the great hall that Hrothgar the Dane has built; and who has slain and devoured all who ventured into the hall at night. Adventure stirred in his heart to set Hrothgar free from this curse, and his war-comrades whetted him to the deed. So helped by a sea-crafty man who knew the ocean-paths, he sought his ship drawn up on the beach under the high cliff.

> There the well-geared heroes
> Stepped upon the stem, while the stream of ocean
> Whirled the sea against the sand. To the deep ship-bosom

> Bright and carvèd things of cost carried forth the heroes,
> And their armour well-arrayed. Then outpushed the men
> On desired adventure their tight ocean-wood !
> Likest to a fowl, the Floater, foam around its neck,
> Swiftly went the waves along, with a wind well-fitted,
>
> .   .   .   .
>
> Till at last the seamen saw the land ahead
> Shining sea-cliffs, soaring headlands,
> Broad Sea-Nesses—So the Sailer of the sea
> Reached the sea-way's end.

And the Weder-folk, at the end of the low bay between the cliffs, beached the ship, slipped down the plank ashore, and their battle-sarks rang on them as they moved. They tied up their bark, thanked the gods the wave paths had been easy to them, and saw on the ridge of the hill above the landing-place the ward of the Scyldings sitting on his horse, and his heavy spear in his hand. He shook it, and cried :—

> " Who are ye of men, having arms in hand,
> Covered with your coats of mail, who, your keel a-foaming,
> O'er the ocean-street, thus have urged along,
> Hither on the high-raised sea? Never saw I greater
> Earl upon this earth than is one of you.
> 'Less his looks belie him, he is no home-stayer.
> Glorious is his gear of war, ætheling his air."

Beowulf explains his coming, and is bid to go on to Heorot. As he tops the hill, he finds the well-paved road leading to the town, and sees the hall below among its homes on a strip of cultivated land, reclaimed from the moor; and on the sea-side of it the ground sloped upwards to the cliffs. The hall is a long, rectangular building; its gables are sharp, with stags' horns on their points, and the ridge of its roof glitters in the sun. Outside of the hall the houses clustered, each with its garden ; and in the midst of the town was a wide meadow, where in the morning the Queen walks with her maidens, and the poet muses apart, and the young men breathe their horses. This is an island of tilled and house-built land between the edge of the sea and a wild waste of moorland which stretches away towards the horizon. Over this the dark mists rose and fell, and in them at night, Grendel, the monstrous growth with eyes of fire, stalked, and thought to devour men. It is the image of a hundred settlements such as the Angles built along the margins of the sea; and the monster, originating in a tale of elder days, is now clothed by the poet with their thoughts about the terror-haunted wastes beyond their dwellings.

And now Beowulf and his men have reached Heorot, in their grisly war-gear, their swords ringing as they walked. Sea-wearied, they set down their shields; their spears of gray ash stood like a grove where they struck them on the ground, and Hrothgar asked their names and their wishes. His Queen Wealtheow and his daughter Freaware sat with him, and at his feet Unferth lay, the boon companion; all of them on the dais, where the table ran from east to west. The other tables stretched for nearly the length of the hall, laden with boars' flesh and venison and cups of ale and mead. In the midst on the paved floor, and between the tables, were the long hearths for fire, and in the roof above, openings for the smoke. The walls and supporting shafts, adorned with gilding and walrus-bone, were hung with shields and spears and tapestries. When Beowulf tells of his wish to fight with Grendel there is a great welcoming, and then the feast begins.

Unferth, jealous of Beowulf, tells of Beowulf's rival Breca, and that he beat Beowulf in swimming; but Beowulf, wrathful, defends himself. When his mocking is over, the Queen greets the guests, brings the cup first to her lord, and last of all bears the cup to Beowulf, who swears that he will slay Grendel. And his boast pleased the Queen, who sat down again beside her lord. Then the Scôp chants clear in Heorot the ancient sagas, and the feast is over. Night has come, the feasters depart; only Beowulf and his men are left in the hall, and Beowulf, knowing that the monster is charmed against all weapons, lies down with naked hands.

Now Grendel enters on the tale—the ancient man-beast of the

folk-tale, the death-bringing winter of the myth to wrestle with the life-bringing summer of the early year. The colours are grim in which he is painted. So strong is he that the strength of thirty men can scarcely overcome him; four men must carry his huge head when he is slain; he smites in the great doors of the hall with a single blow of his hand; his nails are monstrous claws. He is the fiend of the morass and the moor, "lonely and terrible, a mighty mark-stepper who holds the fastnesses of the fells." Night is his native air. "In ever-night Grendel kept the misty moors," and the pools where the marsh-fire burns are his refuge. He is also the fiend of the weltering and furious sea. His companions are sea-monsters, and he lives with his fearful mother in a deep sea-cave, in a ghastly hollow of the rocks, where the billows tumble together and roar to heaven. Like his shape, like his dwelling, is his character; greedy of blood, ravenous, furious, joyless, hating men and their festive music, pleased with evil, always restless, roaming for prey—the creature of the winter and its fury, of the sunless gloom and its despair. If he find sleeping or drunken men in Heorot, he rends them to pieces, breaking the bones and drinking the blood, or bears them away to consume alone in the caverns of the moor or the sea. And he came this night. "In the wan darkness, while the warriors slept, the shadow-stalker drew near from the moorland; over the misty fells Grendel came ganging on; under the clouds he strode." He smote the door in, and when he saw the heroes sleeping his heart laughed and loathsome light flared from his eyes. He tore a warrior into shreds, and then he met the grip of Beowulf. Fear fell on him; the hall cracked and cried with the wrestling and the whoop of the beast; but Beowulf held on, and at last rent Grendel's arm from its socket; "the bone burst, the blood streamed," and the fiend fled to the sea-cave to die.

So in the morning there was wondrous joy in Heorot, games, horse-racing, poets making songs. The king and queen come to see Grendel's arm hung over the dais; fine gifts are given to the rescuers; the feast is set, the hall is cleansed; the bards, even the king, sing old sagas; night comes again and all once more sleep in the hall; each under his shield and spear and coat of woven rings.

Then begins the vengeance of Grendel's dam. This was originally a separate and later lay, and is now woven into the poem by the poet of the whole. The monster is described over again; new qualities are added to him, but Grendel's mother is a fresh creation. The details of the scenery are so particular that it is probable this second lay actually described the cliff scenery of the place where the maker of the lay lived. But the tale is another version of the original folk-tale and myth. Grendel's dam is like her son, only she belongs especially to the furious sea. She is greedy, restless, a death-spirit, a scather of men, a creature also of the mirk and mist. She swims the sea; clutches to Beowulf like a sea-monster; she is a "sea-wolf, a sea-woman, a wolf of the sea-bottom." Her hands are armed with claws; her blood is so venomous that even the magic-tempered blade which alone can slay her melts in her blood like ice in the sun. Wrath for her son drives her to Heorot, and she bursts into the hall, where Beowulf is not that night, and rends Æschere, Hrothgar's dearest friend, limb from limb, and bears him away to her cave. "Hast thou had a still night," asks Beowulf of Hrothgar in the morning. "Ask after no happiness," answered the king, "Æschere is dead, Yrmenlaf's elder brother, my rede-giver, my shoulder-to-shoulder-man in war. All is ill." He tells the tale of the night and of the place where Grendel's mother lives. "Seek it, if thou dare it; I will pay thee with old treasures." "Life is nothing," answers Beowulf. "Better vengeance for a friend than too much of sorrow for him. Who can win honour, let him do it before he die, for that is best for him when he is dead. Have patience of thy woes to-day; I look for that from thee. Neither in earth's breast, nor deep in the sea, shall Grendel's kin escape from me."

So they rode to the cliffs, and found themselves above a deep sea-gorge with a narrow entrance from the sea, where many "nickers" or sea-monsters were stretched upon the rocks, and in which the waves, beaten from side to side, made a mad whirlpool which flung its welter, black and ulcerous, into the sky. Landward the moor sloped downwards, and a stream fell over an arm of gray rock, under ice-nipt trees, into the pool below. The description, often quoted, is the first of those natural descriptions for which English poetry is famous, and which, frequent in Old English poetry, are so remarkable at this early time. It seems to have impressed the English writers, for there is a passage in the Blickling Homilies of the tenth century which reads almost like a quotation of this description.[1]   Secret in gloom is the land

> Where they ward ; wolf-haunted slopes ; swept with wind its nesses ;
> Fearful is its marish-path, where the mountain stream,
> Underneath the nesses' mist, nither makes its way.
> Under earth its flood is flowing, nor afar from here it is,
> But the measure of a mile where its mere is set.
> Over it, outreaching, hang the ice-nipt trees ;
> Held by roots the holt is fast, and o'er-helms the water.
> There an evil wonder every night a man may see—
> In the flood a fire.
> None alive is wise enough that abyss to know.
> If the heather-stepper, harried by the hounds,
> If the strong-horned stag seek unto this holt-wood,
> Put to flight from far, sooner will he flee his soul,
> Yield his life-breath on the bank—ere he will therein
> Try to hide his head.   Not unhaunted is the place !
> For the welter of the waves thence is whirled on high,
> Wan towards the clouds when the wind is stirring
> Wicked weather up, and the lift is waxing dark
> And the welkin weeping.

---

[1] It occurs in the sermon on the Archangel Michael : "As Paul looked towards the North from which all the floods came down, he saw a gray rock over the water and north of it were woods hung with icy rime. And dark mists were there, and under the cliff the dwellings of nickers and other monsters. And he saw how on the ice-clad trees many black souls were hanging with bound hands and the devils in shape of wolves seized on them like hungry wolves, and the flood under the cliff was black. And twelve miles beneath the cliffs was this water, and when the branches on which the souls hung, broke off, the souls fell into the water, and the water-monsters gripped them."

They ride down to the shelving rocks, and find Æschere's bloody head, and the water is red and troubled. One of the strange sea-dragons, imaged by the poet from the walrus and the tusked seal, is slain with arrows and spears, and the men gaze on the grisly guest; but Beowulf, arming himself, and taking Unferth's sword, Hrunting, one of the old treasures of the world, plunged into the ocean surge. But the sea-wolf saw him, and bore him upwards into her dwelling, a cave where water was not. A weird light was there, and the hero struck at the mere-woman. But the war-beam would not bite, and Grendel's dam seized Beowulf and flung him down as he stumbled, and drew her seax, brown-edged, and drove at his heart. His war-sark withstood the blow, and Beowulf leaped to his feet. And he saw, hanging on the wall, an old sword of the Eotens, hallowed by victory, doughty of edges, a pride of warriors, and, seizing the gold-charmed hilt, he smote at the sea-wolf's neck. The brand gripped on her throat, broke through the bone into the body, and she fell dead on the sand. Again he looked round, rejoicing in his work, and there by the wall lay Grendel, lifeless and weary of war; and his body sprang far away as the hero smote off his head. The blood streamed into the water and Hrothgar's thegns saw it and crying, "We shall see him no more," went their way to Heorot. But Beowulf's thegns sat on, and at last the hero rose through the bloody sea, bearing the golden hilt and Grendel's head. Proudly they marched back to Heorot, and the four men who bore on spears the head of Grendel flung it at the feet of Hrothgar. Beowulf told his tale of victory; feasting brought on the night, and night the morning, "over shadows sliding." Great gifts were given and alliance sworn; and Beowulf went home, over the meads and over the sea, to Hygelac, and gave his gifts—horses and gray war-shirts, and a collar like the Brising collar—to Hygelac and Hygd his queen. And Hygelac gave Beowulf a gold-inlaid sword, and seven thousand in money, and a country seat and the dignity of a prince—and so the first part of the poem is at an end.

The second part opens some sixty years afterwards, when Beowulf has succeeded Heardred, Hygelac's son, and has reigned for fifty years. He has outlived all enmity, and dwells in peace, worshipped by his people, till he is past eighty years of age. The summer of his life has died, late autumn has come, and the sun-king now goes forth to his last fight with the dragon of the winter, and to secure for his people the golden fruits hidden in the earth. He wins the treasure, but in the battle dies.

The myth twists itself, through a folk-tale, into the following story. One of Beowulf's thegns found a high barrow on the cliffs, where a dragon watched a treasure laid by three hundred years ago, and stole a cup therefrom. At which the drake, furious, flew forth at night to avenge his wrong, vomiting flashes of fire. The palace-hall, the homes, the country, were all aflame, and Beowulf, hot as of old, let an iron shield be made, under which to slay the ravager. The cave where the dragon lurks is in a valley-dip between two headlands whose cliffs plunge into the sea. These have their names, Hronesnæs and Earnanæs, the Ness of the Whale, the Ness of the Earns. The dell between them has low cliffs on either side, and on the ridge of the right-hand cliff is a wood, where Beowulf sits and sings his death song before he goes down into the meadow below, and where his frightened thegns take refuge. It is on this side that Beowulf, with his back to the rocks, is brought to bay by the dragon. On the other side, but higher up the dell, the great barrow stands, and near it the cave, entered by a rocky arch; and here is the lair of the worm. A stream breaks from the mouth of the cave, and runs down the dell to lose itself in the gray heath which from the inland rises to the cliffs. This is the place where Beowulf finds his last foe and his death. And he sat down, and sang the deeds of his life. "I remember all, since I was seven years old." He bade his men farewell, and armed himself, for he has to fight with fire. "Not a foot will I fly the ward of the hill; but at the rock wall it shall be as Wyrd wills, Wyrd, the measurer of the lives of men. Wait ye on the hill, clad in your byrnies. Then the fierce champion, brave under helm, bore his mail sark down to the rocks." And he shouted, seeing the cave and the stream smoking with the dragon's breath, and his shout was like a storm. Now the ward of the hoard knew the voice of a man, and rolling in curves, and his fiery breath burning before him while the earth roared, he struck at Beowulf with his head. And the king smote hard, but Nægling, his sword, slid off the bone, and in a moment Beowulf was wrapt in flame. Then all his thegns fled, save one, Wiglaf, his kinsman, who, wading through the deadly reek, stood beside his lord. "Ward thy life, loved Beowulf, think on fame, I will stand by thee." And the hero smote again, but Nægling broke, and the drake clasped his paws round the king's throat till the life-blood bubbled forth in waves. But Wiglaf struck lower into the belly of the beast, and the fire abated; whereat Beowulf drew his deadly seax, bitter and battle-sharp, and clove the worm in two. So the battle ended.

But the king had got his death. The venom boiled in his breast, and he sat down to think, and to look at the arch of the cave, while Wiglaf unloosed his helm. And he spoke his death-words: "Would I could give to a son this war-weed of mine, but I have none sprung from my loins. Fifty winters I held my sway over my folk; nor durst any king greet me with his war-friends or press on me the terror of war. I tarried at home on the hour of my weird; I held mine own fitly; I sought no feuds; I swore no oaths which I did not keep, and I swore few; so I may, for all this, have comfort, since the Master of men may not charge me with murder-bale of kinsmen, when life flies from my body. Now hasten, dear Wiglaf, and bring the hoard out of the hollow rock, that I may see the ancient wealth, so that, after sight of it, I may the easier give up my life, and the peopleship I have held so long."

And Wiglaf, hastening, saw in the worm's den the glittering gold, and many treasures; and, greatest of wonders, an all-golden banner, curious in handiwork, woven with magic songs, and shedding a wizard light over all things in the cave. And he brought forth the treasure. "I thank the glorious king," cried Beowulf, "that, ere I die, I have won these things for my people; have paid my old life for them. But do thou supply the need of my folk, I may no longer be here."

> Bid the battle-famed build a barrow high,
> Clear to see when bale is burnt, on the bluffs above the surge.
> Thus it may for folk of mine, for remembering of me,
> Lift on high its head, on the height of Hronesnæs;
> So that soon sea-sailing men, in succeeding days,
> Call it Beowulf's Barrow; when, their barks a-foam,
> From afar they make their way through the mists of Ocean.

And he did off from his neck the golden collar, and gave his helm and ring and mail-coat to Wiglaf. "Use them well," he said. "Thou art the last of the Wægmundings. Wyrd swept them all away; strong earls they were; each at the weirded hour. I must go after them. This was the last of the thoughts of his heart." So Wiglaf sat alone, with his dead lord in the green dell between the two cliffs; and on the meadow lay the fire-drake, fifty feet of him, and the broken sword, and the gold cups and dishes, rings, and jewels: swords rusted with three hundred winters; and above them, as was Scyld's honour when he died, the golden banner glistened. And all the host, and the twelve thegns who had fled, came down to see the sight and their dead king. And Wiglaf reproached the faithless who had deserted their lord; and the passage marks one of the main Teutonic conceptions:—

> Now shall getting gems, and the giving too of swords,
> And the pleasure of a home, and possession of the land,
> Be no more to kin of yours! Every man of kin to you
> Shall bereft of land-right roam, when the lords shall hear
> Of your deep damnation. Death is better far,
> For whatever warrior, than a woeful life of shame.

And the messenger who tells of the king's death to the host prophesies that because of it the old feud with the Sweons will break out again. "The leader of our battle has ceased from laughter, from sport and the joy of song. The treasures will be borne away, the maidens shall walk in alien fields, the hands (of ghosts?) shall lift the spear, morning cold, and the harp shall never more

> With its ringing rouse the warriors, but the Raven wan,
> Eager, fiercely, o'er the fated, shall be full of talking,
> Croaking to the sallow Earn how it sped him at the gorging,
> When he, with the wolf, on the war-stead tore the slain.

So the three beasts, like the Valkyrie, shall speak of their bloody work.

Then Wiglaf told of the battle, and of the burial the king wished for; and they laded a wain with the treasures, and heaved the drake over the cliff, and carried Beowulf to the further edge of Whale's Ness; and Wiglaf sang, while he laid with care the gray-headed warrior on the bier:—

> Now the Gleed shall fret,
> And the wannish flame wax high, on this War-strength of his warriors—
> Him who oft awaited iron showers in the battle,
> When the storm of arrows, sent a-flying from the strings,
> Shot above the shield-wall; and the shaft its service,
> Fledged with feathers, did, following on the barb.

So they made a great barrow, labouring for ten days, timbered-up on high, to be seen far and wide by those who fared the main; and did into it armlets and bright gems and the ashes of their lord, and hung it with shields and helms and shining shirts of war.

> Then about the barrow rode the beasts of battle,
> Twelve in all they were, bairns of Æthelings,
> Who would speak their sadness, sing their sorrow for their king.
> So, with groaning, grieved, all the Geät folk,
> All his hearth-companions for their House-lord's overthrow!
> Quoth they, that he was, of the world-kings all,
> Of all men the mildest, and to men the kindest,
> To his people gentlest, and of praise the keenest.

With these words of farewell *Beowulf* closes; and this carefully-wrought conclusion and the summing up of the hero's character go far to prove that, however many ancient lays were used by the writer, the poem was composed as a whole by one poet who had the keenest sympathy with the heathen traditions of his people, and who may himself have been, like many folk in the eighth century, half heathen at heart. The Christian interpolations, I have already said, may have been made, not by him, but by the Wessex editor of the saga in the tenth century. At any rate, they are few, and of slight importance. Some, who have not, it seems, read the poem, make a great deal of them, and say they spoil the poem. They are, it is true, quite out of place and jarring when they occur. But they are curiously brief, with the exception of the sermon of Hrothgar about pride; and they are easily set aside. The poet was remarkably merciful, and thought too well of his original material to do much of this Christianising work. I have, however, sometimes thought that the second part of the poem, the fight with the dragon, may have been frankly heathen, and that the later editor made omissions in consequence, for this part is much broken up and confused. Whatever may be said of this conjecture, it remains true that the form of the first part is good and clear; that of the second not. Loose lays are introduced into it without any just arrangement; and the story of the theft from the dragon is told twice over. But when that is said, criticism has but little left to say but praise, especially when we think of the early date at which the poem was made. Its lays go back to the seventh, perhaps to the sixth century; its composition as a whole to the eighth. No other extant modern poem—the Welsh poems of the sixth century and some Irish verse being excepted—can approach its age, save, perhaps, that fragment of *Hadubrand and Hildebrand* found at Fulda, said to date from the eighth century, and to have been sung as a lay in the seventh. But this is a mere fragment; *Beowulf* is a complete poem. Its age dignifies it, excuses its want of form, and demands our reverence.

What poetic standard it reaches is another question. It has been called an epic, but it is narrative rather than epic poetry. The subject has not the weight or dignity of an epic poem, nor the mighty fates round which an epic should revolve. Its story is rather personal than national. The one epic quality it has, the purification of the hero, the evolution of his character through trial into perfection—and Beowulf passes from the isolated hero into the image of an heroic king who dies for his people—may belong to a narrative poem. Moreover the poem is made up of two narratives with an interval of some sixty years, an interval which alone removes it from the epic method, which is bound to perfect the subject in an ordered, allotted, and continuous space of time. But as a narrative, even broken as it is, it attains unity from the unity of the myth it represents under two forms, and from the unity of the hero's character. He is the same in soul, after fifty years, that he was when young. There is also a force, vitality, clearness and distinctiveness of portraiture, not only in Beowulf's personality, but in that of all the other personages, which raise the poem into a high place, and predict that special excellence of personal portraiture which has made the English drama so famous in the world. Great imagination is not one of the excellences of *Beowulf*, but it has pictorial power of a fine kind, and the myth of summer and winter on which it rests is out of the imagination of the natural and early world. It has a clear vision of places and things and persons; it has preserved for us two monstrous types out of the very early world. When we leave out the repetitions which oral poetry created and excuses, it is rapid and direct; and the dialogue is brief, simple and human. Finally, we must not judge it in the study. If we wish to feel whether *Beowulf* is good poetry, we should place ourselves, as evening draws on, in the hall of the folk, when the benches are filled with warriors, merchants and seamen, and the Chief sits in the high seat, and the fires flame down the midst, and the cup goes round —and hear the Shaper strike the harp to sing this heroic lay. Then, as he sings of the great fight with Grendel or the dragon, of the treasure-giving of the king, and of the well-known swords, of the sea-rovings and the sea-hunts and the brave death of men, to sailors who knew the storms, to the fierce rovers who fought and died with glee, to great chiefs who led their warriors, and to warriors who never left a shield, we feel how heroic the verse is, how passionate with national feeling, how full of noble pleasure. The poem is great in its own way, and the way is an English way. The men, the women, at home and in war, are one in character with us. It is our Genesis, the book of our origins.

CHAPTER V

SEMI-HEATHEN POETRY

WE are still in heathen times when we accompany the Jutes across the sea to the conquest of Kent. Other Jutes, a good time afterwards, took and colonised the Isle of Wight and a small piece of the adjacent mainland. News of the conquest of Kent reached the Saxons, and the first band of them, landing near Chichester, completed the conquest of Sussex in 491. Wessex began to be made by a second band of Saxons under Cerdic, but it was not till 577, after the battle of Deorham, that the West Saxons, having previously conquered Dorset and Wilts, secured the north of Somerset, reached the Bristol Channel, and seizing the valley of the Severn, occupied our Herefordshire and Worcestershire. The third tribe, the Angles, left Denmark about 547. They settled in the district they named Norfolk and Suffolk; they seized the coasts of Yorkshire and subdivided it westward to the Pennine chain. They subdued the northern coast as far as the Firth of Forth and the land westward to the valley of the Clyde and Cumberland. The Yorkshire part they called Deira, "the southland," and the northern Bernicia, "the land of the Braes," and these two, when they were afterwards united, made Northumbria. Then all the rest of the Angles poured across the sea, leaving their old lands so totally uninhabited that the Angles are never mentioned again among the German tribes; and these belated invaders, passing through the East Anglian lands, turned south and west and won the middle of England as far as the Vale of the Severn. As these English called the borderland between them and the Welsh the March, they called themselves the Mercians. Meanwhile, other Saxon bands conquered Middlesex where London was, and Essex where was Colchester. So all England, save the three Welsh kingdoms—the Kingdom of Devon and Cornwall, that is, West Wales; the Kingdom of our North and South Wales; and the Kingdom of Cumberland with the Clyde valley—belonged to the English. This conquest—for the Brythons fought with desperate and steady courage, unlike the English against the Normans after Senlac—took about 150 years. During this period the poetry of England was altogether heathen, unbroken by a single Christian voice. But there is no doubt that every famous fight and the deeds of kings and warriors were sung by the English bards in ballad form, and grew into sagas of the Conquest of England.

The only English poem which has any relation to the Conquest is the fragment called the *Ruined Burg*. It is now generally allowed to be a description of Bath (Bathanceaster), which was sacked and burnt by Ceawlin after the battle of Deorham in 577.[1] The Saxons left it, for they scorned to dwell in towns, and the wild forest grew in the colonnades and porches of the hot springs, over the Forum and the public buildings of the Romans. It was not till a century after, in 676, that Osric, an under-king of the Hwiccas, founded a monastery among its ruins; and more than a century later, in 781, that Offa, seeing the importance of the place, encouraged the new town into a vigorous life. Some poet, coming in a chieftain's train to visit the place—we may say in the eighth century—and wandering on a frosty morning among the fallen buildings, was smitten to the heart by the sorrow of so much ruin, and made this poem, which has no Christian elements in it, but much humanity. Its motive—imagin-

[1] It is possible that the Roman buildings may have fallen into ruin before Ceawlin attacked the town. It is also possible that the poem may describe not Bath, but Camelot.

ative sadness for the departure of splendour and life—became common in early English poetry.

Wondrous is this wall of stone; Weirds have shattered it!
Broken are the burg-steads, crumbled down the giants' work!
Fallen are the roof-beams, ruined are the towers:
All undone the door-pierced turrets; frozen dew is on their plaster.
Shorn away and sunken down, are the sheltering battlements,
Under-eaten of Old Age! Earth is holding in her clutch
These, the power-wielding workers; all forworn and all forlorn in death are
    they.
Hard the grip is of the ground, while a hundred generations
Move away. . . .
Long its wall abode
Through the rule that followed rule, ruddy-stained, and grey as goat,
Under storm-skies steady. Steep the Court that fell;
Brilliant were the burg-steads; burn-fed houses many;
High the heap of hornèd gables; of the host a mickle sound.
Many were the mead-halls, full of mirth of men,
Till the strong-willed Wyrd whirled that all to change.
In a slaughter wide they fell, woeful days of bale came on;
Famine-death fortook fortitude from men!
All their battle-bulwarks bared to their foundations are;
Crumbled is the castle keep! . . .
                . . . Many a brave man there
Glad of yore, a-gleam with gold, gloriously adorned,
Hot with wine, and haughty, in war-harness shone;
Saw upon his silver, on set gems and treasure,
On his welfare and his wealth, on his well-wrought jewels,
On this brightsome burg of a broad dominion!

Then the baths are described—the steam surging hotly through the courts of stone and whirling round and round, the waves filling the great circle of the bath, "a kingly thing," or a place where a "Thing" might assemble.

There is no trace of Christian sentiment in the poem, and this want seems remarkable. But we must remember that Christianity, after its introduction in 597, took nearly a century to conquer the whole of England, and left, even after the last heathen district was christianised in 686, a great part of the wild country and its farmers all but heathen. It is not strange then that a good deal of poetry among the people was scarcely touched by Christianity. It is probable that many laymen, who, like Cynewulf in his youth, lived as poets in the train of chieftains, had, though nominally Christians, little or no Christian feeling. Even when they were "converted" they easily recurred, at least whenever they sang of war, or of the sea, or of personal sorrow other than that for sin, to the old heathen lays for inspiration. The *Riddles* of Cynewulf, the *Elegies*, the passages concerning war in the Cædmonic poems and in the Christian poems of Cynewulf are all heathen in tone and manner. The same may be said of even so late a poem as the *Song of Brunanburh*. It is not till we come to the *Battle of Maldon*, 991, that we meet with a poem of war which mingles Christian prayer and inspiration with the noise of arms and the passion of fame. Therefore, before we discuss the poetry which is distinctively Christian, it will be well to consider that poetry of war, of nature, and of daily life which has no Christian elements in it, even when it occurs in Christian poems.

War was the chief business and the chief glory of the Germanic tribes. And being waged for the sake of home and fame, adventure and revenge, it became, through the ideality of these things, the chief subject of song. Everything that belonged to it was clothed in imaginative dress. All weapons, and chiefly the sword, were glorified; and the great smiths, like Weland, were the themes of legend. Battle was attended by spiritual beings, by Wyrd, by the Shield-Maidens, by Woden in his coat of gray, by the spirits who became at one with the famous swords and spears of heroes. Even the creatures of the wood and the air who devoured the dead, the gray-eagle, the raven, the kite, the hawk from the cliff, the wolf and the hill-fox, were impersonated. They screamed, croaked, howled their battle-song, they talked with one another as they rent the dead, and the note of their cries foretold the issue of the battle. They are rarely absent from the poetry of war.

Cynewulf conceives the sword in one of his *Riddles*, and with all his impersonating power, as a warrior wrapped in his scabbard as in a coat of mail, going like a hero into battle, hewing his path into the ranks of the foe, praised in the hall by kings, and eyen mourning, when it is laid by, for its childlessness and for the anger with which women treat it as the slaughterer of men. Impersonation can scarcely go further, yet it is not too far among men who conceived of a living being in the sword. In another *Riddle* Cynewulf impersonates the shield, and in others the helmet, the spear, and the bow. The shield is sick of battles, no physician can heal its wounds, it is weary of the sword-edges, notched day and night with the mighty strokes of the sword, that "heritage of hammers." The helmet mourns the bitter weather it has to bear, and as the lines sketch a northern storm I quote them :—

> On me, still upstanding, smite the showers of rain ;
> Hail, the hard grain, beats on me, and the hoar-frost covers me ;
> And the flying snow (in flakes) thickly falls on me.

The spear wails that as a sapling it was taken from the green fields and forced to bow to a slaughterer's will ; but as it comes to know its master better, it learns to love his fame as its own, and to be happy. Then it is proud of its small neck and fallow sides: rejoicing when the sun glitters on its point and a hand of strength is on its shaft, when it knows its way in battle. The bow exults, singing with savage joy when out of its bosom fares forth an adder, hot to sting, venomous against the foe.

> Then a drink of death he buys,
> Brimming sure the beaker that he buys with life.

The coat of mail cries that he was brought out of the bosom of the dewy meadowland, and woven into rings, not with the shuttle, not through the crafts of the Fate goddesses, but to be the honoured web of fighters, famous far along the earth. The horn boasts that he is kissed of warriors, that he summons comrades to battle, that the horse on land and the ocean-horse on sea bear him on adventure, that he calls the haughty heroes to the wine-feast and makes the plundering pirates fly to their ships with his shouting. These are all sketches from Cynewulf's hand, and were written while he was a wild boon-companion of his lord. No touch of Christian thinking intrudes on their heathen hardihood. They tell us how the ancient English thought of their war-weapons, and they have abundant literary power.

Then, many of the finest passages in Old English poetry are descriptions of battles. They occur in Christian poems, but they recollect in every line the spirit of the heathen poetry. When the Jews in *Judith* pressed towards the Assyrian host, making a shield-burg as they went, they sent spear and arrow over their yellow shields.

> Letten forth be flying shower-flights of darts,
> Adders of the battle, arrows hard of temper,
> From the horn-curved bows! Loud and high they shouted,
> Warriors fierce in fighting.
>
> . . . .
>
> Then rejoiced the gaunt Wolf,
> Rushing from the wood; and the Raven wan,
> Slaughter-greedy fowl! Surely well they knew
> That the war-thegns of the folk thought to win for them
> Fill of feasting on the fated. On their track flew fast the Earn,
> Hungry for his fodder, all his feathers dropping dew:
> Sallow was his garment, and he sang a battle lay;
> Horny-nebbed he was.

When in the *Exodus* Pharaoh's host draws nigh, the poet sees

> Forth and forward-faring Pharaoh's war-array,
> Gliding on, a grove of spears! Glittering the hosts!
> Fluttered there the flags of war, there the folk the march trod.
> Onwards surged the war, strode the spears along,
> Blickered the broad shields, loudly blew the trumpets.
>
> . . . .
>
> Wheeling round in gyres, yelled the fowls of war,
> Of the battle greedy! Hoarsely barked the Raven,
> Dew upon his feathers, o'er the fallen corpses;
> Swart was that slain-chooser! Loudly sang the wolves
> At the eve their awful song, eager for the carrion!

When in the *Elene* Constantine joins battle with the Huns, Cynewulf's description is pagan:—

> Forth then fares the Fyrd of folk, and a fighting lay
> Sang the wolf in woodland, wailed his slaughter-rune.
> Dewy-feathered, on the foes' track,
> Raised the Earn his song. . . .
> . . . Loud upsang the Raven,
> Swart and slaughter-fell. Strode along the war-host,
> Blew on high the horn-bearers, heralds of the battle shouted;
> Stamped the earth the stallion, and the host assembled
> Quickly to the quarrel!
> There the trumpets sang
> Loud before the war-host, and the raven loved the work.
> Dewy-plumed, the earn looked upon the march;
> . . . Song the wolf uplifted
> Ranger of the bolt! Rose the Terror of the battle!
> There was rush of shields together, and the crush of men together;
> Hard was the hand-swinging there, and the dinging down of hosts,
> After they had first encountered flying of the arrows.
> Full of hate, the hosters grim, on the fated folk
> Sent the spears above the shields, and the shower of arrows.
> Strode the stark of spirit, stroke on stroke they pressed along,
> Broke into the board-wall, plunged their bills therein.
> Where the bold in battle thronged, there the banner was uplifted;
> Victory's song was sung round the ensign of the host;
> And the javelins glistened, and the golden helm
> O'er the field of fight; till there fell the heathen,
> Dead in ruthless slaughter.

These are but a few examples of the pagan keenness in the war-song lasting on into the Christian poetry, and they probably belong to the eighth century when Christianity had been fully established in England.

When we turn from war to that natural description which is so remarkable in Old English poetry, we are neither in a specially heathen nor in a specially Christian world of thought. Where the descriptions are connected with the nature-myths, the heathen elements of course exist, but the natural description in early English poetry goes far beyond the phrases derived from the myths.

Where the descriptions occur in poems on Christian subjects, they are as it were apart from the theme; the poet steps aside, as if led by a personal fondness, to describe the things he sees in sea or sky. The only set description of nature which is intimately inwoven with Christian thought is that of the sinless and lovely land in the *Phœnix*, and it is not done from nature, but from imagination. Moreover, its origin is in the poem of Lactantius which the poet was adapting, and which itself had a far-off origin in the Celtic myth of the Land of Eternal Youth. Independent, however, of these descriptions, the *Riddles* of Cynewulf insert deliberate and careful descriptions of natural scenery, not as a background for human interest, but for the sake of nature alone, and this is quite singular in early modern poetry.

The chief natural things of which the English poets wrote were the forest-land, the sky, and the sea. The forest-land was all the wild uncultivated country, on the outskirts of which, and continually scooping their way back from the river valleys into it, the English lived and set up their hamlets. Scattered records of this forest-land occur in the poems. The moor, roamed over by the wolves, the grizzly heath-tramplers; in the pools and caves of which dwelt the water elves and the dragon of the English imagination; does not fill so large a place as the fens, where the anchorites built their hermitages, and the fisher watched the "brown-backed billow" come in with the tide, and the wild birds came to St. Guthlac's hand. But the woods were nearest to the English life. The various trees are described in verse—the yew, the oak, the holly, and the birch. "Laden with leaves is the birch, high is its helm, decked out with beauty its branches, in touch with the air." A wild refuge in a forest hollow for the outlaw or the exile is closely described:—

> Men have garred me dwell in a grove of woodland,
> Under an oak-tree, hidden in an earthen cave.
> Old is this earth-hall; I am all outwearied;
> Dark are these deep dells, high the downs above;
> Bitter my burg-hedges, with wild briars overwaxen.

> When in early dawn all alone I go
> Underneath the oak, round about my lair,
> There I sit and weep through the summer-lengthened day.
> Wife's Complaint.

The animals which haunt the wood are described—the wolves, the swine, the wild cattle, the stag tossing his head "while the gray frost fled from his hair," the badger on the slopes of the forest hills, the beaver in the river, and the salmon darting in the pools; the eagle, the raven, and the hawk from their homes in the recesses of the woods; the falcon on the noble's fist, brought from the wild sea cliff; the cuckoo shouting in the glen and announcing the spring, the starlings rising and falling in flocks among the village roofs [Riddle lviii.] :—

> Here the air beareth wights that are little,
> O'er the hill-summits, and deep black are they,
> Swart, sallow-coated! sweet is their song,
> Flocking they fly on, shrilly they sing,
> Roam the wood-cliffs, and at whiles the town-dwellings
> Of the children of men.

So also Cynewulf sings the nightingale, and paints the hamlet as the bird pours its song on the air, and the men sitting at their doors listening in silence [Riddle ix.] :—

> Many varied voices voice I through my bill;
> Holding to my tones, hiding not their sweetness—
> I, the ancient evening-singer, bring unto the Earls
> Bliss within the burgs, when I break along
> With a cadenced song. Silent in their dwelling
> They are sitting, leaning forwards.

But the most charming of these descriptions is that of the wild swan, whose feathers, like those of the swan-maidens, sound in flight [Riddle viii.] :—

> Voiceless is my robe when in villages I dwell,
> When I fare the fields, when I drive the flood along.
> But at times my glorious garment and the lofty air
> Heave me high above all the houses of the heroes.

> Wheresoe'er the craft[1] of clouds carries me away,
> Far the folk above—then my fretted feathers
> Loudly rustling hum, lulling, sound along,
> Sing a sunbright song—then, restrained to earth no more,
> Over flood and field I'm a spirit faring far!

This is of a quality almost unimaginable in poetry of the eighth century. It is like poetry of our own time. The "power of clouds" is a phrase Wordsworth might have used.

The poetry of the sky, of sun and moon, and of the sea is equally remarkable. The northern English were close observers of these great Creatures, and one proof of this lies in the number of words they invented to express their different aspects. The changes of the dawn from the first gray tinge of the east to the upward leap of the sun, the noonday light, the changes of the evening from the light left by immediate sunset to the last glimmer of it before dead night, have each their own special words. The fiercer phases of the weather are drawn with a rough observant pencil. Cynewulf describes three different kinds of storms. But no natural object engaged them so much as the sea, and they have at least fifteen different names for it, to express their conceptions of its aspect and its temper. Then they have coined a multitude of phrases to represent the appearance of its waves, and its movements in calm, but chiefly in storm, most of which I have given an account of elsewhere. There can be no doubt from his poetry that Cynewulf lived constantly near the sea and a rocky coast, and that he watched it with all the care of Tennyson. But the temper of mind in which he and his school, after the settlement, considered the sea was very different from the temper of the sailors of the heathen time. Beowulf and his comrades have the spirit of the sea-dogs of Drake and Nelson. They rejoice in the storms, the ocean is their playmate; they are its masters, or they fight with it as with a monster for their lives. Five nights in all (and if the story be a myth yet the spirit of the swimmers is not), Breca and Beowulf swam in rivalry through the

[1] *Power.*

ocean in the bitterest of weathers and fought with the tusked nickers of the deep [*Beowulf*, ll. 546-548].

> Swoln were the surges, of storms 'twas the coldest;
> Dark neared the night, and northern the wind,
> Rattling and roaring, rough were the billows !

till in the morning the heaving of ocean bore them up on the land of the Heathoraemes.

This fearlessness ceased when they settled down and passed from pirates into agriculturists. There is not a trace in the poetry after Cædmon of their old audacious lordship over the sea. The *Seafarer* tells of his voyages, and how he outlived hours of pain and dread, sailing his ship through frosty seas: "No man on land can tell all he suffers who fares on the wanderings of the deep." The crew in the *Riddle* on the Hurricane are aghast with fear. The companions of Andreas on his voyage are terrified when the storm begins. It is always the merchant sailor and not the Viking who speaks in the later poems. But the imaginative representation of the sea, and especially in storm, is all the greater perhaps for this temper of dread. Here are a few lines out of the *Andreas* [ll. 369; 441] :—

> Then was sorely troubled,
> Sorely wrought the Whale-mere. Wallowed there the Horn-fish,
> Glided through the great deep; and the gray-backed gull
> Wheeled in air, of slaughter greedy ! Dark the storm-sun grew :
> Waxed the wind in gusts, grinded there the waves together.
> Stirred the surges high; and the sail-ropes groaned,
> Wet with washing waves. Water-Horror rose
> With the might of troops.
>
> . . . .
>
> Ocean-streamings then
> Beat upon the bulwarks ! Billow answered billow,
> Wave replied to wave. And at whiles uprose
> From the bosom of the foam to the bosom of the boat
> Terror o'er the wave-ship.

Along with this vivid description of a storm at sea we may place, and also from the *Andreas*, this description of the coming of winter on the land [ll. 1257-1264]:—

        Snow enchained the earth
With the whirling winter-flakes, and the weather grew
Cold with savage scours of hail; while the sleet and frost,
Gangers gray of war were they—! locked the granges up
Of the heroes, and folk-hamlets ! Frozen hard was all the land
    With the chill of icicles ; shrunk the courage of the water ;
    O'er the running rivers ice upraised a bridge,
    And the sea-road shone.

Cynewulf's imagination of nature is perhaps highest when, in the thirty-fourth *Riddle*, he paints the iceberg plunging and roaring through the foaming sea, and shouting out, like a Viking, his coming to the land, singing and laughing terribly. Sharp are the swords he uses in the battle, grim is his hate; he is greedy to break into the shield-walls of the ships. Nor is he less vigorous when he describes the storm on land in the second *Riddle*, and the storm at sea in the third, and the whole progress of a hurricane in the fourth, from its letting loose, like a delivered giant, from the caverns under the earth, to its driving of the flood of sea, gray as flint, upon the cliffs; from the thunder of the mountainous advance of ocean under its impulse, to the shipwreck it makes and the terror of the seamen. Then he brings the tempest from the sea into the air, and then on the works of men, and finally lulls it to sleep again in its cave. There is no finer description of a great northern gale than this in the whole of our literature. I have translated it fully in an appendix, but it ought to be read in its own language. I may give one more example of this nature-poetry, of a fine poetical quality. It uses one of the old nature-myths with remarkable skill, and fills it with vivid natural description. The first two lines describe the old moon with the young moon in her arms long before Sir Patrick Spence saw it. The rising of the sun over the roof of the world, his setting, the dust and dew and the advent of night are done with the conciseness and force of Tennyson.

Cynewulf saw the crescent moon like a boat of air and light sailing up the heaven, and the old myths came into his mind. So he likened the moon to a young warrior returning with his spoil, and building a fortress in the height of heaven. But another and a greater warrior, even the Sun, was in hot pursuit, who, coming over the horizon wall, took the moon's booty and drove him away with great wrath. Then the Sun, full of his vengeance, hastened to the West, and then Night arose and overwhelmed the Sun. It is a true piece of nature-poetry, built on an ancient nature-myth [Riddle xxx.] :—

> Of a wight I've been aware, wonderfully shapen,
> Bearing up a booty in between his horns !
> 'Twas a Lift-ship, flashing light, and with loveliness bedecked,
> Bearing home his booty brought from his war-roving ;
> All to build a bower for it, in the burg on high,
> And to shape it skilfully if it so might be !
> Then, all wondrous, came a wight, o'er the world-wall's roof ;
> Known to all he is of the earth's indwellers ;
> Snatched away his war-spoil, and his will against,
> Homeward drove the wandering wretch ! Thence he westward went,
> With a vengeance faring ; then he hastened further on !
> Dust arose to Heaven, dew fell on the earth,
> Onward came the Night ! And not one of men
> Of the wandering of that wight ever wotted more.

That there should be so much deliberate nature-poetry, written for the sake of nature alone, and with an evident and observing love, is most remarkable in vernacular poetry of the eighth century, and very difficult to account for. There is nothing that resembles it, even in the later Icelandic sagas. It is only partly derived from nature-myths. We may say in explanation that the Celtic influence was very strong in Northumbria where these poems were written, and the Celtic feeling for natural scenery is always strong. But the feeling here is different from the Celtic; and it is rather in the imaginative quality of the verse and in certain charmed expressions that we detect the Celtic spirit. It has been said, again, that these *Riddles* were nothing more than imitations of the Latin *Ænigmata* on the same subjects. This is no explanation. Cynewulf took the subjects, but he transformed the treatment; whatever he takes he makes original. Ealdhelm's Latin *Riddles* have not a trace of imagination, Cynewulf is impassioned with it. Ealdhelm writes like an imitator of the late Latin poets, Cynewulf writes out of his own delight and from the sight of his own eyes. We cannot mistake his personal love of nature. Where, at this time, did he gain it? How does he happen to have it in a way which scarcely appears again until the nineteenth century?

Perhaps the best answer is that he was a man of genius, but then genius moves in the groove of its own time, and this is not a groove which belongs to the time. The one thing I can think of in the way of explanation is that he was a reader of Vergil, and there are passages in his poems and in the *Andreas* which seem directly suggested by Vergil. We know that Vergil was commonly read by literary men in Northumbria, and no one, with a natural tendency to the observation of nature, could long read Vergil without being put into the temper of love of nature, and of a close observation of her ways. Once the temper was gained, the original genius of Cynewulf would use it on the natural scenery which surrounded him. But then, other men read Vergil and did not write like Cynewulf. There must have been something singular in the man. At any rate, it is interesting, considering the magnificent work which the English poets have done on nature, to find at the very beginning of our poetry one who was so filled with pleasure by her doings, and who had the power to put his pleasure into noble expression.

These poems then, poems of war and poems of pure nature, may be called half-heathen, though written in Christian times. What changes Christianity wrought in poetry is now our subject.

CHAPTER VI

THE COMING OF CHRISTIANITY

THE English literature written of in the previous chapters has been heathen or secular. The passages about war and those dealing with the natural world, taken from poems written when England had become Christian, show clearly how long the temper of heathendom clung to the English, even to those who had warmly accepted the new religion. Long after the last conquest of Christianity, heathenism retained its power over the superstitious farmers and folk of the remoter hamlets. Even in the days of Cnut, the laws forbid the worship of heathen gods, of sun and moon, of rivers and wells, of fire, stones, and trees. For a long time, then, Christianity and heathendom mingled their influences together, and they did so in comparative peace. The growth of Christianity was left to the will of the people. It was not forced upon them by the sword. There was so much wisdom and tolerance on the part of the kings and nobles that the two faiths scarcely ever persecuted one another during the many years they existed side by side. Even Penda, that sturdy Mercian pagan, did not prevent the preaching of the faith in his kingdom, and allowed his son to become a Christian.

The result of this long intermingling was that heathen ideas were not so much rooted out in literature as changed. There was a continual interpenetration of Christian and heathen elements, of Christian and heathen legend, which had no small influence upon the early Christian poetry of England. The mythical representations of Nature—the Sun hasting up the sky like an eager youth, the march of my lord Darkness over the earth, the Moon building his burg in the topmost vault of heaven against the onset of the Sun, the vast "Chasm of chasms" out of which the worlds were made, the all-covering, swart ocean—are mythical conceptions which endure. We find them in the poems of *Genesis* and *Exodus*, and in the poems of Cynewulf. The great nature-festivals of Yule- and Eostra-tide were taken into Christian service, and bound up with the story of the birth and resurrection of Jesus. The festival of Midsummer lives in many Christian observances. New Christian feasts were made to fall on heathen holidays. The Church took the place of the heathen temple, the Holy Rood of the sacred tree; the groves of the Nature God became the groves of the convent. The hills, the wells, the river islands, once dedicated to deities of flood and fell, were called after the saints and martyrs. The minor gods and heroes which the various wants of men created to satisfy these wants were replaced by saints who did precisely the same work. The gracious and beneficent work done by the gods kind to man was now done by Jesus and the Virgin; while the cruel and dreadful monsters of frost and gloom were embodied in Satan and his harmful host. In this way the emotions of the past and their pleasant poetic joy, the primitive imaginations and their popular influence, were retained unimpaired, though all the names were changed. The ancient heathen stuff endured, but it was Christianised. The same things happened, under the wisdom of the Roman Church, over all freshly converted lands, but they happened with persecution. In England they happened without it. The *Charms* to which I have drawn attention are an example of this intermingling. Other things also passed over from heathenism, with a change, into Christian poetry. The belief in the Wyrd—the goddess who presided over the fates of men or who overcame them in the end —became belief in the will of God. Even the name was at times transferred. "The Wyrd is stronger, the Lord mightier than any man's thought," is a phrase in the *Seafarer*, and it may be matched in many Anglo-Saxon poems. But though the sadness of destiny remains, it is no longer grim. The Wyrd is now the will of a just God who keeps eternal joy and peace for the Christian warrior.

Another heathen motive was the regret for the passing away of the splendour and mirth and fame of men. It is the note of the Prince's lay in *Beowulf* and of the *Ruin*; it continues after Christianity in the *Wanderer* and the *Seafarer* and in all the poems of Cynewulf. Mingled with this is the regret for the loss of youth, of dear companions, and of personal happiness, such regret as we find in *Deor's Complaint*. This too continues, but it was changed and modified by the Christian hope. "One thing is sure," cries the Epilogue to the *Wanderer*, "the Fortress in Heaven"; and Cynewulf in many a poem, when he has mourned for earth and loss, and the storms in which all he loved has perished, thinks of the "Haven which the Ruler of the Ether has established," where all "his friends are dwelling now in peace and joy." These are new feelings for the English, and they are the foundations of all our religious poetry. The note of Cynewulf, of Vaughan, of Keble is much the same.

The added gentleness and grace of these thoughts and of many others concerning life which Christianity instilled into the English character, but the germs of which we see in the heathen character of Beowulf, brought many new elements of poetry and of poetic feeling into English literature. The *Ecclesiastical History* of Bæda is full of lovely and tender stories. But with all this new mildness, the war-spirit of our ancestors lived on in literature with as keen a life as it had in heathen times. The battle in the *Genesis* with the kings of the East might serve to describe the pursuit of some Pictish plunderers by a Northumbrian host. The advance of Pharaoh's army in the *Exodus* is the exact image of the going forth to war of the Fyrd of Æthelfrith or Penda. The overthrow of the Huns in the *Elene* might serve for the war-song sung by Oswiu's bard after the destruction of the Mercians at the fight of Winwæd.

The battle in *Judith* is sung with the same delight with which Hengest would have sung his first victory. There is no change in the fury of war-poetry.

But there is even more to say. The distinctively Christian poetry, the poetry about the fall and the redemption of man, the last judgment, the Nativity, Death, Resurrection and Ascension of Christ, and the spread of the Gospel, is all sung in terms of war. The heathen rapture in battle is transferred to the Christian warfare. The contest between Light and Darkness, between Summer and Winter, becomes the contest between Christ and Satan, between the Christian and his spiritual foes. The original spirit of the myth is preserved. It was made not less but more imaginative in Christianity. The Christian war began before the creation of man; it would only end at the last judgment. It took in all the history of the world. Satan was the great foe who was gripped by God as Grendel was by Beowulf, and hurled into the dark and fiery burg of hell. When man was made, a new phase of the war began, of which Jesus is the divine king. It is by his being the great warrior that he becomes the great Saviour; and round his victory the force of the Christian poetry was concentrated. In the *Vision of the Rood*, the young Hero girded himself for the battle. He was almighty God, strong and high-hearted, and he stepped up on the lofty gallows, brave of soul in the sight of many, for he would save mankind. All creation wept, mourned the fall of its king, as all created things wept for Balder. Sore weary he was when the mickle strife was done, and the men laid him low, him the Lord of victory, in his grave, and folk sang a lay of sorrow over him—as his comrades did for Beowulf. It is the death and burial of an English hero.

Then in this vast epic comes the Harrowing of hell; and it is always told in the spirit of the war-song. The hero, Christ, came "like a storm, loud thunder roaring, at the break of day. The war-feud was open that morning, the Lord had overcome his foes; terrible, he shattered the gates of hell, and all the fiends wailed far and wide through the windy hall." The women who go to the tomb in the poem on the *Descent into Hell* are Ætheling women. Christ's tomb and death are those of an Ætheling. He is "the joy of Æthelings, the victory-son of God." John the Baptist, the great thegn whom Jesus has armed with sword and mail, welcomes his Lord to the gates of hell. "Then high-rejoiced the burghers of Hades,"—that is, the Old Testament saints—"for the Hero had risen full of courage from the clay. Conquest-sure was he, and hastened on his war-path. For the Helm of Heaven willed to break and bow to ruin the walls of hell, he alone; none of byrnie bearing warriors would he lead with him to the gates of hell."

> Down before him fell the bars ;
> Down the doors were dashed, inward drove the King his way.

In triumph the hero returns to the burg of heaven. The feast of the Lamb is laid in the long hall, amid the singing of the angels who are the bards of the battle; and the king makes his speech of welcome and victory to his assembled warriors. But he has left an army on earth to carry on the war, and he gives them, like an English leader, weapons and courage for the fight. The apostles are Æthelings known all over the world. Great proof of valour they gave; far spread was the glory of the King's thegns. "What!" cries the poet in the *Andreas*, "we have heard from ancient times of twelve heroes famous under the stars, thegns of the Lord. Never did the glory of their warfare fail when the helms crashed in fight. Far-famed folk-leaders were they, bold on the war-path when shield and hand guarded the helm upon the battlefield." "Bold in war was Andreas; not tardy was James, nor laggard on his way. Daring was the venture of Thomas in India; he endured the rush of swords. Simon and Thaddeus, warriors brave, sought the Persian land; not slow were they in the shield-play." Andrew is "the hero hard in war, the beast of battle, the steadfast champion." Round about these heroes stand their thegns, sworn by baptism, as the English warrior was by his oath, to keep unfailing truth to their Lord. All the devotion which tied the thegn to his chief, all the disgrace which befell him if he broke his bond by cowardice or by betrayal was transferred to the relation of the apostles and saints to Christ. And the fame given to the heathen fighter who was true in war was now given to the warrior of Jesus who fought faithfully to the death. Then, at the end, was the consummate triumph. The Christian poetry of early England exhausts itself in the joy of the great day, when, after the judgment of evil, the King returns with his warlike hosts to the city of heaven. Little then of the imaginative poetry, little of the spirit of war was lost. Saga changed its name, but not its nature.

These, then, are the ideas which, altered, passed on into Christian out of heathen poetry. But there were also other ideas, new to the English, which are rooted now in poetry. The first of these was the sorrow for sin, the personal cry for release from it, and the rapture which followed the conviction of forgiveness. This, of course, belongs in its depths to personal poetry, and poetry in Old England did not become personal till it came into the hands of Cynewulf. In his verse it reaches a profundity of pain and of joy, of prayer and of exulting praise, the fulness of which is scarcely equalled in the whole range of sacred song in England. And this is true of the praise especially. The very first hymn of English poetry, which Cædmon sang, was an outburst of praise. The rushing praise of Cynewulf in the *Crist* has the loud uplifted trumpet note of Milton; and the later poems, entitled *Christ and Satan*, break their divisions with impassioned hymns of joy. English sacred poetry has never lost the music and the manner of its first raptures.

One other element was quite new—the love of fair and gentle scenery in contrast with the fierce weather, the bitter climate and the stormy seas which heathen poetry described so well. The Christian poets also painted in words the tempest and the frost, but they had the vision of sweeter scenery, of a more tender air, and a grave delight therein. The gentleness of Christ disposed their minds to this love of happy nature. Here are a few lines— the first from the *Genesis*; the second from the *Azarias*—

> Winsomely the running water, all well-springs that be,
> Washed the happy lands, nor as yet the welkin
> Rose above the roomful land, nor dispersed the rains that are
> Wan-gloomed with the gale; yet with growing blooms
> Was the earth made fair.
>
> Lord Eternal, all the river springs
> Laud thee, high exalted! Often lettest thou
> Fall the pleasant waters, for rejoicing of the world,
> Clear from the clean cliffs.

The "bubbling streams that run through the woods, the fountains that well through the soft sward"; the "spreading plain, fresh with green grass that God loved"; the "blossoming earth, the flowers, honey-flowing and rejoicing, the fragrant woods"; "the sweet song of birds; the cuckoo announcing the year"; "the dew dropping at the dawn and winnowed by the wind; the cool winds in the summer-tide when the sun is shining"; "the calm and shining sea when the winds are still"; are described with distinction, and the phrases bear with them the proof of a contemplative pleasure in lovely and gracious scenery which was not known or felt by the heathen English.

It is in the description of the happy land where the Phœnix lives that this new delight is best expressed. The writer took a great part of it from the poem of Lactantius which he adapts. But he added largely to that poem, and I think that into the Northumbrian mind had grown, from its long connection with Celtic feeling, the elements at least of the Irish myth of the land of eternal youth and beauty set far among the western seas—the myth which we find in varying forms among nearly all peoples, but nowhere more vividly wrought than among the Celtic tribes. Far away the island lies;

> Winsome is the wold there, there the wealds are green;
> Spacious-spread the skies below; there nor snow nor rain,
> Nor the furious air of frost, nor the flare of fire,
> Nor the headlong squall of hail, nor the hoar-frost's fall,
> Nor the burning of the sun, nor the bitter cold,
> Do their wrong to any wight; . . .

> Calm and fair the glorious field, flashes there the sunny grove :
> Happy is the holt of trees ; never withers fruitage there !
> In the winter, in the summer, is the wood for ever
> Hung with blossomed boughs ; nor can ever break away
> Leaf below the lift ! . . .
>   . . . but the liquid streamlets,
> Wonderful and winsome, from their wells upspringing,
> Softly lap the land with the lulling of their floods !
> Welling from the woodland's midst are the waters fair,
> Which, at every moon, through the mossy turf of earth,
> Surge up as the sea-foam cold,
> That the mirth of rivers, every month that goes,
> All about the fame-fast land, should o'erflow in play.

This was the new element which, in pleasant contrast with the bitter weather and frost-bound land, the Christian poet introduced into natural description, and it completed the range of that subject of poetry. The Welsh poetry of soft nature was much later. It was, as I have said, remarkable that wild nature should be made in England a separate subject for song; it is still more remarkable to find—however much influence we allot to the study of Vergil—the gentleness of nature treated distinctively. And this is all the more interesting when we think that the poetry of natural description has been in England continuously mingled up with the poetry of the love of God, of Christ, of the Virgin Mary ; with the devotion of the human spirit in worship, repentance, and joy. Such a mingled harmony is indeed to be found in Italian, German, French, and Spanish poetry, but it is found most closely knit together in English poetry, most happily expressed, and most fondly realised.

CHAPTER VII

LATIN LITERATURE

From the Coming of Augustine to the Accession of Ælfred

THE history of literature written in Latin prose in early England might, if we were rigid, be justly excluded from our history, but it is scarcely possible to shut out from our view the School of Canterbury and the School of York, or men like Ealdhelm, Bæda, Ecgberht, and Alcuin, who, if they did not write English, at least spread knowledge; who stimulated the production of English; and who sent, when it was most needed, English education and learning into the Continent. The whole of our earliest prose is contained in their Latin work. There were no books of any importance in English prose till Ælfred sent forth his translation of Gregory's *Pastoral Care*.

Rome was the origin of this Latin prose, and it was written by monks, in monasteries established by the Latin Church. The history of it lasts from 597, when Augustine landed in England, to the destruction of the monasteries by the Danes in the ninth century; or, if we wish to be more accurate, from the founding of the Canterbury School by Theodore in 671 to the battle of Ashdown in 871. By 871 almost every centre of learning in Wessex, Mercia, and Northumbria had been destroyed. The story, then, is the story of 200 years, and it may best be told by dividing it into three parts—Latin literature in Wessex, in Mercia, and in Northumbria.

1. The story begins in Wessex, or rather in Kent, which was then a separate kingdom. Gregory the Great, before he was Pope, saw, according to a well-known story, some blue-eyed and fair-haired children standing to be sold for slaves in the forum of Rome, and was told that they were Angles. "Not Angles," he said, "but Angels"; and he was moved to bring the people from whom these lovely ones came to the faith of Christ. So, when he was Pope, he sent Augustine to England, who, though delayed on his way, landed in Thanet in 597, and sent messengers to King Æthelberht of Kent. Æthelberht, partly influenced by his Christian wife Bertha, daughter of Chariberht of Paris, graciously gave him leave to preach the Gospel. Bertha had already set up a Christian service at St. Martin's Church, and, when the King and his people were baptized, St. Martin's, freshly restored, became the first Christian Church in England, as Canterbury was the first Christian town. In 601 Augustine was made archbishop, and the bishopric of Rochester was founded. Not long after Augustine's coming the Witan was held which enacted the first code of laws that we possess in our mother tongue, and this is the title of the code: "This be the dooms that Æthelbriht, King, ordained in Augustine's days." They were written in Roman letters; but we do not possess them in the Kentish dialect, but in a West Saxon translation, and in a register of the twelfth century. In 673 the *West Kentish Code* appeared, and in 696 King Wihtræd "set forth more dooms." The Kentish dialect is, then, the first vehicle of English prose, and the schools of Kent the rude cradle of English learning.

The first bishops of Canterbury had, however, no sympathy with the English tongue. They were all Italian up to the death of Honorius in 653. Frithona (*Deus-dedit*) succeeded him, and then Theodore of Tarsus was enthroned in 669. He had brought with him from Rome an Englishman, Benedict Biscop, who soon, leaving Canterbury, led the choir of Latin learning in the North. Hadrian, Theodore's deacon, and an excellent scholar, joined him in 671, and with his help Theodore resolved to make the English clergy into a body of scholars. A school was established, and from month to month disciples from Ireland as well as England gathered into Canterbury. "Streams of knowledge," said Bæda, "daily flowed from Theodore and Hadrian to water the hearts of their hearers."

This was the true beginning of literature in the south of England. The teaching of the school included theology, arithmetic, medicine, astronomy, rhetoric; Greek and Hebrew composition and Latin verse were not neglected; the Latin poets, grammarians, and orators were read, and careful instruction was given in caligraphy, illuminating, and ecclesiastical music. Theodore's fame for learning in the canon law soon spread over Europe. Some record of this learning appeared in the *Penitential of Theodore*, drawn up from Theodore's oral answers to questions about discipline. Canterbury had thus begun to produce books of her own; learned foreigners soon ceased to be needed in England; she had her own bishops and scholars, and before long taught her foreign teachers. Brihtwald, the next archbishop, "was a man," Bæda declared, "whose knowledge of the Greek, Latin, and Saxon tongues and learning was manifold and thorough." Tatwine, who followed him, was "splendidly versed in holy writ," and his *Ænigmata* were studied by Cynewulf. By this time, that is, by 731, many bishoprics had been set up in Wessex. They were served by men of learning, of whom Daniel, Bishop of Winchester, 705-744, was the most famous. He helped Bæda in his *Ecclesiastical History*; foreign missions grew under his fostering care, and the whole West Saxon Church was deeply indebted to his work. But the scholar of Theodore who gathered into himself all the learning and ability of the time was Ealdhelm. He was born about the middle of the seventh century, and was a kinsman of Ine, King of Wessex. Eager for the new learning, he joined himself to Mailduf, an Irishman, who set up a hut and hermitage, a school and a small basilica at a place which afterwards took his name, Malmesbury, Mailduf's burg. Ealdhelm thus joined the Irish to the Latin learning, for he was also a scholar of

Canterbury. He loved Hadrian with the deep affection which belonged to his character. "My father," he writes, "beloved teacher of my rude infancy, I embrace you with a rush of pure tenderness: I long to see you again." He took up the school at Malmesbury after Mailduf's death; it rose into a monastery of which he became abbot; he was made Bishop of Sherborne, and travelled continuously through his diocese, preaching, founding monastic schools, building churches (for he was a good architect), and playing on all kinds of instruments, as eager a musician as Dunstan. He founded two monasteries, one at Bradford-on-Avon, another at Frome, and he assisted Ine in his plans for the restoration of Glastonbury. It is not impossible that he had something to do with the compilation of the *Laws of Ine*, the oldest West Saxon laws. They date from about 690, and we possess them in an appendix to the *Laws of Ælfred* in a noble parchment of the *Chronicle* now at Cambridge. They are in English, and have this much literary interest that "as the foundation," Earle says, "of the Laws of Wessex, they are also at the foundation of the laws of all England." Ealdhelm is the first Englishman whose Latin writings are those of a scholar. His classical knowledge was famous. He wrote Latin verse with ease; he composed a long treatise on Latin prosody, and he showed what he could do in this way by his transference into hexameters of the stories told in his treatise, *De laudibus Virginitatis*. He knew Horace, Lucan, Juvenal, Persius, Terence, and Vergil; he read the Old Testament in Hebrew; he spoke Greek, and it is supposed he wrote on Roman Law. He concocted Latin *Riddles*, which went to the North with his *Prosody* to Acircius (Aldfrith), King of Northumbria, and these kindled the genius of Cynewulf in after-days. His Latin is fantastic, alliterative, swelling, and pedantic, but the spirit in which he writes is tender, keen, and gay. He corresponded with Gaul, with Ireland, with Rome, with English and Welsh kings; but his most charming letters are to the abbesses and nuns who knew a little Latin—*flores ecclesiæ*, he calls them, *Christi margaritæ, paradisi gemma*. Nor did he wholly neglect the literature of his own tongue. He made songs in English, some of which Ælfred had, and one of which was still commonly sung in the twelfth century. And as he travelled on his preaching tours from town to town, it was his habit to stand, like a gleeman, on the bridge or in the public way, and sing to the people flocking to the fairs in the English tongue, that by this sweetness of song he might lure them to come with him and hear the word of God. He died on one of his journeys in 709, but he had lived long enough to fill Wessex with the desire of learning, to build up its Church into strength, and to link into spiritual harmony the North and the South. Even the Welsh owned his charm. His letters to Gerontius, King of the Damnonian Britons, converted both king and people to the observance of the Roman Easter.

Ealdhelm was the last man in the south of England before Ælfred to whose work we may give the name of literature. The learning and energy of Wessex were more displayed in building up the church, in teaching, in policy, and in missionary work than in literature. Winfrid (Boniface), Willibald, and Lullus were Wessex men. Boniface was, from 719 to 755, the chief apostle to the heathen of Central Europe. Willibald, famous in the history of travel, journeyed through Sicily, Ephesus, Tortosa, and Emessa to Damascus. Thence he visited the whole of Palestine, and reached Constantinople in 725. His voyage was written by a nun, it is supposed from his own dictation. Lullus, who left England about 732, and succeeded Boniface as Archbishop of Mainz, never forgot his country. His correspondence, as well as that of his predecessor, was constant with England. There is no better example, not even that of Boniface, of the continual intercourse between the English kings and bishops and the Continent than the letters of Lullus.

But after the middle of the eighth century, the literary life of Wessex passes away. The ceaseless wars troubled even the monasteries; ignorance succeeded to knowledge, and the schools decayed. The ecclesiastical struggle of Canterbury with the new metropolitan See set up at Lichfield by Offa left no leisure for the work of its school. Archbishop Æthelhard won back the supremacy of Canterbury in 803, but he did not win back any of the learning which Theodore had originated. Alcuin begs him "to restore at least the reading of the Scriptures." Ecgberht, great king as he was, who came to the throne in 802, was too much employed in establishing his overlordship in Mercia and Northumbria to do anything for learning; and, worst of all, he had to fight the Vikings, who had begun their raids by a descent on Dorsetshire in 787. In 833 they endangered the very life of his kingdom. They fell on London in 839 and plundered Rochester. They had the year before descended on East Anglia. In 845 they were defeated in Somersetshire. These were desultory raids. But in 851 Rorik sacked Canterbury with furious slaughter, and penetrated into Essex. Then the Vikings regularly camped for the winter at Sheppey in 855. In 860 they plundered Winchester, and in 865 devastated Kent. In 866 "the army," as the Danish host was called, came no longer to raid but to settle. They conquered Northumbria, they marched into Mercia, and in 871 crossed the Thames into Wessex. There "the army" was met at Ashdown by Æthelred and Ælfred, and defeated with great carnage. But in the course of this raiding and invasion the centres of literature in Wessex were destroyed, and there is no more to say of learning and literature in the south of England till they rose again to life at the call of Ælfred.

2. There is but little to tell of Latin learning in Mercia. Mercia had been heathen during the reign of Penda, who had slain Oswald of Northumbria in 642. But Penda met his death at Winwæd's stream of which it was sung:—

> At the Winwede was vengèd the war-death of Anna,
> The slaughter of Kings—of Sigbert, of Ecgrice,
> The death of King Oswald, the death of King Edwin.

In 655, then, the date of this battle, Mercia became Christian. Penda's son, Wulfhere, 657-675, established some monasteries, and fable has made him the builder of many more. Under Æthelred, who followed him, the Mercian Church was organised and under Æthelbald, his successor, Mercia seems to have established a reputation for literature and learning. When Canterbury wanted archbishops, it drew them from the Mercian priests. Ecgwin, Bishop of Worcester, who founded Evesham, was one of Æthelbald's bishops, and is said, in the questionable report of two later biographers, to have written his own life and to be our first autobiographer. The king himself patronised learning, and his name is mixed up with that of St. Guthlac. In his days, Felix of Crowland wrote in a swollen Latin prose the *Life of St. Guthlac* for an East Anglian king. The book formed the foundation of the second part of the English poem of *St. Guthlac*, and was translated into Anglo-Saxon prose in the tenth or eleventh century. Crowland, where Guthlac had his hermitage, became the site of a great abbey which owed its splendour to the munificence of Æthelbald. Offa, the next Mercian ruler, 757-796, was so great a king that we should expect literature to flourish in his reign. Many have conjectured that it did flourish then; *Beowulf* has even been allotted to his court; but we have no evidence of any Mercian literature in his time. The king, however, became himself a subject of literature. The legendary tales told of Offa the son of Wermund, who ruled the Engle on the Continent, were imputed to our Offa, and obscure all his early history. But after his death the supremacy of Mercia perished. Ecgberht annexed it to Wessex in 828, and shortly after Ecgberht died the great abbeys of East Anglia and Mercia were swept away by the Danes. In Middle England, then, as well as in Wessex no Latin literature was left.

3. Northumbria was the chief English home of Latin literature, and its beginnings were contemporary with the coming of Theodore. The history of it is fuller and longer than that of Mercia or of Wessex, for it contains the tale of a great scholar whom at one point we may call a man of genius, and of a great

hool—the tale of Bæda, and the tale of the University of York. begins indeed at York, and in that city it also ends.

Christianity reached York, the capital of Deira, in the year 627, when Eadwine and his people were baptized by Paullinus. But when the king died in 633, the kingdom relapsed into heathenism, and Paullinus, fleeing away, left the conversion of the country to the Celtic missionaries whom Oswald summoned from Iona to his help in 634. Aidan, the gentle Irish monk whom Oswald loved, set up his bishop's seat on the wild rock of Lindisfarne, and in many missionary voyages Christianised both Bernicia and Deira—provinces which Oswiu, a few years after, made into the one kingdom of Northumbria. Twenty-six years after Aidan took root at Lindisfarne, Wilfrid, who followed the Latin rule, led its cause against that of the Celtic Church. He introduced the Benedictine rule at Ripon, under the patronage of Alchfrith, son of Oswiu, 661. Some years later he built with great splendour the Priory of Hexham, and made it, as well as Ripon, a centre of Latin learning. In 664, at the Synod of Whitby, he succeeded in establishing the Roman instead of the Celtic Church as the mistress of Northumbria, though the Celtic influence lasted for many years. But Benedict Biscop, who had been in Rome with Theodore and afterwards with him at Canterbury, was, rather than Wilfrid, the real founder of Latin learning. He came north, bringing with him the methodical teaching of Canterbury, and set up in 674 the monastery of St. Peter's at Wearmouth, and in 682 the sister monastery of Jarrow. In the course of five journeys to Rome, this indefatigable collector brought back to his two monasteries enough books, images, relics, and pictures, to furnish both of them with large and decorated libraries. To these libraries we owe Bæda and the school of York and Alcuin, and all the continental learning that flowed from Alcuin. A famous school grew up around them, and Bæda led it to a greater fame. Benedict was as active in the cause of art as of learning. Architecture, painting, mosaic, music, glass-making, embroidery, belonged to his religion. But his chief love was his books.

I

"Keep them together," he cried, as paralysis brought on death,—"keep them with loving care. Never injure them, never disperse them." He died in 690. Aldfrith was King of Northumbria at the time, and Aldfrith, educated in Ireland and at Canterbury, and the friend of Ealdhelm and Wilfrid, may be called a scholar. He too was a collector of books, and gave to Abbot Ceolfrid, Benedict's successor at Wearmouth and Jarrow, support and affection. Ceolfrid's school became famous. Men as far asunder as the Pope and Naiton the King of the Picts asked his advice on ecclesiastical and theological subjects. Bæda himself wrote his Life, and there is no better picture than this brief biography of the daily life of a great English monastery. Moreover, these two men, Ceolfrid and Aldfrith, touched the literature of a Celtic monastery. They were both connected with the celebrated book in which Abbot Adamnan of Iona gave at this time an account of Arculf's journey to the Holy Land. Arculf, shipwrecked on the west coast, found his way to Iona and dictated his adventures to Adamnan, and the abbot brought the book to Aldfrith, who had been his pupil and who sent it eagerly on to Ceolfrid.[1] Many copies were made of it and dispersed throughout Northumbria. It was also popular in Europe through Bæda's abridgment of it, and through the extracts he made from it in the *Ecclesiastical History*.

Some years later, after 709, Wilfrid's biography was written by his friend, Eddius Stephanus. This book, in an excellent style, is of the greatest use for the history of the Northumbrian Church in the seventh century. Moreover, it is the first biography ever written in England. It had a companion, composed about the same time, in the *Life of St. Cuthbert* by a nameless writer, which Bæda borrowed from Lindisfarne when he was inditing his genial story of St. Cuthbert. Another well-known name must not be

---

[1] "These two men, Adamnan and Ceolfrid, met at Wearmouth. Ceolfrid converted Adamnan to the Roman Easter, and Adamnan probably showed Ceolfrid his new book, the *Life of St. Columba*, which he made at the end of the seventh century."

forgotten—John of Beverley, who had studied under Theodore and Hild, who ordained Bæda, who became Bishop of York and of Hexham. He loved magnificence as a great ecclesiastic, but he loved still more the life of the anchorite. The Celtic pleasure in a solitary life with God often drove him from the grandeur of Hexham to his hut on the summit of the Howe of the Earn, a hill above the flowing of the Tyne. Beverley, where the fair minster now claims our admiration, was then a lonely meadow in the midst of the waters and trees of Underwood, round which the river Hull, delaying its speed, had been dammed by the beavers who gave the place its name. There, round the little church, John kept a school, to which a number of persons, lay and clerical, resorted. Among this circle of learned men, Acca, Wilfrid's closest friend and supporter, is not the least famous. Abbot, and then Bishop of Hexham in 709, he increased the monastic library. Like Benedict Biscop he was an architect and musician. He finished the three churches near Hexham that Wilfrid had begun. If he was not a writer himself, he urged others to write. It was he who caused Eddius to compose the *Life of Wilfrid*. He pressed Bæda to write his *Commentary on St. Luke*, and Bæda dedicated to him his *Commentary on St. Mark*, a poem on the *Last Day*, and perhaps the *Hexameron*.

These are the chief names among a number of persons who made Northumbria famous for Latin learning in the seventh and the beginning of the eighth century. That learning was as yet scattered; it needed to be gathered together and generalised by a man of genius, and the man who did this work was Bæda of Jarrow. He mastered all the learning of Northumbria; he gathered new learning from the rest of England and from the Continent, and he threw the whole into form in a series of books which his quiet life and his unwearied industry produced year after year. These books became the teachers, not only of England, but of Europe. They were the text-books of the school of York to which students came from Gaul, Germany, Ireland, and Italy; and they went with Alcuin to the court of Charles the Great.

As to the means of education in Bæda's power and the learning which he collected, I quote the summary of them which the Bishop of Oxford gives in the *Dictionary of Christian Biography*, and more especially as it illustrates the extension of learning all over England at this time: "Under the liberal and enlightened administration of Benedict Biscop and Ceolfrith, Bede enjoyed advantages which could not perhaps have been found anywhere else in Europe at that time; perfect access to all the existing sources of learning in the West. Nowhere else could he acquire at once the Irish, the Roman, the Gallican, and the Canterbury learning; the accumulated stores of books which Benedict had bought at Rome and Vienne, or the disciplinary instruction drawn from the monasteries of the Continent, as well as from the Irish missionaries. Amongst his friends and instructors were Trumbert, the disciple of St. Chad, and Sigfrid, the fellow-pupil of St. Cuthbert under Boisil and Eata. From these he drew the Irish knowledge of Scripture and discipline. Acca, Bishop of Hexham and pupil of St. Wilfrid, furnished him with the special lore of the Roman school, martyrological and other; his monastic learning, strictly Benedictine, came through Benedict Biscop, through Lerins and the many continental monasteries his master had visited; and from Canterbury, with which he was in friendly correspondence, he probably obtained his instruction in Greek, in the study of the Scriptures and other more refined learning."

Then Bæda himself mentions, as his authorities for the *Ecclesiastical History*, Albinus, Hadrian's pupil; Nothelm, who worked for him among the libraries at Rome; Daniel of Winchester, and Forthhere of Malmesbury, who brought to him, I suppose, the works of Ealdhelm which had their own influence on Northumbrian literature; Esi from East Anglia; Cynibert from Lindsey; the monks of many monasteries, and chiefly those of Lastingham, who told him the stories of Cedda and Ceadda. All these, from so many diverse parts of England, poured their knowledge into Bæda's reservoir. Kings gave him their friendship—Aldfrith, and Ceolwulf to whom he dedicates his *History*;

his own pupils were great scholars; he had correspondents in many parts of Europe; and a host of visitors came to the silent cell at Jarrow with the experience of many men and many lands.

As to the books he wrote, the first probably were the *Ars metrica*, the *De Natura Rerum*, and the *De Temporibus*, written between 700 and 703. These scientific manuals were followed by the *De sex aetatibus saeculi*, an admirable epitome of the history of the world, written for Wilfrid about the year 707. The commentaries on the books of the Old and New Testaments, the composition of which ranges over many years, come after 709, for they are dedicated to Acca as Bishop of Hexham, and Acca succeeded Wilfrid in that year. The *Lives of St. Cuthbert and the Abbots of Wearmouth and Jarrow* date between 716 and 720. The *De temporum ratione* was in 726. The *Ecclesiastical History* was finished in 731. After this, shortly before his death in 735, is his *Epistola ad Egbertum*, and on the day of his death he was still employed on his translation into English of the Gospel of St. John. Many other things, including *Homilies*, he wrote, but these are the chief. Most of them are studious epitomes, of great learning, of little originality, but all suffused with his gentleness and brightness. The scientific works are mostly derived from the elder Pliny; the grammatical and rhetorical from the then known classical writers on these matters. He possessed Greek as a scholar, and he knew "all the Hebrew he could learn from the writings of Jerome." The *Commentaries* are a mixture of a calm, clear, sensible, and unaffected teaching of Christian conduct and love with an extravagance of allegorical interpretation. They preserve that steady piety which has made the practical religion of the English people, "seeking," as Bæda said Cuthbert and Boisil did while they read St. John's Gospel, "that simple faith which works by love, not troubling themselves with minute and subtle questions."

The chief information we have of his life is given by himself at the end of his *Ecclesiastical History:* "Bæda, a servant of God, and priest of the monastery of the blessed Apostles, Peter and Paul, which is at Wearmouth and Jarrow; who, being born in the lands of the same monastery, was, at seven years old, handed over to be educated by the most reverend Abbot Benedict and afterwards by Ceolfrid; and passing all the rest of my life in that monastery, wholly gave myself to the study of the Scriptures and to the observance of the regular discipline, and of daily chanting in the Church, and had always great delight in learning and teaching and writing. When I was nineteen years old, I received deacon's orders, and when I was thirty those of the priesthood, and both were conferred on me by Bishop John, and by order of Abbot Ceolfrid. From which time till I was fifty-nine years of age I made it my business, for the use of me and mine, to gather together out of the writings of the venerable fathers, and to interpret, according to their sense, the following pieces:"—And here follows a list of his works, at the end of which is this gracious sentence: "And now, good Jesus, I pray that to whom thou hast granted of thy grace to share in the words of thy wisdom, thou wilt also grant that he may come to thee, Fount of all wisdom, and stand before thy face for ever, who livest and reignest world without end, Amen." These are the last words of the book. "Here ends," he says, "by God's help, the fifth book of the *Ecclesiastical History* of the English nation."

It is his greatest work, the book in which he showed he was not only an industrious compiler, but also a writer who had gained those powers of choice of what to say, of arrangement, of rejection of needless material, of imaginative form, which are needful for a capable historian. The pains also he took to get at the truth, the host of assistants he employed to procure for him contemporary information at first hand, the quotation of all his authorities, permit us to call him the leader of modern history, one whom a careful writer like William of Malmesbury might be proud to follow. "I have not dared," he said in his preface to his *Life of St. Cuthbert*, "to transcribe what I have written without the most accurate examination of credible witnesses, without inserting the names of my authorities to establish the truth of my narrative." But the qualities which add literary charm to his history and biographies, and often to his commentaries, arose out of his happy, joyous, gentle, and loving nature, which kept to the end, like Arthur Stanley, a childlike simplicity, charm, and love of beauty. The stories which animate and ornament the *History;* their peculiar lucidity and grace; the vivid sketches of characters and persons, the pervading tenderness, the delight with which he entered into those legends especially which breathed of human affections, make us love the writer, and there is no greater proof of a book being fine literature. It seems a pity we know so little of him, but had he been more personal, he had not been so enchanting a story-teller.

That no imaginative work full of his personality exists seems to set him apart from those who feel the poetic impulse, and his long home-staying agrees with this judgment. But though he sat at home, he knew the world. I have said that his quiet cell received many travellers; men of all ranks of life were his correspondents, and he had many pupils in high places in Church and State. One of these, Ecgberht of York, seems to have been nearest to him. Almost the only visit he paid in his long life was to Ecgberht, when for a few days they consulted about the condition and welfare of the Church in Northumbria. The year after he sent to the bishop his well-known *Letter*. Few pastoral letters have been more weighty with wisdom and piety, with love for the souls of men, and with love of his country, with soundness of ecclesiastical advice, and with knowledge of the needs of the Church. It is firm and gentle, authoritative and courteous, and the style is worthy of the thoughts and emotions with which it is charged.

Not long after, on the eve of the ascension, in 735, the time of his departure came. "I have not lived among you," he said, "so as to be ashamed, nor do I fear to die, since we have a gracious God." Even to the last breath he drew, he laboured to complete two works—*Collections out of the Notes of Bishop Isidorus*, and a *Translation of the Gospel of St. John* into the

English tongue. "Go on swiftly," he said to his scribe as he dictated the words of the gospel, "I know not how long I can continue." And the boy said, "Dear master, there is yet one sentence unwritten." He replied, "Write quickly," and the boy said, "The sentence is now finished." At which he answered, "It is well, it is ended. Take my head into your hands, for I am well pleased to be facing my holy place, where I was wont to pray." And so singing the "Gloria in Excelsis" he breathed his last in his cell, among his books, and entered the kingdom of heaven. It is well to think of him as the "Light of the Church," as the "Father of English Learning," but it is pleasant also to remember that he began English prose in his translation of St. John; that he loved English poetry, and told, with a personal pleasure in the story, of its origin with Cædmon; and that even in death, "he said," as his scholar Cuthbert tells, "many things—for he was learned in our songs—in the English tongue. Moreover, he spoke this verse, making it in English.

> Before the need-faring, no one becomes
> Wiser in thought than behoves him to be,
> To the out-thinking, ere his hence-going,
> What to his ghost, of good or of evil,
> After his death, shall be doomed in the end."

When Bæda died in 735, the seat of letters was transferred from Jarrow to York, where Ecgberht, Bæda's pupil, had already established a school, which before long rose to so high a position, and was directed by so excellent a staff of teachers, that we may call it a university. Canterbury, under Theodore, was not more than a brilliant monastic school, and when Theodore died, its light departed. But the heads of York provided for the continuance of the school, and for an organisation which may be called corporate. The teaching was systematised, subdivided, specialised; pupils were trained into professors; the library, famous over Europe, was added to every year; and the whole organisation was handed on intact and in good working order for fully fifty years. The long history of York, from the Roman time when it took rank almost as an imperial city to the years when it was the seat of the supremacy of Eadwine, and the capital shortly after of the Northumbrian kings; the fact that the first Christian king of Northumbria was baptized within its walls; the fame of the little chapel of wood set up by Eadwine and Paullinus, over which rose the rich cathedral of Æthelberht; its becoming again in the days of Ecgberht the seat of an archbishopric; its crowded and wealthy population; its active commerce, and the beauty of its site between the rivers—these, one and all, added to the repute of its school in England, and to its fame in Europe. It became the centre of European learning. Scholars flocked to it from Germany, Gaul, Italy, and Ireland. European schools sought for their teachers at York. Its certificate secured their reputation.

Ecgberht, the Archbishop, was brother of Eadberht, King of Northumbria, 738-758, and his life was as princely as his birth. He loved the arts of gold and silver working, of figured silk, of rich embroidery, of church music, and applied them to the decoration of the minster. Round about the minster rose the schools. The education began with grammar and continued through classical literature. The Roman poets, orators, and grammarians were read, and some of the Greek fathers. Rhetoric, logic, law, astronomy, arithmetic, the natural history of Pliny, and the Scriptures were studied; and Ecgberht himself kept in touch with the pupils through their whole course. His chief work there was educational, but he wrote a few books—a volume of *Episcopal Offices*, *Extracts on Church Discipline*, a *Penitentiale*—standard authorities in the Anglo-Saxon Church. It is probable that he translated these into English, and that we may class him among the earliest writers of English prose. When he died, he was succeeded in the archbishopric by his friend and chief assistant in the school, Æthelberht or Ælberht. A better scholar than Ecgberht, he was the chief administrator and improver of the famous library. Alcuin, his fellow-scholar, travelled with him to Gaul and Rome, seeking for manuscripts, and in 770 no library outside of Rome could be compared with that of York. Under their direction the number of students increased, and missionary enterprise was not forgotten. Nor was art neglected. In 741 the minster was burnt. Æthelberht remade it; embellished the little oratory in which King Eadwine was baptized; enriched the whole with gold, silver, gems, and decorated altars; made it glow with coloured ceilings and windows, and dedicated it before he died—leaving all men in love with him—

> O pater, O pastor, vitae spes maxima nostrae,
> Te sine nos ferimur turbata per aequora mundi,

wrote his greatest friend, Alcuin, who, born about 735, and brought up from childhood at York, had taught the school during Æthelberht's latest days.

Of all these men Alcuin was the finest scholar. Ecgberht and Æthelberht gave him their knowledge. The arts and sciences, especially astronomy, engaged him as well as theology. He mastered all the classics in the library at York, and formed a Latin style so good that he has been called the Erasmus of the eighth century. He loved Vergil so well that he sometimes neglected for him the services of the Church. His fame spread, and England was soon deprived of him. He left York in 782, the date of Æthelberht's death, and from that date the school decays. He had met Charles the Great at Pavia about 780, and again at Parma in the following year; and in 782 he joined Charles, and remained with him for eight years, taking charge of the Palatine schools. In 790 he was again in England, but in 792 he rejoined Charles, and from that year, or perhaps we may say from 782, Alcuin belongs, not to English learning, but to the planting of learning in the Continent by the hands of English scholars. He took with him a number of men trained in York; he constantly sent to York for fresh men and for books; English scholars visited him and many remained with him. It is not too much to say that Alcuin drained York of its best, and hastened the paralysis of its learning. He remained with Charles till 796, and then, wearied with work, retired to the abbey of St. Martin at Tours, where he lived till his death in 804. He left behind him an extensive series of books, most of which, of great value for the extension of learning, of theological knowledge and discipline, are of little value as literature. The longest of his Latin poems—*De Pontificibus et Sanctis Ecclesiae Eboracensis*—is also the most attractive, and is our best authority for the history of the school of York from the consecration of Ecgberht to the death of Æthelberht. But the most important of his writings, both as literature and for the uses of history, is the collection of his *Letters*, more than three hundred of which exist. The most interesting of these are those between Charles and Alcuin, letters which reveal many charming traits in both men. But they all prove his wide influence, "as the success of his work is proved by the literary history of the following century." Alcuin, bringing to Europe English learning, is the chief source of the revival of classical learning which has been, with much justice, called the *Carolingian Renaissance*. None of this work belongs to English literature in England, but it is pleasant and interesting to know that an English scholar carried off all the learning of Northumbria, exactly at the right time, before the invasion of the Danes destroyed it, to fertilise therewith the Empire which Charles the Great had ploughed out of Europe. Of this revival of learning Charles himself was the driving power. It was he that chose Alcuin, Peter of Pisa, Paul the Lombard, and Einhard to be his literary friends and courtiers, who kept them to their work, who made them read to him, who set up a court school which became an academy for learned men such as was set up afterwards at Florence and Paris; who took care that good schools should be founded at Tours, at Utrecht, at Fulda, at Würzburg and in other places. No one can read the account that Einhard gives of his master without comparing Charles, as a patron and founder of literature, with Ælfred. They pursued the same aims, they worked on similar lines. But Charles had more power to enforce his will. Where Ælfred failed, he succeeded.

Unhappy fates had now fallen on Northumbria. It could no longer shelter or cherish literature. The kingdom was the battlefield of anarchy from 780 to 798. Then six years of quiet followed, quiet in which Northumbria was expiring. The school of York sank into silence, and in 827 Ecgberht of Wessex annexed the north. Meanwhile, a terrible blow was dealt on learning from without. In 793 the Vikings made their first raid on the coasts of Northumbria, and "God's Church at Lindisfarne was ravaged with rapine and slaughter by the heathen." "St. Cuthbert could not save his own," cried Alcuin; "the most venerable place in Britain, where Christianity first took root among us after Paullinus left York, is a prey to the heathen men. Who thinks of this and does not cry to God to spare his country has a heart of stone and not of flesh." The next year Jarrow and Wearmouth suffered. The mother of all Northumbrian learning was defiled. But the monks took arms, the pirates were driven off, and the repulse saved for a time monastic life from Coldingham to Whitby.

There was an interval of seventy-four years between the attack on Lindisfarne in 793, and 867 when "The Army" came to invade and settle in Northumbria. During that time, uneasiness, dread, preparations for defence, absence of quiet and hope, weakened everywhere the health of learning. At last "The Army," coming from East Anglia, had, after a fruitless English rally, an easy conquest of York. Then the Danes, setting out from York, utterly destroyed every monastery in Deira. A few years afterwards they rooted out all the abbeys of Bernicia. There was not one home of learning left from the Forth to the Humber. Bishoprics perished, even so great a one as Hexham. The libraries, the schools, the knowledge of two hundred years were swept away. Northumbria thus shared the same terrible fate which had fallen on Mercia and Wessex.

In Western Mercia, which alone now retained the name of Mercia, one poor school of learning lingered still in Worcester after the peace of Wedmore; in Wessex Ælfred's victory enabled him to build the foundations of a new learning; but Northumbria, where learning in England had reached its highest excellence, was so exhausted and dismantled, that no literature of any worth issued from it till long after the Norman Conquest. York, however, may have retained some faint show of learning. As the Danish capital of Northumbria, it was not ruined; nine years after its capture the invaders settled down in it. Commerce began to return; the place grew in population; the archbishop still ruled the churches. The city sat again as a queen upon its river, and it may be that into its library flowed whatever manuscripts had been saved by the fugitives from Wearmouth, Whitby, Tynemouth, Lastingham, Ripon, and Hexham. We can distinguish nothing amid the gloom, but when it was known that Ælfred welcomed any one who had a grain of learning, or could bring him a manuscript of Bæda, or a collection of Northumbrian verse in English, many sad-faced scholars may have set out from York to Worcester, and from Worcester to Winchester, to bring to the wise and generous king the fragments that had escaped from the Danish hurricane of fire.

This then brings to a close the history of the literature of Latin prose before the time of Ælfred. When it arose again in England, it arose in Wessex with the revival of monasticism by the scholars of Dunstan and by the kings he influenced. But before its rebirth, English prose had grown under King Ælfred, and a century after him under Ælfric, into a vigorous and fruitful life.

CHAPTER VIII

CÆDMON [660-680]

THE Christian poetry of England began in Northumbria, and the story of its origin is told by Bæda. The place of its birth was the double monastery of Hild. Hild was a princess of the royal blood, grand-niece of King Eadwine, by whose side, when she was a girl of thirteen, she was baptized by Paullinus. The monastery was founded by her in 658, high above the fishing village and the little harbour where the Esk, coming down from the wild moors, meets the stormy sea. Streoneshalh was the name of the village, and in after-years the Danes called it Whitby. A paved road, even then, led straight up the steep ascent to the lofty summit of the black cliff, which, stretching out towards the north-east, looks from its gusty edge over the German Ocean. The remains of the abbey, built long afterwards, now stand on its highest point, dark against the evening sky, and are reflected in the long pool which alone breaks the desolation of the meadows, humped and ridged with the grass-grown ruins of the monastic buildings. In the same place where this abbey church still draws the seaman's eye, rose of old the wooden and wattled church of Hild, surrounded by its halls, dormitories, refectories, and out-buildings. A number of small oratories were scattered over the hillside, and many of them no doubt occupied the long and narrow platform where St. Mary's Church stands now among the tombs of drowned sailors. It was a fitting home for the first poet of the nation which has ruled and loved the sea. Cædmon was his name, and he was attached in a secular habit to the monastery —one of its dependents, and living in the village at the foot of the cliff. Whence he came we cannot tell, but he may have come to Whitby with Hild from Hartlepool. He was born a heathen, and the heathen note rings clear in some of the poems attributed to him. His name is scarcely English, and this, and the similarity of his story to other stories of shepherds suddenly gifted with song, have made some persons deny his real existence. But Bæda's account makes it clear, by evidence almost contemporary, that he was himself, and not a mere name. Whether he was truly an Englishman is an undecided question. His name seems to be Celtic, and Dr. Sweet is of this opinion, or at any rate he does not believe it to be Teutonic. The name in Welsh is Cadvan, and in earlier spellings Catman, and in a Latin inscription Catamannus. I cannot, however, trace any Celtic elements in *Genesis A;* but there are clearly Teutonic elements. But then, it is not proved that he wrote *Genesis A*. His personality eludes us. We know nothing of him beyond that which Bæda tells us.

He was well advanced in years when he began to make poetry, and as he died in 680, we may fairly think that his first verses were written between 660 and 670. He was only a dependent of the monastery, for he took care of the cattle in his turn, but lowly birth and a poor education do not prevent Apollo. The gifts of the god are no respecter of persons; and though they lingered long before they spoke in the man, they spoke at last. Moreover, though Cædmon had only received the slight monastic education given to the dependents of a monastery, he lived in a place where great events took place and to which great personages came; and the higher education which flows from national emotion was received by him. He often heard the story of the baptism of King Eadwine and of his mistress Hild, and the tale of the first conversion of Northumbria. He saw the long procession and heard the solemn service with which Eadwine's body was re-buried at Whitby, a burial which made Whitby the Westminster Abbey of Northumbria. In 670 he saw Oswiu laid in the same church, and probably his wife Eanfleda — great burials charged with history. Ælfleda, the daughter of Oswiu, was dedicated to Christ by her father and sent to Hild at Hartlepool after the battle of Winwæd, where Oswiu slew the heathen Penda and avenged the death of Oswald. Ælfleda—whose very presence spoke of the glory of Northumbria—lived all her life at Whitby. She was about twenty years old when Cædmon began to write, and she listened to his first hymn. Oswiu the victorious king; Ecgfrith, who in 670 worthily carried on the noble traditions of Northumbria; were both seen by Cædmon, and from the sight of these high princes flowed into the poor man's soul the deep emotion of national glory.

Nor did he want the impression of a spiritual glory. Paullinus had baptized the abbess; Aidan was her friend, Aidan, who, when Paullinus fled, reconverted Northumbria. After 664, Cædmon saw the "angel face" of Cuthbert who died seven years after Cædmon, and whose romantic life was common talk at Whitby. Great ecclesiastics, like John of Beverley and Bosa of York, were educated at the monastery. Cædmon lived at a centre whence spiritual life radiated over England. In 664 he saw one renowned event at Whitby which brought together the national glory of Northumbria, the splendid memories of the Celtic mission, and the intellectual power, the spiritual unity and the awe of Rome. The Synod of Whitby was presided over by King Oswiu, and Alchfrith his son came with him. Colman of Lindisfarne, Hild, Cedda, represented the Celtic evangelisers; Wilfrid, with Agilberht Bishop of the West Saxons, Romanus, chaplain of Oswiu's wife, James the Deacon, one of Paullinus's companions, represented the overmastering Church of Rome. It was a great occasion, a sight to be always remembered by a man in whom poetry was as yet hidden; nor could any one who heard Wilfrid, speaking English with a "sweet soft eloquence," ever forget that keen and passionate partisan. These things would work even on a dull spirit; they would certainly have their kindling power on Cædmon.

The story of his awakening is told by Bæda. It was Cædmon's

habit, when a feast was held and all were called on to sing in turn, to return to his house when the harp came to him, for he knew nothing of the art of song. "But on an evening when he had the care of the cattle he fell asleep in the stable; and One stood by him, and saluting him, said, 'Cædmon, sing me something.' And he answered, 'I know not how to sing, and for this reason I left the feast.' Then the other said, 'Nevertheless, you will have to sing to me.' 'What shall I sing?' Cædmon replied. 'Sing,' said the other, 'the beginning of things created.' Whereupon he immediately began to sing in praise of God, the world's Upbuilder, verses which he had not heard before; "and Bæda gives in his Latin prose the sense of the words of this first English hymn."[1] "When Cædmon awaked, he remembered

---

[1] A happy chance has left us at the end of an old MS. of the *Historia Ecclesiastica* the words of this hymn of Cædmon's, in their native Northumbrian. As it is the most ancient piece of extant Christian song in English, I give it here, and translate it.

Nu scylun hergan hefœnricæs uard,	Now must we greet with praise the guard of Heaven's realm,
Metudes mæcti end his modgidanc,	The Maker's might, and of His mind the thought,
Uerc uuldurfadur; sue he uundra gihuæs	The glorious Father's works, and how to wonders all
Eci Dryctin or astelidae.	He gave beginning, He, the Eternal Lord !
He ærist scop ælda barnum	He at the very first formed for the bairns of men,
Heben til hrofe; haleg scepen !	He, Holy Shaper ! Heaven for their roof;
Tha middungeard; moncynnæs uard !	Then Middle-garth He made: He, of mankind the Ward !
Eci Dryctin ! Æfter tiadæ	Lord everlasting He ! And then He let arise
Firum foldu; frea allmectig !	The earth for man; He is Almighty God !

This is from "Sweet's Old English texts."—"The hymn is written," he says," at the top of the page in a smaller hand than that of the list of kings which follows it. It is not impossible that the hymn may have been written later than the list, to fill up the blank space. But the hand is evidently contemporary." "The list must have been written either in 737, or between 734 and 737, most probably in 737, which is of course the date of the Moore MS. of Bæda's history."

what he had sung, and added words in the same fashion worthy of God. In the morning he told the Town-Reeve of his gift, who brought him to Hild. And she, in the presence of learned men, ordered him to tell the dream and sing the verses, which they approved, and said that heavenly grace had been given him by our Lord. And he sang again for them a holy history in excellent verse, and the abbess, loving this grace of God in the man, urged him to take the monastic habit, which he did, and in time was taught the whole series of sacred history. Then Cædmon, ruminating like a clean animal all he had heard, turned the whole into the sweetest verse, and sang the Creation of the world and man, all the history of Genesis, and of the departure of Israel from Egypt and their entrance into the Holy Land, and of many other stories in the Scriptures; and of the Incarnation of the Lord and his Passion, Resurrection, and Ascension, and of the coming of the Holy Ghost, and of the doctrine of the Apostles. And of the terror of future judgment and of the sweetness of the heavenly kingdom he made many songs." "So he lived, always desiring to stir men to despise the world and to aspire to heaven. A devout and humble man, but inflamed with fervent zeal against those who were not minded to follow the regular discipline, wherefore he brought his life to a fair end. For on the night he was about to depart he went to the house where the dying were borne, and having talked in a right joyous fashion with those who were there, asked whether the Eucharist were nigh. 'What need of the Eucharist,' said they, 'since you talk as merrily as a man in health?' 'Nevertheless,' he replied, 'bring me the Eucharist,' and saying, 'I am in charity, my children, with all the servants of God,' strengthened himself with the heavenly viaticum and made ready for the other life. 'Is it far from the time,' he then asked, 'when the brethren shall sing the Nocturns?' 'Not far off,' they said. 'Well,' he replied, 'let us wait that hour,' and signing himself with the sign of the Cross, he laid his head on the pillow, and falling into a slumber, ended his life in silence and as he had served God with a pure and simple mind and with tranquil devotion, so also he left the world by as tranquil a death; and he seemed indeed to have foreknowledge of his death."

We know, then, that he sang, in a series, like some of the later mysteries, the whole story of the fates of men, from the Creation and the Fall to the Redemption and the Last Judgment, and, within this large framework, the Scripture history. This would be a long and steady piece of work; it cannot have taken less than ten, and may have taken twenty years. His poems, we may surely infer, went from monastery to monastery over the whole of Northumbria, not only to the Celtic, but to Latin monasteries like Wearmouth and Jarrow. Where they went, they kindled other men into poetry. Among those who wrote English verse in Cædmon's manner we may count Bæda himself, who was most learned in English songs—*doctissimus in nostris carminibus*—and who himself, as we have seen, made verses in English. Cædmon then made, as it were, a school. "Others after him," said Bæda, fifty years after Cædmon's death, "tried to make religious poems in the English nation, but none could compare with him, and no vain or trivial song came from his lips." He was the first and best of his school. If this view of Bæda be worth anything, we can scarcely accept the opinion of those who look upon Cædmon as a rude and uncultivated writer, or that of those who think that he produced nothing but hymns of a quality similar to the verses with which he began. A man of some genius, as Bæda certainly represents Cædmon to be, who continually writes poetry and practises his art for fifteen years makes steady advance in that art, and is capable of writing in various manners, not only in one. And to deny that he could have written the *Genesis A* pushes criticism beyond the bounds of literary sense. I do not say he wrote it; I know nothing about it; but it is not wise to say that he could not have written it. It is archaic in feeling; it uses the old nature-myths. When it comes to tell of war, it borrows with frank simplicity the terms of the ancient war-songs; when it does touch the scenery of sea or land, it is such as

Cædmon might have seen from the lofty and storm-swept fields on which the monastery of Hild was built; and though the beginning of *Genesis A* differs in words and form from the verses given above, it is just such a difference as one who has become a good poet would make out of an early sketch which, nevertheless, from his fondness for his first verses he retained. It pleases me then (though I record the view of some critics who say we have nothing of Cædmon's in the Junian manuscript, and of others, who think that Cædmon wrote, not long poems like the *Genesis*, but short, hymn-like songs) to believe that we have in *Genesis A*, with the changes that time and recitation make in a poem, some of the work of Cædmon himself. That piece consists of paraphrase of the Biblical narrative, interspersed with episodes in which the poet lets his imagination play freely with the story of the Creation, the Flood, the war of Abraham, the tale of Hagar, and the sacrifice of Isaac. The paraphrase is as it were the dull background before which the scenic tales are represented, and it is as sleepily written as the tales are vividly written. In fact, two kinds of poetry appear in *Genesis A*. The one resembles the mere monotonous narrative of a homiletic monk, the other is the heroic lay of the heathen saga transported into a Christian frame, and having at its root a poet's clear individuality. Cædmon, then, if he made this poem, had two manners. It is probable that he had others. No poet is contented with one fashion of writing. He certainly made hymns in the same manner as his first song, but better—lyric outbursts of praise; and this kind of poetry was likely to become fashionable in the monasteries.

It is probable that he attained another manner. He may have created the heroic Christian lay, in which Christ takes the place of the saga-hero; and the battle for world-victory, fought between him and Satan, is deeply tinged with the colours of the nature and the hero myths. This conjecture—it is nothing more—is based on the possibility, which some critics suggest, that he wrote the poem quotations from which are carved in runes upon the Ruthwell Cross in Annandale close to the Solway Firth.

The cross itself dates from the first half of the eighth century, and the lines, which from their situation and language belong to the north, are believed to be of the latter end of the seventh. Stephens translated the runic inscription on the top of the cross, " Cædmon me fawed," as " Cædmon made me," and explained this phrase as an assertion that the verses were by Cædmon. This it does not say, but criticism of the language and manner of the lines tends to make the authorship of Cædmon more and more probable. They sing how " Jesus, the young hero, who was God Almighty, girded himself, and stepped up full of courage on the gallows for the sake of man." Then the Rood itself speaks and tells how, " lifted on high, it bore the Lord of the heavenly realm, and how it trembled, all besteamed with blood." " Christ was on the Rood," it cries, " but I, pierced with the spears, and sore pained with sorrows, beheld it all. They laid him limb-wearied in the grave, they stood at the head of his corse." This is part of a lay, written in the old heroic manner, and belongs to a time when heathendom lay close to Christianity. Cædmon himself was born a heathen, and his work bridged the river between the pagan and the Christian poetry. He showed how the new material of Christianity could be assimilated by the English poets. High honour is due to his name. Though perhaps of Celtic descent, his tongue was English and his poems English. He wrote—*in suâ, id est, Anglorum linguâ*, says Bæda. But the monks of Whitby who taught him and helped him in his work, were some of them Irish, and all of them under Irish influence; and Wülker conjectures that they laid before him, as a pattern for his poetry, or as an incitement, existing Celtic hymns, such as Colman's, of the seventh century. Thus, as the English learned the arts of writing and of illumination from the Irish, so Cædmon may also have received from them an impulse to the making and form of his poetry. But it was no more than an impulse. What he wrote, he wrote in his own original way; and that way was English not Irish, Teutonic not Celtic.

CHAPTER IX

POEMS OF THE SCHOOL OF CÆDMON

THE poetry which we may collect under the name of the *School of Cædmon* belongs to the end of the seventh and the beginning of the eighth century. Men were as yet close to the heathen lays of war and to the heroic sagas; and in the hymnic songs of praise which formed one kind of the poetry of this school, and in the half-epic poems like *Exodus* and *Judith* which formed another kind, the close influence of heathen models and heathen thought is clearly felt. In yet another kind of poetry, the narrative poem, like *Genesis A*, with episodes like lays inserted into it, the episodes retain many of the qualities of heathen poetry. Of the poems of this character and date some are preserved in the *Exeter Book*. Three long ones—*Genesis A*, *Exodus*, and *Daniel*—are in the Junian manuscript. Another considerable fragment is the last three books of the *Judith*. Whether we can add to these the poems in the Junian manuscript entitled *Christ and Satan*, is still, I think, a matter under judgment.

In the *Exeter Book* (to take these sources in turn) there is a seventh-century adaptation of the *Song of the Three Children in the Furnace*. That hymn of praise comes from the Apocrypha, but being in the Liturgy for Sunday, would be one of the first things chosen by a versifying monk to put into English. The *Prayer of Azarias* soon followed it, composed from an ancient original. It was joined on to the previous song, and both were, but much later, furnished with a conclusion—a hymn of praise for the glorious deliverance of Shadrach, Meshach, and Abednego.

Meantime, at the end of this seventh century, we find some traces of poetry in the south of England. Ealdhelm, we know, made songs and sang them to the people, and no one doubts that the family lay and the war-song were made and sung all over the south. It is conjectured, on slight grounds, that some of the Anglo-Saxon *Riddles* may be Ealdhelm's translations of his own Latin Riddles. His Latin Verse and Riddles are said to have some traces in them of folk-poetry. It is difficult to find them. Whatever may be said of the probabilities of English poetry flourishing in the south, one thing is plain : no such school of Christian poetry existed in the south as did exist in the seventh and eighth centuries in Northumbria. Bæda is silent on the subject, and though his silence does not prove the absence of southern poetry, yet it means something. Moreover, had Ealdhelm, who did care for English verse, known of a school of poets in the south, he would scarcely have left it unnoticed. We may say, I think, that there was no school of English Christian poetry in the south during the seventh and eighth centuries.

The next poems belonging to this time, and of the school of Cædmon, are some of those contained in the Junian manuscript. That manuscript, of which a short account is necessary, was found in England by Archbishop Ussher, and was sent to Francis Du Jon (whose name in literature is Junius), a scholar of Leyden, and librarian to Lord Arundel. When Junius left England, in 1650, he had the manuscript printed at Amsterdam, and published it as the work of Cædmon. He based this opinion on the substantial agreement of its first lines with Bæda's abstract of the verses sung by Cædmon in his dream, and on the harmony of its contents with Bæda's account of Cædmon's work. It is a small folio of 229 pages, and it rests in the Bodleian. The first part, in fine handwriting of the tenth century, and illustrated with rude pictures, contains the *Genesis*, the *Exodus*, and the *Daniel*. The second part, in a different and later handwriting, includes poems and fragments of poems—the Fall of the Rebel Angels, the Harrowing of Hell, the Resurrection, Ascension, Pentecost, and the Temptation. They are generally classed under the title of *Christ and Satan*. Since the time of Junius, the critics have found in the separate parts of the manuscript so many diverse elements and differences of style and thought that they have allotted the various poems to separate and nameless authors, and have hesitated to attribute a single line of it to Cædmon. However, we will take, without guessing at their authorship, those poems in the manuscript which belong to the close of the seventh or the beginning of the eighth century. They are that portion of the *Genesis* which is now called *Genesis A;* the *Exodus;* and the *Daniel.*

Genesis A consists of the first 234 lines of the *Genesis*, and then of the lines from 852 to the close. The lines from 235 to 851 (*Genesis B*) contain a second account of the Fall of Man, and are a late insertion into the original. They will be discussed in their proper place. Our poem begins with an ascription of praise to God, which resembles but is not the same as the hymn sung by Cædmon in his dream. The action of the poem is opened by the rebellion of the highest of the angels, who, swollen "with pride and of malicious hatred all athirst," strove with God for the wide clearness of heaven, and for empire in the north.[1] But God made "a woful dwelling for the false spirits, howls of hell and hard pains, a joyless deep; furnished with eternal night and crammed with sorrows, filled full of fire and frightful cold, with reek of smoke and ruddy flame." And he "beat down their courage and bowed their pride," and, like Beowulf with Grendel, "gripped, stern and grim, his foes

With cruel clutch and crushed them in his grasp.

---

[1] Deep malice thence conceiving and disdain.
. . . . .
Homeward with flying march where we possess
The quarters of the North.—*Par. Lost*, Book V.

So they sang no more their lofty song, shamed for their lost beauty, and knew exile and broken boast, and were decked with darkness as with a garment."

But as ever, there was "soft society in Heaven," thegns who loved their Lord, and manners fair and mild. But God, grieved for the empty seats of heaven, looked forth on the vast abyss—the Norse *ginnûnga gap*, the chasm of dark mist, where broods the *heolster-sceado*, the shadow that hides the unfathomable caverns, Milton's *hollow dark*—and filled it with creation. The antique lines I here translate are full of heathen conceptions, of nature-myths :—

> Nor was here as yet, save a hollow shadow,
> Anything created ; but the wide abyss
> Deep and dim, outspread; all divided from the Lord,
> Idle and unuseful. With His eyes upon it
> Gazed the mighty-minded King, and He marked the place
> Lie delightless—(looked and) saw the cloud
> Brooding black in Ever-night, swart beneath the heaven,
> Wan, and wasteful all,[1] till the world became.
> Then the ever-living Lord at the first created—
> He the Helm of every wight—Heaven and the Earth ;
> Reared aloft the Firmament, and this roomful land
> Stablished steadfast there.

---

[1] They viewed the vast immeasurable Abyss,
Outrageous as a sea, dark, wasteful, wild,
Up from the bottom turned by furious winds
And surging waves.—*Par. Lost*, Book VII.

This whirling of the winds in the unutterable depths of darkness is not in the Teutonic conception. That chasm of chasms is silent. But Milton has other phrases for chaos. He calls it "the wasteful Deep," "the waste, wide anarchy of chaos, damp and dark," "the unvoyageable gulf obscure," "the dark, unbottomed, infinite Abyss," "the vast Abrupt"—a splendid phrase—

> The void profound
> Of unessential Night receives him next,
> Wide-gaping, and with utter loss of being
> Threatens him, plunged in that abortive gulf.
> *Par. Lost*, Book II.

Most of these phrases—so receptive was Milton—belong to the Teutonic and not to the classical conception of the dark beyond.

> But as yet the Earth—
> E'en the grass[1]—ungreen was now! Gloomed in Ever-night
> Far away and wide, waters rolling wan,
> Ocean veiled the world. Then the wondrous-bright
> Spirit of the Heaven's Ward o'er the heaving sea was borne
> With a mickle speed. . . .
> Then the Lord of triumphs let a-sundered be,
> O'er the lake of Ocean, light apart from gloom,
> Shadows from the shining. . . .
> And of days the first saw the darkness dun
> Fading swart away o'er the spacious deep.
> Then that day departed o'er the ordered world
> Of the midmost earth, and the Measurer drove
> After the sheer shining—He our shaping God—
> Earliest Evening on. On its footsteps ran,
> Thrust along, the gloomy Dark. That the King Himself
> Named the Night by name. . . .
> After that stept swiftly on, striding o'er the Earth,
> Bright, the third of morns.

There is now a gap of three leaves in the MS., and we come at once on the Creation of Man. God is "blithe of heart" as he blesses them; in the breast of both is burning love of God: and the phrases are full of the new English passions of joy and love which had come with Christianity. Nor is the love of quiet nature which follows in the description of Eden less new to the English. It marks that feeling towards nature on which I have dwelt, and which the novel tenderness of Christianity had induced. The fierce weather and storm-tossed seas and ice-clad trees of *Beowulf* stand alone no longer: I quote a second time

> Winsomely the water, running, all well-springs that be,
> Washed the happy lands; nor as yet the welkin
> Bore above the roomy ground all the rains that are
> Wan-gloomed by the gale; yet with growing blooms
> Was the Earth made fair.

At this point the work of the elder poet finishes, but it is taken up again at the story of Cain and Abel. There is no interest

[1] "A yawning gap was there, and nowhere was the grass."—*Volospá*.

in it; it is only a dull paraphrase till we come to the episode of the Flood. This pleased the poet who knew the ways of the sea, and he describes the black heaven and the whelming waves with so much eagerness that we are ready to think that he lived at Whitby. Dialogue, with even a dramatic touch in it, is here, as afterwards through the whole poem, introduced to enliven the tale. The sea is the dark, "flint-gray" sea of the Eastern coasts, the "swart water, the wan waves," wherein dwells that strange creation of the English poets—the Terror of the Water. The ship is called by the old names of the heroic poems—"the ocean-house, the foam-bark, the wood-fortress." God bids Noah build his ark, and the lines in which the poet tells of the wrath of God, and in which the flood is described, might well have been sung in the great hall of the abbey while the storm roared outside, and the sound of the waves kept company with the clanging of the harp and the roll of the verses. "And God said:—

> Now I'll set a feud of war, for the space of forty days,
> 'Gainst (the souls of) men; and with surging troops of waves,
> Owners and their ownings, quell them all, in death,
> . . . .
> When the swart cloud-rack upward swells (in heaven).
> . . . Then sent forth the Lord
> From the heavens heavy rain; eke he hugely let
> All the welling water-springs on the world throng in
> Out of every vein of earth, and the ocean-streams
> Swarthy, sound aloud! Now the sea stepped up
> O'er the shore-stead walls! Strong was He and wroth
> Who the waters wielded, who with His wan wave
> Cloaked and covered then all the sinful children
> Of this middle-earth.
> Then afar and wide rode on, all the welkin under,
> O'er the Ocean-ring, that excelling house:
> Faring with its freight; and this faring ship—
> That swift sailer through the seas—durst no surge's terror
> Heavy, heave against:

The northern sternness of this is soon relieved by the northern tenderness when the poet begins to play with the story of the dove. Sympathy with animals belongs to the quietude of the monastic life, and he describes her sorrow—for she could find no resting-place — in gracious lines, and then her joy when she perched at last on a gentle tree; how she plumed her feathers, and brought to the sailor an olive-twig of green. The lines, in their love of animals, in their new sympathy with rest and joy, are a strange contrast to the pagan poetry. And they have a quality in them which makes us think that here, if anywhere, the Celtic touch is felt :—

> Far and wide she flew,
> Glad in flying free, till she found a place,
> Fair, where she fain would rest! With her feet she stept
> On a gentle tree. Gay of mood and glad she was.
>
> . . . . . .
>
> There she fluttered feathers; went a-flying off again,
> With her booty flew, brought it to the sailor,
> From an olive wood a twig; right into his hands
> Bore the blade of green.

"Then the chief of seamen knew that gladness was at hand."

After this episode, the poem hurries through another desert of paraphrase to the Abraham story, and the invasion of the kings of the East is made into a well-invented lay of war. It is developed with great freedom through 200 lines. It is English war, full of English terms and customs; it might be a piece out of an heroic saga. The raid into the Jordan valley exactly represents a raid of the Picts into Northumbria. "The country side is overspread with foes; many a maiden, pale of cheek, passes, trembling, to the embraces of a stranger; the shielders of the brides fall, sick of wounds"; but the folk gather under their kings and the battle is joined. Then the poet becomes all heathen, all heroic :—

> Loud were then the lances,
> Savage then the slaughter hosts ! Sadly sang the wan fowl,
> With her feathers dank with dew, midst the darting of the shafts,
> Hoping, (crying) for the carrion.

> Then was hard play there,
> Interchanging of corpse-darts, mickle cry of war;
> Loud the hurtling clash of battle.

And the folk of Sodom went, for their life, from that encampment, and "fell on their track, eaten by the edge of the sword: and all the wives and maidens fled with them." But "the war-wolves exulted in their triumph and their booty." Then a man, "a sparing of the spears," brings the news to Abraham, the Hebrew earl; and the hero told it to his war-comrades Aner and Mamre and Eshcol, and they "give him their troth that they will wreak his wrong or fall with him on the war-stead. And the hero bade the host-men of his hearth take their weapons, and they gather of head-warriors eighteen, and of the rest three hundred, loyal to their lord. Of them all he knew that on the fighting Fyrd they could well bear the fallow linden." This is as close to English history as the poet could make it. Nor, after the battle, where the "sharp ground spears grisly gripped at the heart of men," is the talk between the war-leader of Sodom and Abraham less true to English life. "Give me the maidens," cries the king, "the bairns of the æthelings, the widows of those who were good folk-fellows in the fight; let me lead them home to their wasted dwellings—but keep the twisted gold and the cattle and the beauteous ornaments of horse and man. These are yours."

And Abraham answered, as a great English earl might have answered: "Nothing will I take, lest thou shouldst say—'I have been enriched by Sodom'; all the booty mine by battle thou shalt keep—all except the share of my æthelings. Never will I take from my warriors their right." These are the words of the Bible, but they exactly fitted the temper of a great ealdorman. Then the poet passes to his own time and his own temper, and ends with a piece of pure heathen fierceness—of the Northumbrian impassioned against the Pict:—

> Go, and bear with thee
> Home the gold enchased, and the girls embraceable,
> Women of thy people! For a while thou needest not

> Fear the fighting rush of the foes we hate—
> Battle from the Northmen! For the birds of carrion,
> Splashed with blood, are sitting on the shelving mountains,
> Glutted to the gullet with the gory corpses.

The paraphrase begins again, but vivid dialogue illumines it in the story of Hagar, so vivid that one might almost say that the dramatic genius of the English people begins to show itself in this early poem. This quasi-dramatic method is again introduced in the tale of the sacrifice of Isaac with which *Genesis A* abruptly ends. Homely northern touches enter into it—the bale-fire for the bairn; the swart flame ready to burn the body; the holy man, the white-haired gold-giver, girding his gray sword upon him; the golden spear-point of the sun showing its wondrous brightness over the deep sea; the high downs towering above the roof of the land; the wolds where the pile of wood is upbuilt—till the father heaves the child on the bale and grasps and lifts the sword. It is almost an actual picture of a northman's human sacrifice, and the poem ends with the cry of God:—

> Pluck the boy away living from the pile of wood.

The poem called *Exodus* stands alone, a united whole. It is taken up with one event, the beginning, progress, and close of which it records; it moves swiftly and moves well. The triumph of the death of the first-born begins it; the triumph over Pharaoh at the Red Sea concludes it. In the midst is the march of the Israelites and the passage of the sea. Dialogue is not so common as in *Genesis A*, and when used it is brief and dry. On the other hand, the descriptions are long and very elaborately worked, through many repetitions of the same things in different words; they are, however, full of force, even over-forcible. We are by no means so close to human nature as we are in *Genesis A*. The naïveté of the earlier production of the school is gone. The writer is too conscious of his art to be simple, and on the other hand, he has none of the intellectual subtlety which we find in later work, for instance, in *Genesis B*. There is no actual battle as in *Genesis A;* but war and the circumstance of war give great pleasure to this poet. The gathering of hosts, the march, the pomp of ensigns and music and cavalry, the appearance and speeches of the chiefs, the array of warriors, are described with so much personal interest that we feel the writer had seen war and loved it. The real battle of the poem is the battle of God and of the fierce storm and charging waves He wields with Pharaoh and his host, and a fine piece it is of early heroic work, done on a Scriptural subject. A great number of curious, vigorous, pictorial expressions, not used by other poets, individualise this writer from the rest of the Anglo-Saxon poets. His style is also more desirous of effect; it tends even towards that fresh sensationalism which is so often connected with exuberance of life. The literary audacities of the poem suggest a young man as its writer.

The poem, after a short celebration of Moses as the law-giver, passes into its subject with a bold image which carries with it the central matter :—

> Then in that old time, and with ancient punishments,
> Deeply drenched with death was the dreadest of all folk.

The fate of the first-born follows, and it sometimes reads as if the poet had read *Beowulf,* as if he used some of the phrases of the lays in that poem, especially that of the prince who hid the dragon's treasure. Certainly the whole passage is in the heroic manner :—

> By the death of hoard-wards, wailing was renewed,
> Slept the song of joy in hall, spoiled of all its treasure !
> God had these manscathers, at the mid of night,
> Fiercely felled.
> Broken were the burg-defenders, far and wide the Bane strode ;
> Loathly was that people-Hater ! All the land was gloomed
> With the bodies of the dead ; all the best were dead.
> Far and wide was weeping, world-delight was little ;
> Locked together lay the hands of the laughter-smiths !
>   Famous was that day,
> Over middle-garth, when the multitude went forth.

The journey follows through narrow ways, past the fortresses of the March, underneath the blazing sun. But God overtented the sky with "a sail of cloud by day, and by night the cloud stood above the shooters, a fiery light." The shields shimmered in its flame, the shadows slunk away. It was their watchman, to guard them from "the terror of the wan-gray heath, and its tempests like the ocean":—

> Fiery flaming locks had that Forward-ganger;
> Brilliant were his beams; bale and terror boded he!

The poet had probably seen the great comet of 678, which "shone," the *Chronicle* says, "like a sunbeam every morning for three months."

The host arrives at the Red Sea shore, and they heard with hopeless terror of Pharaoh's Fyrd a-forward ganging. This is a fine opportunity for the poet, and he takes full advantage of it to describe an English army going into battle. Flags are flying, trumpets sounding, horses stamping. The ravens circle above the march, the wolves are howling on its skirts; haughty thegns are prancing in the van; the king with his standard rides before them, fastening down his visor, shaking his sark of mail. Close beside him are his comrades, hoary wolves of war, thirsting for the fray, faithful to their lord. The well-known horn gives order by its notes how the host should march. Then with all this glory the poet contrasts the dark fate that was at hand. This "battle-brilliant" host was doomed.

Nor is the Israelites' call to arms and their march less English. With the blare of brass, at the break of day, all the folk are gathered, bid to don their war-sarks, to think of noble deeds, to call the squadrons to the shore with the waving of their banners. Swiftly the watchmen bethought them of the war-cry, and the sailors struck their tents to the sound of shawms. The tribes are marshalled under their leaders, their numbers are counted, the gray-haired warriors and weak youths are put aside. The host-banner is displayed, and the war-chief leaps to the front of the heroes, and upheaves his shield, bids the folk-leaders silence the host that all may hear. It is the image of the English Fyrd at the moment of marching. Tribe by tribe, each in order, each with its device, they raise their white linden shields and wade into the greenish depths of the sea-paths between the wondrous walls of water. First came Judah, and above his host shone his banner, a lion all of gold. The greatest of folk bore the boldest of beasts. No insult to their leader did they ever bear in war. They ran to onset in the van:—

> Bloody were the bill-tracks, rushing was the battle-strength,
> Grind on grind of visored helms there where Judah drove.

After them the sons of Reuben marched, sailors proudly treading! Shields these Vikings[1] bore over the salt-marshes. Next came the sons of Simeon: their ensigns waved over their spearfaring, their shafts were wet with dew. Then the rustling murmur of the dawn reached them from the moving of the ocean: God's beacon rose, bright shining morn.

Here a dull episode has been pushed into the poem, but it soon recovers itself, and tries, by repeated descriptions, to realise the overwhelming by the sea of the host of Pharaoh. Vigour, even fury, fills the pictures; startling images obscure them, but the artist does not get home to the horror and madness of the hour. Nevertheless he reaches a certain power, a power far beyond that which we should expect from early poetry. "Wyrd wrapt them," he says, "with her wave."

> Where the paths had lain
> Mad of mood the sea was. Drowned the might of Egypt lay!
> Then upsurged the streaming sea, and a storm of cries arose,
> High into the Heavens—greatest of host-wailings!
> Loudly howled the hated foes, and the heaven grew black above;
> Blood was borne the flood along, with the bodies of the doomed.

---

[1] The Israelites are "seamen," as above; the children of Reuben are Vikings, the pillar of cloud is like a sail spread from a great mast. Was the writer a seaman?

> Shattered were the sea shield-burgs! This, of sea-deaths greatest,
> Beat against the vault of sky!
> . . . . . .
> So the brown upweltering overwhelmed them all;
> Highest that of haughty waves! All the host sank deep!

"God, with his death-grip, decided the battle. With his sword of old he smote down on Egypt the foam-breasted billows, and the host of sinners slept."

This is the end of the overthrow, and the poem closes with the joy of the Israelites. "The trumpets of victory sang, the banners rose to that sweet sound. The men looked on the sea. All stained with blood was the foaming wave through which they had borne their sarks of battle. They sang of glory, and the women sang in turn.

> Then was easily to see many an Afric maid
> On the Ocean's shore all adorned with gold:
> And the sea-escaped began from their seines to share
> On the leaving of the waves,[1] jewels, treasures old,
> Bucklers and breast armour. Justly fell to them
> Gold and goodly webs, Joseph's store of riches,
> Glorious wealth of warriors! But its wardens lay
> On the stead of death, strongest of all peoples."

Judith is probably of the same cycle as the *Exodus*. Like the *Exodus*, the subject is conceived in a saga fashion. Both these poems addressed not only the monk but the warrior. The king, the thegns, and the freemen listened to them as they sat in the hall at the mead. The poems, half war, half religion, touching heathendom with one hand and Christianity with the other, equally excited and instructed the feasters. This poem was probably written towards the middle of the eighth century, after the death of Bæda. It belongs to the joyous, unself-conscious time, before the Muse became melancholy in Cynewulf, full of regrets for the past, of hopes only for a world beyond this earth, and of self-introspection. We are placed in the midst of an eager life, in

---

[1] That is, the shore.

full sympathy with liberty, battle and patriotism, with bold and heroic deeds. Judith is a fine creature, even finer than she is in the Apocrypha; and I do not doubt that there were many Englishwomen of the time capable of her warlike passion, and endowed with her lofty character. The manuscript exists along with the MS. of *Beowulf*. It seems to have been in twelve books or sections, for we only possess fourteen lines of section ix., and the whole of sections x., xi., and xii. Perhaps the beginning was a mere paraphrase of the earlier chapters of the book of *Judith*, and the listeners did not care about preserving it. The scribe therefore only preserved the main interests: the feast, the slaughter of Holofernes, Judith's call to battle, and the overthrow of the Assyrian host.

The feast with which the tenth book begins lasts the whole day, and the drunkenness of Holofernes may be drawn from some English chief. "He laughed and shouted and raged so loudly that all his folk heard how this stark-minded man stormed and yelled, full of fierce mirth and mad with mead." He bids Judith be led to his tent, but she, of plaited tresses, drew the sharp sword, hardened by the scours of battle, and called on the Ward of Heaven with a fierce and passionate prayer: "Let me hew down," it ends, "O God, this lord of murder! Venge thou that which is so angry in me, this burning at my heart,"—and the slaying of the heathen dog is described point by point with careful joy. *Book xi.* takes Judith and her pale-cheeked maid to the walls of Bethulia. And the folk raced, old and young, to meet the divine maid. Then she bade her women unwrap the bloody head, and calls on them, like Joan of Arc, to strike for freedom. "I have wrenched life from this loathliest of men; fit ye for the fighting. When God makes rise the blaze of day, bear your lindens forward:—

> Shield-board sheltering your breast, byrnies for your raiment,
> Helmets all high-shining midst that horde of scathers;
> Fell in death the folk-chiefs with the flashing swords,
> Doomed for death are they!"

Then again the English battle is described with all its attendants. Din was there of shields, loud they rang; and the gaunt wolf of the weald rejoiced, and the black raven, thirsty for slaughter, and the earn flew on their track, dusky-coated, horn-nebbed, dewy-feathered, hungry for fodder, singing his battle-song. Swift was the step of the chiefs of war to the carnage; and they let fly, sheltered by their shields, showers of arrows, battle-adders, from their bows of horn. Right into the host of the hard ones they sent their spears, and their cries were like a storm. So the Hebrews showed their foes what the sword-swing was.

Book xii. tells of the dread waking of the Assyrians, of their finding of Holofernes headless, of their headlong flight. Then is told the gathering of the spoil. " Proud, with woven tresses, the Hebrews brought to Bethulia helms, hip-seaxes, bright-gray byrnies, panoplies inlaid with gold." And to Judith they gave the sword and bloody helm of Holofernes and the huge war-sark embossed with gold and his armlets and bright gems. For all this she praised the Lord—and the poem makes a fair ending, gracious and touched again with that new rejoicing in the tenderness of nature which is so great a contrast to the fierce, storm-shaken natural scenery in *Beowulf:*—

> To the Lord beloved, for this,
> Glory be for widening ages ! Wind and lift He shaped of old,
> Sky above and spacious earth, every one of the wild streams,
> And the Æther's jubilation—through His own delightfulness.

To pass from the brilliant heroism of Judith to the dull monotony of the *Daniel* is sorrowful indeed. It shows how the impulse Cædmon gave, how the heroic imagination, had died away. A long poem of 765 lines, its end is wanting. It closes abruptly with the story of Belshazzar (Daniel v.), as if the writer thought the rest of the book uninteresting. The beginning seems to wish to connect itself with the *Exodus,* for it sketches the history of the Hebrews from the Exodus to Nebuchadnezzar.

When he comes to the book of Daniel, his alliterative verse is nothing more than a dull paraphrase of the Latin version which lay before him on his desk. The writer was some monk, with a dreary turn for homiletic verse. He had, however, the good taste to recognise better work than his own, and when he came to the story of the three men in the burning fiery furnace, he inserted the old poem of the seventh century on that subject, as well as the *Song of the Three Children* and the *Prayer of Azarias*, without taking any pains, says Wülker, to reconcile the contradictions between this insertion and the previous part of his poem.

The *Daniel* closes the cycle of the earliest Christian poetry—that which belongs to the end of the seventh and the first half of the eighth century. It is a poetry which passes, as we have seen, through paraphrase, hymns, heroic Christian lays like that on the Ruthwell Cross, and heroic pieces of saga worked on the Genesis stories, into poems of a quasi-epic character like the *Exodus* and the *Judith*. At last it dies, as in the *Daniel*, in mere paraphrase, and in imitation of the good work of the past. It was also a poetry which drew nearly all its materials from the Old Testament history, and left untouched the stories of the Saints and the legends of the Church. Though it celebrated Christ as God Almighty, it celebrated Him, with one exception, only as the God of the Jews, as the great Shaper who made the world and man, as the great Warrior who overthrew the rebel angels, who destroyed the kings of the East and the Egyptians, and who subdued the pride of Assyria. It was, moreover, a poetry eminently English; it clothed the events and personages of the Old Testament in an English dress. It was also eminently objective, historical, unmeditative. The personality of the poet, his sorrow or joy, his own thoughts about the subject on which he writes, never intrude. And finally, as we have seen, it was so close to heathendom, that it shares in the myths, the manner, the thoughts, the war-customs and expressions of the heroic sagas before Christianity.

The Christian poetry which succeeded it in the latter half of the eighth century is clearly distinguishable from it; and it marks the exuberance of early Anglo-Saxon literature, first, that this new poetry is more copious than its predecessor; and secondly, that it is as good in its own literary way. Many critics say that it is better, and in one sense that is true. It is more literary; its form is more carefully considered; it has greater command of language and of metrical movement; it has a finer faculty of comparison, a livelier fancy, a more cultivated imagination; in one word, the art of the poetry is higher. However, more of the materials of poetry were in the hands of this second band of writers. They had studied Vergil, Ovid, and the Latin Hymns.

In Cynewulf, the leader of this later school of poetry, all these finer elements are found. But we miss, with some regret, the bold, unconscious heathen note, the rude heroic strain. We miss the sublimity given—as in the *Genesis* account of the Creation—by the nearness of the nature-myths; we miss the youthful audacity of the *Exodus*, and even its furious wording; we miss the absence of self-consciousness. To compare these small things of poetry with very great, we feel as if we were reading Euripides instead of Æschylus.

But this is only a distinction of art; in other matters the new poetry is even more clearly to be distinguished from the old. Its subjects are now drawn from Christianity rather than from Judaism. The New Testament replaces the Old; the stories of saints and martyrs and the legends of the Church replace the stories of Abraham and Isaac, of Daniel and Judith. The Roman Church has laid its power on poetry. The influence of the Latin, not of the Celtic, Church is now dominant. Again, Christ is celebrated now as the Saviour rather than as the Warrior-God. His victory is the victory He wins for all mankind upon the Cross; and the poetry of it is a poetry of sorrow before it becomes a poetry of triumph. Earthly life is all sorrow in it; only in the life to come is rapture. The elder poetry lived in the present, this in the future. Then, too, the special English note decays. It is there, but it sounds ever weaker and weaker; it is succeeded by the more international note of the Roman Church. And finally, the poetry almost ceases to be objective. The personal passion of the poet, especially in Cynewulf, always intrudes; it colours everything that is written—hymns, stories of martyrdom, legends of anchorites and of saints, allegorical poems, and even natural description. The inward feeling overtops that outward vision of the thing which was dear to the writers of the *Genesis*, the *Exodus*, and *Judith*.

All these new elements were raised in Cynewulf's work to the highest value they could then attain. He added to them the shaping and surprising imagination of a true poet; he added—and it is the natural companion of imagination—a personal passion which in his outbursts of praise, in his strong crying of prayer, in his feeling for human affections and for divine love, lifts his religious poetry into a lofty place in the record of the sacred song of England. Moreover, he added to these elements, if we allot the best of the *Riddles* to him, so vivid an imagination of the things he describes that he not only saw them as they were, but also, driven by his own strong personality, saw them as if they were persons, and attached to them, as he did, for example, to the Hurricane, the Sword, the Swan, the Nightingale, the Iceberg and the Sun, human passions and human intelligence.

CHAPTER X

THE ELEGIES AND THE RIDDLES

WE have closed the last chapter with the name of Cynewulf as the chief of the new Christian poetry. But before we speak of that poetry, we must notice poems which have few if any connections with Christianity, and may have been written, as far as I can judge, in the first half of the eighth century. These are the Elegies, the *Ruined Burg*, the *Wanderer*, the *Seafarer*, the *Wife's Complaint*, the *Husband's Message*. They are not of the Cædmon school, nor have they any close relation to the known poems of Cynewulf. They stand apart on a platform of their own. The Cædmon poems seem to belong to a time of youth and of national exultation. These Elegies are steeped in regret for the glory of the past, they speak of exile and slaughters and ruin; they love nature, but love in it sorrow; the writers belong to a nation in distress — such distress, if we may guess, as prevailed in Northumbria during that parenthesis of bad government and national tumult which filled the years between the death of Aldfrith in 705 and the renewed peace and order under Ceolwulf in the years which followed 729. The *Ruined Burg*, which I have already partly translated (p. 86), swells with impassioned sorrow for the passing away of the splendour and fame and work of men. The Wyrd has "whirled their glory into change." This too is the motive of the *Wanderer*, but mixed up with it is the poet's personal sorrow for vanished friendship and good fortune. Then the personal cry becomes universal again: Woe is me, this fate of mine is the fate of all the world of men :—

> All is full of trouble, all this realm of earth ;
> Doom of weirds is changing all the world below the skies.

The *Wife's Complaint*, the *Husband's Message* are the laments of exiles. The *Seafarer* is the wailing of the worn-out seaman who thinks of the dread and misery of the ocean, and yet of the fierce Weird which makes him long to put out to sea again—the very note of Tennyson's *Sailor Boy*. The internal evidence of them all, except the *Seafarer*, points to a time when the halls of nobles were desolated, when war and exile were common ; but neither this nor the mournful motive can date the poems or place them in any special part of England. Ruined cities and ruined chieftains, exile, and the fates of war, were common everywhere and at every time in ancient England.

Their date can best be conjectured from their want of Christian sentiment, and from the presence in them of certain heathen elements, especially the dominance of the Wyrd, elements which have all but disappeared in Cynewulf and his followers. It is true, the *Seafarer* ends with a Christian tag, but the quality of its verse, which is merely homiletic, has made capable persons give it up as a part of the original poem. It is true, the *Wanderer* has a prologue into which the name of God is inserted and an epilogue which is distinctly Christian, but the whole body of the poem, full of pagan sentiment, suggests that these are later additions; and even these additions are not made by a person who cared, as one of the Christian school would have done, for specialising doctrine. I believe these poems were written by laymen, men who were only Christians in name, who cared for poetry not for religion—poets who, like Cynewulf in his youth, had lived and feasted with great chieftains, who had loved, had sailed the seas, and suffered exile. It is probable that there were many poems of this kind. But they would not have been written in this semi-heathen manner in the later part of the eighth or in the ninth century. Their proper place, it seems to me, is in the earlier part of the eighth century, when, especially in Northumbria, heathenism was still close at hand.

As to where they were written, we cannot tell. Wülker says they belong to the ninth century, and were written in the south of England. I cannot agree with him. It is probable enough that the *Ruined Burg* was written by a Mercian guest in the monastery of Osric. But the *Wife's Complaint* and the *Husband's Message* have no special note, they are both imaginative poems, they have a clear eye for natural scenery; and neither in Wessex nor Mercia have we any evidence, at present, of a school of English poetry capable of producing such good work, or of any person, unless we except Ealdhelm in the conventionalisms of his Latin verse, who had a care for nature. In Northumbria we have a fine school of poetry, and that poetry has a love of nature. As to the *Wanderer* and the *Seafarer*, they have the note of the North. The seas, the cliffs, the seamanship, the wild and desolate coasts they describe are not southern. Seamanship had died out in the South, but it was kept up in the North by the incessant traffic between the monasteries of Northumbria from Coldingham to Whitby. The *Seafarer* should be a northern poem, and I should be inclined to say the *Wanderer* also. But we can attain to no certainty on these matters.

What is most remarkable in the Elegies, as in many of the *Riddles*, is their pleasure in the aspects of wild nature. And it may serve to help us to date these poems that, with the one exception of the coming of spring, the nature they describe is the savage nature which we find in the heathen poem of *Beowulf*. The tenderer, lovelier aspect of field and glade and river which belongs to the poems of Cynewulf has not become common in poetry. The *Seafarer* could scarcely describe better the fierce doings of the tempest and of the frost on the German ocean, the wild birds which haunt the gale, and the plunging waves; or, in contrast, the soft incoming of the spring and the cuckoo crying sorrow. The *Wanderer* paints the fallow waves and the interweaving of their crests, the sea-birds bathing and broadening out their plumes, the driving sleet and the snow sifted through with hail, the storms lashing on the ruined fortress, the whirling of the snow when the drift of it—that terror of the winter—comes black from the North, and the night darkens down, bringing harm to men. The *Wife's Complaint* describes the wild wood cave in the steep downs overgrown with briers and sheltered by the roots of a great oak; the overhanging cliff, storm-beaten, white with frost; and the *Husband's Message* sings of the cuckoo crying of his grief from the woods that fledge the mountain steep.

This is a remarkable love of nature, but what is more remarkable and modern in these poems is that the natural objects are seen, not as *Genesis A* saw them—as they are—but in accordance with the mood of the poet. Even the modern passion of being alone with nature is not unrepresented. The young man in the *Seafarer* longs to be away from the noise of men upon the far paths of the deep. Nor do these poems want a psychological element which is startling in poetry 1100 years old. The young seaman, eager for the ocean, sees his spirit pass from his body and go before him:—

> O'er the surging flood of sea now my spirit flies,
> O'er the homeland of the whale—hovers then afar,
> O'er the foldings of the earth! Now again it flies to me,
> Full of yearning, greedy! Yells that lonely Flier,
> Whets upon the whale-way irresistibly my heart,
> O'er the storming of the seas!

The Wanderer, remembering his friends, sees them as ghosts floating before him in the ocean-mist. He cries to them, "but they are silent. They sing none of the old familiar songs, but swim away in the mist as in a sea, and his sorrow is deepened." These are passages steeped in our modern spirit, and they show, at least, how constant are the roots of English song, and how needful it is, if we would fully understand it, to go back to the ground from which it has grown.

As to the poems themselves, the *Husband's Message* begins with an introduction of eleven lines describing the slice of wood on which the message is carved in runes. The rest is the message itself, and the word-tablet is the spokesman,—an awkward experiment of the poet. The message is a love-message from the exile imploring her to join him: "Bethink thee of the troth we plighted of old, take sail to meet thy lover :—

> Soon as ever thou shalt listen, on the edges of the cliff,
> To the cuckoo in the copsewood, chanting of his sorrow—
> Then begin to seek the sea, where the sea-mew is at home,
> Sit thee in the sea-bark, so that, to the south-ward,
> Thou mayst light upon thy lover, o'er the ocean pathway—
> There thy Lord with longing, waits and looks for thee."

And the poem ends with the binding together of the runes of their names to symbolise a love till death. It has a distinct note of passionate love and tenderness which does not occur, save here and in the *Wife's Complaint*, in Anglo-Saxon poetry.

The *Wife's Complaint* is a much more involved piece, subtle in feeling, better written than the last, and also unique in Anglo-Saxon poetry. It may be a story out of an old saga belonging to the time of Offa, King of the Engle, the son of Wermund, but it is best to think of it as a separate poem. It tells its own story fully.

The foes of the woman have made bad blood between her and her husband; he has exiled her into the wild wood, and she sings her grief. She recalls how they were parted by treachery, how much she loved him, how deep were the vows they made that death alone should divide them—and now "in this cavern, overrun with briers, under-the oak, is my dreary dwelling. Other lovers there are who live and sleep together, but I am alone with uncounted sorrows." Then she thinks of her husband, and pictures his lonely life while he thinks of her and his home. "He who thinks her guilty, and yet loves her, what sorrow must be his!

> For my friend is sitting
> Under the o'erhanging cliff, overfrosted by the storm :
> O my Wooer, so outwearied, by the waters compassed round

> In that dreary dwelling! There endures my dear one;
> Anguish mickle in his mind; far too oft remembers him
> Of a happier home! Woe is his, and woe,
> Who with weary longing, waits for his Beloved!"

The *Seafarer* is still more modern in feeling, and contains the two motives which have underlain so much of our sea-poetry—pity for the sailor's dangers on the deep, and the passion which drives the sailor into the secrets of the sea. It has been divided into a dialogue between an old mariner who represents the first motive, and a young one who represents the second; or it has been taken as a dramatic soliloquy in which the poet contrasts these two views of a seaman's life, and ends by saying that whether the life be hard or not the attraction to it is irresistible. Whatever it be, it is the work of a fine poet, and there is little reason why its motive and sentiment should not belong to the nineteenth century. I have placed a translation of it in the Appendix, along with a translation of the *Wanderer*, for both belong to the fine flower of old English song.

The *Wanderer* is the best in form of all Anglo-Saxon poems. The Prologue is, I think, as ancient as the body of the poem. "The grace of God" is a phrase which may have slipt in; we feel the full remembrance of pagan thought in the phrase—"Wyrd is fully wrought." Wyrd and the doom of her weirds stands throughout instead of the will of God. The duty of a great earl to bind up the coffer of his breast is described. The gold-friend from whose treasure-giving the poet is exiled, the feast in the hall, the heroes, the man-lord on the gift-stool, the tie of comradeship, the drawing of the character of the wise man, the picture of the ruined fort and hall, the fates of war, the hero lost in the ship or torn by wolves, or hidden in the earth by his weeping friend, tell us the story of English life in stormy times, and are followed by the long cry of desolation—

> Whither went the horse, whither went the man, where has gone the treasure-giver?
> What befell the seats of feasting, whither fled the joys in hall?

> Ea la! the beaker bright, Ea la! the byrnied warriors!
> Ea la! the prince's pride! How departed is that time!
> Veiled beneath Night's helm it is, as it ne'er had been.

This reminds us of the heroic age, of those who bore the battle and the tempest, and confessed that Wyrd had her way. Then, when the poet has cried that the foundations of earth itself are of no avail, that doom of weirds changes to fleetingness all that is great below the skies; and has left us unconsoled—some later writer, loving the poem, added a Christian epilogue which brings the consolation. We have the grace of the Father and the eternal Fortress that stands sure.

These are the Elegies. Of a different type of poetry, somewhat later than the Elegies, and related to them not only by a similar affection for the same kind of natural scenery, but also by the absence, for the most part, of Christian, and the presence of heathen, feeling, are the *Riddles*. There are some which have to do with Church and Monastery; with the sacramental paten, chalice and pyx; with the book chest in the scholar's cell, holding things more costly than gold; with the missal and the book-worm; but nearly all those that have to do with natural objects or with war might have been written by a man who had no concern with religion of any kind. A few of them, indeed, are of such primæval grossness that it is quite plain the writer of them was a layman and lived a "Bohemian" life, singing his *Riddles* from hall to hall, at the Chieftains' feasts, and at the village-gathering. They are also alive with heathen thoughts and manners. The old nature-myths appear in the creation of the Storm-giant who, prisoned deep, is let loose, and passes, destroying, over land and sea, bearing the rain on his back and lifting the sea into waves. With him are the Spirits of lightning and thunder and death. "See, the swarthy Shapes, forward pressing o'er the peoples, sweat forth their fire; and the Thunders that let fall black sap from their womb; and the pale Phantom stalking through the sky, who darts his deadly spears—the Spirit of the rain who wades through the clashing of the clouds." They appear again in the ever-renewed contest between the sun and the moon, in the iceberg shouting and driving his beak into the ships, in the wild hunt in the clouds, in the snakes that weave, in the fate goddesses, in the war-demons who dwell and cry in the sword, the arrow, and the spear; in the swan, who is lifted into likeness with the swan-maiden whose feathers sing a lulling song.

And the thoughts and manners are such as we see in *Beowulf*, and not in the Christian poems. The heroes are painted at the drinking: we share the strife of the drunken warriors, and the lords haughty with wine; the jewelled horns are carried round, the warriors sing; the sword is brought in, displayed, and its master boasts of it; the mighty smiths are exalted; the bower-maidens bedecked with armlets attend the feast, the bards are rewarded with rings and falcons—and all the other business of heathen life, the business of war, of sailing the ocean, of horses, of plundering and repelling plunderers, of the fierce work of battle, is frankly and joyfully heathen. These are the work of a man who, Christian in name, was all but heathen in heart.

We possess the *Riddles* in the *Exeter Book*, scattered throughout it in three divisions. There are ninety-five of them, but, as generally reckoned, they are combined into eighty-nine. There were probably a hundred. Riddles were made in centuries. Symphosius made a hundred of them, so did Ealdhelm. Tatwine, the Archbishop of Canterbury, made only forty; but Eusebius completed them into a hundred. These were all in Latin verse, and vary from four lines to twenty; and Ealdhelm wrote many at a much greater length. But then Ealdhelm had some original fancy, and he knew some of the Classics well.

The collection in the *Exeter Book* is, with the exception of one Latin Riddle, in English verse, and nearly half of it is worthy of the name of literature. All the Latin Riddle-writers of England, who wrote to the end of the seventh century, are used by the writers of the English *Riddles*. They are therefore not written earlier than the eighth century. They are of various lengths, from four to more than a hundred lines. The best of them escape altogether from the Latin convention, and are English in matter and sentiment. Nor is this the only difference. Their writer has the poetic faculty of which his models are destitute. Those who state that these nobler *Riddles* are merely imitations are unable to distinguish between what is and what is not poetry. Of course, this is not said of all the *Riddles*. Some are poor and meagre, and others are close imitations of the Latin. We find a number on common subjects, as if they were made for villagers of the ruder sort; on the ox and dog, the hens and swine; on things in common use, on the cowhide, the leather bottle, the wine-vat, the onion; others on half-humorous persons,—the one-eyed garlic-seller, and the clowns who are led astray by the marsh fires and the night. But those on splendid subjects,—on the fierce aspects of nature, on weapons of war and feasting, on the nobler birds, on instruments of music, on wild animals like the badger, on the plougher, the loom, and old John Barleycorn, are of an extraordinary fine quality. It is plain, then, that if, as some believe, various writers shared in their composition, there was also one poet of youthful imagination and original personality who, loving humanity and nature, made these Riddles which stand out so clearly from the rest. Whether the same man in his more vulgar hours made the others, without caring for his subjects, is possible, and not so very improbable.

Who this man was is still a subject of discussion. There are those who attribute some of these English Riddles to Ealdhelm, translations of his own Latin Riddles. But there is a general agreement that we may attribute the best to Cynewulf. The first Riddle, Leo declared, was a riddle on Cynewulf's name. The name *Wulf* occurs in it, but Mr. Gollancz has explained it, with some probability, as a little story of love and jealousy between two men, Wulf and Eadwacer. The eighty-sixth Riddle, however, the only one in Latin, has the name *Lupus*, and this has been used as the Latin translation of the name Cynewulf. We may, therefore, though this evidence is vague, allow that he was the writer of at least the finest of the *Riddles*. If so, he wrote them when he was a young poet. And his retrospective sketch of himself in the *Elene*, one of his signed poems, paints exactly the youth who could have written these *Riddles*. "He was a singer," he says. "He had taken in the mead-hall treasures of the appled gold. Need had often been his companion; a secret grief (of love) had cramped him when his horse paced the roads and proudly pranced along. Yet he had had his joy; the radiance of youth had long ago been his. But all is vanished now." Then he speaks elsewhere of the "youthful sins in which he had been ensnared, and how he came to tremble for them." This is the portrait of a wild young poet, sometimes a Scôp attached to a chieftain, but for the most part, for he loved his liberty, a "Wandering Singer." And the eighty-ninth Riddle, the solution of which is *The Wandering Singer*, is most probably his own description of himself when he was young. "I am," he says, "a noble, an Ætheling, and am known to the Earls. I rest with the rich, but also with the poor. Amid the Folks I am famous. Loud applause rings through the hall when I sing to the rovers and the warriors, and I win glory in the towns and glittering gold. Men of wit love to meet with me, for I unveil to them wisdom. When I sing all men are silent. The dwellers on earth seek after me, but I often" (with a poet's love of loneliness) "hide from them my path."

This sketches not only the position and temper of the Scôp, but also that of the wandering singer. It is a revelation of Cynewulf's youthful character. But the *Riddles*, if they are his, tell us more about his youth. They make plain that he knew some Latin, that he had received a good education at the convent school. They show that he was a lover of natural scenery and of animals, a close observer of all he saw and heard; that he delighted as much in the song of the dove and the nightingale as in the roaring of the tempest and the sea; that he was imaginative and rejoiced in his imaginations; that he was as ready to verse a coarse song for the peasant as a lay of the sword for a king;

that he had a passion for impersonation, and a keen sensitiveness to beauty which afterwards became a keen sensitiveness to righteousness; that he had fought as a warrior, had sailed the seas, and seen many phases of human life.

Any poet might have had this character and these experiences as well as Cynewulf, but we know of Cynewulf, and that he was a wandering singer when he was young; and we do not know of any other poet who fits so well as he into the character of the man who wrote the best or even the worst of the *Riddles*. Moreover, what he says and suggests about himself in his signed works agrees with the knowledge that the poet of the *Riddles* has of the seas and of war and of the scenery of rock-bound coasts. Cynewulf is at home in all these matters; and when he is writing of them there are certain passages which parallel others in the *Riddles*, not only in wording, which does not make much matter, but in sentiment, which makes a great deal. Finally, whoever reads the *Riddles* and believes them to be Cynewulf's, cannot have much power of impersonating a man if he does not form a clear conception of what Cynewulf was in his wild, radiant, impressionable, gay, and loving youth. But the world soon changed to him, and what he became we know, and with certainty, from the poems he signed with his name.

CHAPTER XI

THE SIGNED POEMS OF CYNEWULF

THERE are four poems signed by Cynewulf,—the *Fates of the Apostles*, the *Crist*, the *Juliana*, and the *Elene*. And this is the fashion in which he signs his name. He puts the runes which spell his name into the midst or at the end of each of these poems. Attached to these quaint signatures there are four personal statements, in which something of his character, feelings, and life are portrayed. We possess then not only his name, but we can also realise him as a man. No other Anglo-Saxon poet has this intimate fashion of talking about himself; and the manner of it is so distinct that when we find it in a poem not signed by himself—in the *Dream of the Rood*—it seems almost as good as his signature.

The question as to where he lived and wrote has been elaborately argued to and fro, and Wülker has decided, against Ten Brink, that Mercia was his home. The inland counties of Mercia seem a strange dwelling for one who was certainly well acquainted with the sea, who himself knew the pains, longing, and trouble of a sailor's life; who describes them and the cliffs beaten by the waves in the *Crist*, who told with such vigour the sea-voyage in the *Elene*. If he wrote the *Riddles*, the improbability of his being a Mercian is doubled. The man who composed the *Riddles* on the *Anchor*, on the *Hurricane*, on the *Tempest at Sea* and the *Tempest by Land*, on the *Iceberg*, is most likely to have lived on the sea-coast, and on a coast fringed by lofty cliffs, and on a coast where a welter of ice and sea was a common phenomenon. It is very improbable that one whose home was in Mercia or in Wessex could have made these descriptions so vivid. A Mercian would scarcely be a seaman; in Wessex seamanship had fallen to the lowest ebb; in Northumbria alone good seamanship was common; and the cliffs and seas of Northumbria realise the pictures of Cynewulf. If he wrote, and it is not impossible, the poem of the *Andreas*, the probability of his being a Northumbrian of the sea-border is increased. The scenery of that poem closely resembles northern coast scenery, even to details; and it would strain credulity to believe that any inland man could have written the voyage of St. Andrew.[1] Again, if Cynewulf wrote the second part of *St. Guthlac*, the probability that he was not a Mercian nor an East Anglian, but a Northumbrian, is also strengthened. The voyage over the fens is turned into a sea-voyage, which an East Anglian would not have done; and the voyage is described with a keenness and pleasure very difficult to find in an inland man. I think the writer tells of what he knew—of a journey made by sea—such as was frequent between Whitby and Tynemouth, between Jarrow and Lindisfarne, between Lindisfarne and Coldingham. In truth, the atmosphere of the *Riddles*, the *Crist*, the *Elene*, the second *St. Guthlac* and the *Andreas*, is entirely northern, and though some may think little of an "atmosphere" as proof, it is thoroughly good literary evidence. Secondly, if Cynewulf lived in Mercia, and had many imitators, why have we never heard of any Mercian or Wessex school of poetry? A poet of the genius of Cynewulf arises out of a long-established school, his work bears the traces of the previous school, and he creates a school. There was such a school in

---

[1] The changes, or rather the additions, made to the original Greek story by the poet are chiefly in the natural description of the coasts and of the sea, and they are realistic, as if written on the spot. The conversation of Andrew with Christ as master of the sea-boat is worked into an English scene with an English sailor, and special English sea-touches are continually inserted.

Northumbria, and the work of Cynewulf touches it at many points. Thirdly, the sentiment of his poems corresponds with the historical conditions of Northumbria at the time in which he wrote. The personal portions are marked with regret and melancholy; the general statements with regard to the fates of men speak of wealth fleeting away like water, or passing like the wind, and of the decay of glory. This note does not suit the life men lived in Mercia under Æthelbald and Offa from 718 to 796, when Mercia, with one brief interval, was lifted into its greatest prosperity; nor the national life of Wessex after the battle of Burford, 754, when Wessex, in fine fighting condition, was looking forward, alert and young, to the conquest of England. But Northumbria was exactly in the state which would produce the half-sad, half-despairing note of Cynewulf from the year 750 to the year 790, when a patriotic Northumbrian looked back from anarchy and misrule to a past time of national glory.

But it was not only the misfortune which troubled his country which now changed the thoughtless joy of the young poet into the thoughtful sorrow of his manhood; it was even more personal misfortune, bringing with it a passionate conviction of sin. His careless happiness passed away "like the hastening waves," he says, "like the storm which ends in silence." And we find him now in the bitterest repentance, fear of the wrath of God lying heavy upon him, so heavily that his "song-craft left him." Then he had a revelation of the redeeming power of the Cross of Christ; and I believe that the *Dream of the Holy Rood* was written in his old age and is his poetic account of this moment of conversion in his youth. He alludes to it also in the *Elene* when, speaking of his past, he says that the "Lord gave him a new learning through His work as a Light-bearer, that the burden of his sin was removed, and his singing-craft restored."

It is a question which was the first of the signed poems written in this new atmosphere. The *Fates of the Apostles* is given this place, and this seems likely, for the poem is short, dull and conventional, such as a man might write when beginning on a changed class of subjects in a changed temper of mind. Moreover, Wülker thinks that the usage of phrases borrowed from heroic poetry, such as the description in the *Fates* of the Apostles as "Æthelings going forth to war, as heroes hard in battle, in the play of shields" are the remains of Cynewulf's youthful period; and that the personal statement mixed up with the runes of his name refers to the overthrow of his youthful happiness and to his exile from his home.

But Cynewulf makes full use of the phrases of heroic poetry in his latest signed poem, the *Elene;* and I think he would, in his miserable remorse, have avoided everything which could recall a poetry which for the time he would consider wicked. It would be more natural for him, when his soul was long afterwards at ease with God, to recur to the manner and expressions of pagan poetry. And he certainly did this in the *Elene*, a poem of his old age. Moreover, if the *Fates of the Apostles* be, as Mr. Gollancz conjectures, not a separate poem but the epilogue to the *Andreas*—and making therefore the *Andreas* a poem by Cynewulf—its heroic manner would belong, as I think it should, to the later life of Cynewulf. Nor is the personal passage in the *Fates*, in which he signs his name, against this view. It has no reference to a time of conversion, to his sins or to his fear of God. His "departure to a land lying where he knows not" is much more applicable to a belief in approaching death than to an exile from his home. And the home he prays for is in "the height with the King of Angels."

I cannot, then, think that the *Fates of the Apostles* was his first signed poem. The *Juliana*, I believe, takes that place. In it the bitterness of sin, the fear of divine wrath are the foremost thoughts. Here is the personal passage, with his signature in runes, and we read the man in it.

Sorrowful are wandering
C and Y and N ; for the King is wrathful,
God, of conquests Giver ! Then, beflecked with sins
E and V and U, must await in fear

>What, their deeds according, God will doom to them
>For their life's reward. L and F are trembling,
>Waiting, sad with care. Sorely I remember me
>Of the wounds of sins wrought by me of old,
>And of late, within the world!
>   All too late I shamed me
>Of my evil deeds.

This fits a time of contrition and change.

The *Juliana* is in the *Exeter Book*. Its source is the *Acta S. Julianae, virginis, martyris.* Cynewulf has worked the legend up with some care for unity of feeling and form. Juliana is led from triumph to triumph, in a series of episodes couched in Cynewulf's favourite form of dialogue, to her final purification in death. There is some tentative art in the poem, but art and work are both poor. Abrupt changes, crude dialogue, tiresome repetition, disfigure the poet's recast of the legend. It is written by a man who was wearied of himself or weary of his subject. A few touches of rough humour, very similar to those which occur in the *Andreas*, an attempt to realise the mingling in Juliana's character of iron resolution and of womanly charm, the turning of the devil into the northern dragon and of Heliseus the persecutor into an English heathen king, are the only things in which the English poet himself appears. It is a transition poem in which the writer is feeling his way into originality.

In the *Crist*, which is the next signed poem, this note of sorrow for sin continues, but with a difference. "How are we troubled," he cries, "through our own desires! Weak, I wander, stumbling and forlorn. Come, king of men, we need thy mercy to do the better things." But there is also another note; of peace almost attained, of modest joy, and these two—sorrow for sin, delight in forgiveness—mix their music, like life and death, throughout the poem. The personal passage in which his name is signed belongs to his sorrow. It is in the middle of the *Crist*, at the end of the second division, when he is about, in the third, to sing the day of judgment. "I dread the sterner doom," he cries, "terror and vengeance for my sins."[1]

> Then the *C*ourage-hearted cowers when the King he hears
> Speak the words of wrath—Him the wielder of the heavens—
> Speak to those who once on earth but obeyed him weakly,
> While as yet their *Y*earning pain, and their *N*eed, most easily
> Comfort might discover.

These shall bear their judgment; but then, turning from his own fate to the destruction of the earth by fire, as of old by water, he sets the three last letters of his name into three other words—omitting the E:—

> Gone is then the *W*insomeness
> Of the Earth's adornments! What to *U*s as men belonged
> Of the joys of life was locked, long ago in *L*ake-floods,[2]
> All the *F*ee on earth.

Thus he records his name in a passage as sad as that in the *Juliana*. But the sadness is no longer unrelieved. Only a few lines farther this lovely strain appears, full of peace; a passage as personal in its pathetic religion as anything in Cowper, and of a

---

[1] The runes in the *Juliana* have only the value of the letters of his name. But here and in the *Elene* and the *Fates of the Apostles* they have also the meaning of the words by which the runes are named; and these meanings are to be read into the text.

C [ᚳ] stands for *Cene*, the keen, the courageful warrior.
Y [ᚣ] stands for *Yfel*, which as a masculine adjective is *wretched;* or as an abstract noun *misery*.
N [ᚾ] stands for *Nyd*, necessity, hardship.
E [ᛖ] stands for *Eh*, horse.
W [ᚹ] stands for *Wyn*, joy.
U [ᚢ] stands for *Ur*, our.
L [ᛚ] stands for *Lagu*, water.
F [ᚠ] stands for *Feoh*, wealth.

I have accepted, it will be seen, Mr. Gollancz's explanation of the runes Y and U as *Yfel* and *Ur*. He discovered *Ur* glossed as *noster* in a Runic alphabet.

[2] *Lagu*—the great water of the Flood.

higher hopefulness. The man who wrote it has passed far beyond the fears in the *Juliana* :—

> Mickle is our need
> That, in this unfruitful time, ere that fearful Dread,
> On our spirits' fairness we should studiously bethink us !
> Surely now most like it is, as if we, on lake of ocean,
> O'er the water cold, in our keels were sailing ;
> And through spacious seas, with our stallions of the deep,
> Forward drove the Flood-wood ! Fearful is the stream
> Of immeasurable surges that we sail on here,
> Through this wavering world, through these wind-swept oceans ;
> O'er the path profound. Perilous our state of life,
> Ere that we had sailed our ship to the shore at last,
> O'er the rough sea-ridges ! Then there reached us help,
> That to win the hithe of healing led us homeward on—
> He the Spirit-Son of God—
> So aware at last we were, from our vessel's deck,
> Where to stay our stallions of the sea with ropes,
> Fast a-riding by their anchors—ancient horses of the wave !
> In that haven then, all our hope we shall establish,
> Which the Ruler of the Æther there has roomed for us,
> When He rose to Heaven—Holy in the Highest.

This is a strain of peace; the change from the temper of the *Juliana* is clearly marked. The *Crist* is full of quiet joy.

In this poem Cynewulf attains originality and his true line of work as a Christian poet. It is not the translation of a legend; it is invented, and out of its freedom springs its excellence. Cynewulf has recovered, with a difference, his youthful imagination, his rushing movement, his exultation and his ease. In his outbursts of exalted praise and his descriptions of great events, he reaches his nearest approach to a fine style, and his style reveals his character. We feel the man's heart, when his trumpet-tongued joy in salvation is succeeded by personal passages full of a profound humility. In praise and prayer, in mournfulness and rapture, he is equally passionate. The half-dramatic turn we find in a *Riddle* like the *Sword* appears crudely in the *Juliana*, but reaches a finer development in the *Crist*, and so does his pictorial power. The ascent from Hades, the four angels blowing their trumpets, the deluge of flame, the blazing Rood streaming with blood, its foot on earth and its head in heaven, are done with the same originality and force as the picture of the Hurricane in the *Riddles.*

The *Crist* is in the *Exeter Book.* Several leaves of it are lost. We owe to Dietrich the proof that the hymnic poems of the sections from 8*a* to 32*b*, which were held to be separate, are one connected whole of three parts. The first part celebrates the Nativity and ends at line 438; the second part the Ascension, and ends at line 865; the third part, the Day of Judgment, ends at line 1637, and the whole poem (if we accept Mr. Gollancz's transference of the last verses to Guthlac i.) at line 1663. The first part uses the Gospel of St. Matthew; the second makes a free use of Gregory's homily on the Ascension; the third relies on the Latin hymn *De die judicii,* to which Bæda refers in his treatise *De Metris.* The tenth homily of Gregory is also used. One can scarcely say these are sources; they are, even when some of their passages are closely followed, rather assistances. The poem is truly original.

The first part is set in hymnic parts, in cantatas. The first is mutilated, but slightly, and begins by a fortunate chance with the word "cyninge," "to the King." It might almost serve as a title to the poem, and the invocation which follows to Christ as the Wallstone, to preserve His Church, to pity His people and make them worthy, introduces the miraculous conception. The second celebrates the place of Christ's birth, and this is a piece of it:—

> See! O sight of peace! sacred Hierusalem!
> Thou, of kingly thrones the choicest, citadel of Christ,
> Native seat of seraphs, of the sooth-fast souls
> That for ever sit, they alone, at rest in thee
> In their splendours, singing joy.

Now the King of Heaven draws near to thee, "Heaven and Earth are looking upon thee." At this moment Mary appears, carrying the babe in her womb. The scene of this third hymn, in which the men and women of Jerusalem meet Mary, is set in a dramatic dialogue—the first seed, in our literature, of the Miracle Play. It may even be probable that this part of the poem was sung in the church, and the parts taken by different persons. A scenic effect is, as it were, made for the entrance of the personages, a choir seems to await them and to close the scene with a choric hymn. We might, then, see in this remarkable passage the first striving of the poetry of England towards the drama in which afterwards it reached such excellence.

As Mary is seen approaching, the dwellers of Jerusalem break into welcome and questioning:—

> " In the glorious glory, hail ! gladness thou of women
> In the lap of every land ; loveliest of maidens
> Whom the ocean-rovers ever listened speech of.
> Make us know the mystery that has moved to thee from Heaven."
> *Mary answers—*
> " What is now this wonder, at the which ye stare,
> Making here your moan, mournfully a-wailing ;
> Thou the son of Solima, daughter thou of Solima !

Ask no more ; the mystery is not known, but the curse is overcome," and a chorus to Christ closes the dialogue. In the sixth cantata the poem becomes for a time a true dramatic conversation between Joseph and Mary. Joseph arrives on the scene, sad and troubled :—

> " *Mary.* Ea la ! Joseph mine, child of Jacob old,
> Kinsman, thou, of David, king of a great fame,
> In our fast-set friendship wilt thou fail me now ?
> Let my love be lost ? "
> *Joseph.* Lo, this instant I
> Deeply am distressed, all undone of honour ;

Sore speeches have I heard, insult to thee, mocking scorn of me. Tears I must shed, and yet God may cure

> Easily the anguish deep, that is in my heart,
> And console me, sad. Oh, my sorrow ! oh young girl !
> Maid Maria ! "

Mary. Why bemoanest thou?
Criest now, care weary? Never crime in thee
Have I ever found; yet thou utterest words
As if thou thyself wert all thronged with sin!

Joseph, on whom the tables are thus turned, replies at some length, and this dramatic form of writing is not again resumed save for a few lines at the opening of the second part. Two other cantatas follow, celebrating the Virgin, Christ and the Trinity, but all are linked to the main subject of the Incarnation, and end with choric praise and prayer.

The second part is taken up with the Ascension; and an episode relates the ascent of the Old Testament saints with Christ after the harrowing of hell. This fine scene is laid in mid-space. The angels in heaven come forth to meet and welcome the ascending saints; and when Cynewulf sees this mighty meeting in his vision, the warrior wakens in him, and the speech the angelic leader makes to his host is such as a heathen chief might make when he saw his lord return victorious. "See," it begins, "the Holy Hero has bereaved Hell, taken back the tribute. Lo, He returns after the war-playing, with this unnumbered folk set loose from prison. O ye gates, unclose, the King has come to His city." Then the whole story is retold; and in the midst, at line 591, there is a passage which needs to be noted, because each limb of the alliterative verse is set in rhyme. Another passage farther on, when he describes Christ's descent with the Spirit at Pentecost, repeats a favourite motive (there is a parallel to it in the *Gifts of Men*)—the description of the various gifts which men derive from God—wisdom, harp-playing, law-giving, star-telling, writing, smithery, tracking, sailing ships, good fortune in war.

The next part of the Ascension is an allegorical exposition of the text in the Canticles—"He came leaping on the mountains, skipping on the hills." Six leaps made Christ, and the first was from heaven into the Virgin's womb; the second, when in the bin He lay, of all majesties the Majesty. The third was the mounting of the Cross, the fourth into the rocky grave, the fifth when He descended into hell, the sixth was the "Holy One's enraptured play when He stept up into His ancient home, to His house of glittering light; and the angels were blithe with laughter upon that holy tide." The last portion of the Ascension contains that personal passage in which Cynewulf signs his name, and suggests his new subject, "The Day of Doom." He sketches, in a rapid study, this third part :—

> Then shall all earth-glories
> Burn within the bale-fire. Bright and swift
> Rages on the ruddy flame, wrathfully it strides
> O'er the out-spread earth. Sunken are the plains,
> Burst asunder the Burg-steads! See the Burning on its way
> Greediest of guests, pitilessly gorges now
> All the ancient treasures, that of old the heroes held.

"O our need is great," he cries, "to bethink us of God's grace before that terror comes," and he closes with the sea-suggested passage which I have already translated.

At line 866, the third part of the poem, *The Day of Judgment*, begins with the gathering of the angels and the faithful on Mount Zion; and Cynewulf, as if suddenly smitten with a vision, breaks into a noble description of the summoning angels :—

> Therewith from the four, far-off corners of the world,
> From the regions uttermost of the realm of earth,
> All aglow the Angels, blow with one accord
> Loudly thrilling trumpets. Trembles Middle-garth;
> Earth is quaking under men! Right against the going
> Of the stars they sound together, strong and gloriously,
> Sounding and resounding from the south and north;
> Over all creation, from the east and from the west;
> Bairns of doughty men from the dead arousing,
> All aghast from the gray mould, all the kin of men,
> To the dooming of the Lord.

A blaze of sun appears, and after the blaze the Son of God, with His hosts. Deep creation thunders, the heavens are broken up, sun and moon depart, and the stars " shower down from heaven, through the roaring air, lashed by all the winds." And then, in words which recall the third *Riddle*, he describes the ocean of fire which devours the world, impersonating, as his way was of old, conflagration :—

> So the greedy Ghost shall gang searchingly through earth,
> And the Flame, the Ravager, with its fire-terror,
> Shall the high uptimbered houses hurl upon the plain.
> Lo, the Fire-blast, flaming far, fierce and hungry like a sword,
> Whelms the world withal ! And the walls of burghs
> In immediate ruin fall. Melt the mountains now,
> Melt the cliffs precipitous, that of old against the sea,
> Fixed against the floods, firm and steadfast standing,
> Kept the earth apart ; bulwarks 'gainst the ocean billow,
> And the winding water. Then on every wight
> Fastens now the flame of death ! On the fowls and beasts,
> Fire-swart, a raging warrior, rushes Conflagration,
> All the earth along.

And the dead rise, "and in them, as through a glass, are seen the figure of their works, the memory of their words, and the thoughts of their heart." This motive, with that of the terror and the fire, is wearisomely repeated, till at line 1081 the theme of the Holy Rood is wrought out. It is a piece of true imagination. The cross is pictured, standing with its root on Zion's hill and rising till its top strikes Heaven. By its light all things are seen and the vast multitude look upon it. It shines instead of the ruined sun ; all shade is banished by its brilliancy. From head to foot it is red, wet with the blood of the King of Heaven. It brings brightness to the souls of the good, torment to the evil. A description of the agony of all creation at the crucifixion follows, and Cynewulf works up this thought, which belongs also to the Balder story, with his curious minuteness concerning nature-changes. The rest of the poem, with the exception of a remarkable speech of Christ concerning His death, who emphasises His words, like a Roman Catholic preacher, by turning to the Rood and pointing to the image of Himself upon it, is an enlargement of the xxvth chapter of St. Matthew's gospel. Homiletic exhortation, the final locking of Hell, and a joyous description, like that in the *Phœnix*, of the saints in the perfect land, conclude the poem.

It is here, but preceded by the *Phœnix* and the second part of *St. Guthlac*, that I place the third of the signed poems, the *Fates of the Apostles*. The personal passage, containing the runes of his name, was discovered by Professor Napier at Vercelli. "Here," Cynewulf says, "the wise in forethinking may find out, whosoever joyeth him in songs, what man it is that wrought this lay." The letters of his name follow, but not, as in the other poems, in order. They begin with F, the last letter of his name. W, U, and L follow; then come C and Y; but N has been obliterated in the manuscript. "Wealth (Feoh) stands at an end, and Joy (Wyn) shall fall away; our (Ur) joy upon this earth. Then drop asunder the fair trappings of the body, as Water (Lagu) glides away. Then the bold warrior (Cene) and the afflicted wretch (Yfel) shall crave for help, but destiny (Nyd) overrules."[1] Then he asks for prayer, for he must "seek for strange dwellings and a strange land, strange to all who hold not fast the Spirit of God. But be His praise great, and His might abide ever youthful, over the universe." These do not seem to me to be the words of a young man, but of one who is looking forward to death, to the strange land beyond. Nor are they the words of a man overwhelmed with sin, as those in the *Juliana*. They close with a strain of praise and faith. This is one reason why I place the poem not at the beginning but towards the close of Cynewulf's Christian poetry. The other reason is the bold use of the old saga phrases, such phrases as are constantly used in the *Elene*. The work of the apostles (I have already quoted the passage) is told as if it were a Viking expedition—"Great proof of valour gave these Æthelings; far spread over earth was the might of the King's thegns. Bold in war was Andreas; not slow was James, nor a laggard on the journey. Daring was the deed of Thomas in India; he bore the rush of swords. Brave in battle, Simon and Thaddeus warred in the Persian lands; they were quick in the shield-play." Wülker, as I

---

[1] These three last are Mr. Gollancz's restoration.

have said, thinks the use of these phrases characteristic of a man who has just left his profane poetry. I think the opposite—that he would have refrained from such phrases at first, and when his soul was at rest recurred to them. It is plain he did recur to them in a poem we know to be written in age, in the *Elene;* and Mr. Gollancz's opinion that the *Fates* belongs to the *Andreas* accords with my view of the place of this poem in Cynewulf's life.[1]

The *Elene* is the last of the signed poems. It comes from the *Vercelli Book;* 1320 lines. Its source appears to be the Latin life of Quiriacus or Cyriacus, Bishop of Jerusalem, in the *Acta Sanctorum* of the 4th of May, but reasons have been alleged that some other life was used by Cynewulf. Cyriacus is the Judas of the poem. Cynewulf uses his source with all his own freedom, expanding and contracting where he pleases. The battle of Constantine with the Huns and the sea expedition of the Empress Helena are original additions of his own. These are the best parts of the poem, and worthy of the pains he says he bestowed on its composition. The subject is the *Finding of the True Cross;* and the action passes on steadily to the close. The Huns gather round Constantine's host as he lies asleep in his tent. He dreams his famous dream of the Cross, and is bid to conquer by that sign. The battle follows; Helena goes to Jerusalem to find the Cross. Her council with the Jews is described; the separate council of the Jews when Judas advises them to conceal the place where the Cross lies; his imprisonment, release, his prayer to Christ; the finding of the three crosses; the discovery of the true Cross by a miracle; the baptism of Judas as Cyriacus, and his appointment to the Bishopric of Jerusalem; the finding of the nails, the return of Helena. The personal epilogue closes.

This epilogue is full of the character of the old man. He recapitulates his life, first in simple verse and then in a riddling

[1] Sievers, however, does not consider that this rune passage is attached at all to the *Fates of the Apostles,* or to any poem in the Vercelli manuscript, but thinks it to be a detached fragment.

representation under the runic letters of his name. "Thus I," so he begins like a careful artist, "old and ready for death in my frail tabernacle,"

> Craft of words have woven, wondrously have culled them out,
> O'er and o'er my art have thought, anxiously have sifted
> Night by night my thinking—

Then he recalls the days of his conversion—"I was stained with sins, tortured with sorrows, till the Lord was my Light-bearer, and for my solace, now I am old, measured to me a gift that does not make ashamed. And straightway my singing-craft returned to me, and I used it with all my heart." This is followed by the closest piece of biography in his poems, though it is somewhat obscured by the runes of his name having each the value of the words by which the runes are called and by some of them, as C, Y and U, also meaning himself:—

> Beaten by care-billows, C[1] began to fail,
> Though he in the mead-hall took of many treasures
> Of the appled gold. Y was wailing sorely,
> N was his companion then; harrowing was its grief,
> 'Twas a rune that cramped him, when before him E
> Paced along the mile-paths, proudly raced along,
> Prankt with woven trappings. W was weakened soon!
> After years, my pleasures and my youth all passed away,
> And my ancient pride. U was in the times of old
> All one gleam of youth! Now the gone-by days,
> Far away, to fading came, when the fated hour rose;
> And delight of living passed, as when L doth glide away,
> Flood that follows flood. F for every soul
> Is but lent below the lift; and the land's adornments

---

[1] C = Cynewulf as *Cene*, the keen warrior.
Y = Cynewulf as *Yfel*, the "wretched one."
N = Nyd, hardship, need.
E = Eh, his horse.
W = Wyn, joy.
U = *Ur*, our—that is, "I Cynewulf."
L = *Lagu*, water.
F = *Feoh*, wealth.

> Vanish all the welkin under, to the wind most like,
> When, before the eyes of men, roaring, it upsteps the sky,
> Hunts the clouds along, hurries, raging onward,
> Till all suddenly again silent it becomes,
> In its clampèd chambers closely prisoned now,
> Pinned with mighty pressure down.

So Cynewulf—with these allusions to the myth in Vergil and to the northern myth of Woden's wild hunt in the sky—strikes his melancholy note. It is natural, for he is old; but he does not support it to the end. He closes his poem with a picture of the righteous, victorious in beauty.

The battle with the Huns has been already mentioned. But here is the voyage, full, like the battle, with the Viking passion, quite unlike the sea-note in the other Anglo-Saxon poems of the Christian poetry. One would think that Cynewulf had been reading the *Beowulf*.

> Quickly then began all the crowd of Earls
> For the sea themselves to ready. Then the stallions of the flood
> Stood alert for going, on the Ocean-strand,
> Hawsered steeds of sea, in the Sound at anchor.
>
> . . . .
>
> Many a warrior proud, there at Wendelsea[1]
> Stood upon the shore. Over the sea-marges,
> One troop after other, hourly urged they on.
> So they stored up there—with the sarks of battle,
> With the shields and spears, with mail-shirted fighters,
> With the warriors and the women—the wave-riding horses.
> Then they let, o'er Fifel's wave, foaming, stride along
> Their sea-rushers, steep of stem. Oft withstood the bulwark,
> O'er the surging of the sea, swinging strokes of waves;
> Humming hurried on the sea! Never heard I now or since,
> Or of old, that any lady led a fairer power
> O'er the street of sea, on the stream of ocean!
> There a man might watch—(who should mark the fleet
> Break along the bath-way)—rush the Billow's-wood,
> Play the Flood-horse on, plunge the Floater of the wave
> Underneath the swelling sails. Blithe the sea-dogs were,

---

[1] The Mediterranean.

> Courage in their heart! Glad the Queen was of her journey,
> When at last to hithe, o'er the ocean-lake fast-rooted,
> They had sailed their ships, set with rings on prows,
> To the land of Greece. Then they let the keels
> Stand upon the sea-marge, driven on the sandy shore,
> Ancient houses of the wave.

Here the heroic terms are in full use. They enliven and strengthen Cynewulf's verse, and seem to inspire the work of his old age with youth. It is curious how tame he is when he does not stray from his text, or whenever he has no opportunity for hymns of praise. He is always far better in invention than in imitation, or as a lyric than as a narrative poet. In this poem also the metrical movement is more steady than in the rest of his work. He rarely uses any other than the short epic line into which English poetry now drifted more and more. Rhyme and assonance are also not uncommon. These things point to a time when the poets had consciously adopted rules in their art, when metrical freedom was strictly limited. Had English poetry lasted, it might have become as rigidly scientific as the Icelandic.

CHAPTER XII

POEMS ATTRIBUTED TO CYNEWULF OR HIS SCHOOL

THE most important of these poems are the *Phœnix*, the second part of the *St. Guthlac*, the *Harrowing of Hell*, the *Andreas*, and the *Dream of the Rood*. They have all been attributed to Cynewulf, but with regard to the two last there has been much difference of opinion, and present criticism tends to remove them from his hand.

The *Phœnix* is in the *Exeter Book*, and runs to 677 lines. Its source is a Latin poem by Lactantius. Cynewulf, to whom almost all the critics attribute the poem, leaves his original at verse 380, and then composes the story he has told into an allegory of the Resurrection. He uses, in this second part, the writings of Ambrose and Bæda. He greatly expands, but sometimes shortens, the original Latin of the first part. His expansions are mostly when he is describing natural scenery or breaking into praise. The ending is somewhat fantastic in form—eleven lines, the first half of each in Anglo-Saxon, the latter half in Latin. The Latin is alliterated with the Anglo-Saxon.

The first canto describes the Paradise—which is related to the Celtic land of eternal youth—in which the Phœnix dwells, and I have already translated a part of this famous piece. The second describes the enchanting life the Bird lives from morn to evening in that deathless land of joy. A translation of them will best express the careful imagination of Cynewulf, and his

CH. XII   POEMS OF CYNEWULF OR HIS SCHOOL   181

delight in the doings of the sun and in the waters of the earth and sea.

> He shall of the Sun see and watch the voyaging;
> And shall come right on 'gainst the candle of the Lord,
> 'Gainst the gladdening gem! He shall gaze with eagerness
> When upriseth clear that most Ætheling of stars,
> O'er the Ocean wave, from the East a-glitter,
> Gleaming with his glories, God the Father's work of old;
> Beacon bright of God!—Blind the stars shall be,
> Wandered under waters to the western realms,
> All bedimmed at dawn, when the dark of night,
> Wan, away has gone. Then, o'er waves, the Bird,
> Firm and feather-proud, o'er the flowing ocean stream,
> Under Lift and over Lake, looketh eager-hearted
> When up-cometh fair, from the East a-gliding
> O'er the spacious sea, the upshining of the Sun.

The next lines repeat the same motive in other words, and as this is one of the characteristics of Anglo-Saxon poetry, and as Cynewulf manages it with excellent skill, I translate them here. They were used to heighten the impression, and when they were sung were perhaps set to different music or to the same in a different key.

> So the fair-born fowl at the fountain-head,
> At the well-streams wonneth, in a winsomeness unfailing!
> There a twelve of times, he the joy-triumphant one
> In the burn doth bathe him, ere the beacon cometh,
> Candle of the Æther; and, as often, he
> Of those softly-joyous springings of the Wells
> Tastes at every bath—billow-cold they are!
> Then he soars on high, when his swimming-play is done,
> With uplifted heart on a lofty tree—
> Whence across the Eastern paths, with an ease the greatest,
> He may watch the Sun's outwending, when that Welkin-taper
> O'er the battle of the billows brilliantly is blickering,
> Flaming light of light! All the land is fair-adorned;
> Lovely grows the world when the gem of glory,
> O'er the going of great Ocean, glitters on the ground,
> Over all the middle earth—mightiest this of stars!

This is the repetition, and very well done it is. Then Cynewulf describes the Phœnix's life till evening falls, and its wondrous song.

> Soon as ere the Sun, o'er the salt sea-streamings,
> Towers up on high, then the gray and golden fowl
> Flieth forth, fair shining, from the forest tree;
> Fareth, snell of feathers, in its flight along the lift;
> Sounds, and sings his way (ever) sunwards on.
>
> Then as beautiful becomes all the bearing of the bird;
> Borne his breast is upwards in a blissfulness of joy!
> In his song-craft he makes changes, in his clear re-voicing,
> Far more wonderfully now than did ever bairn of man
> Hear, the Heavens below, since the High-exalted King,
> He the Worker of all glory, did the world establish,
> Earth, and eke the Heaven.
>   The up-ringing of his voice
> Than all other song-crafts sweeter is and lovelier;
> Far away more winsome than whatever winding lay.
> Not alike to that clear sound may the clarion be,
> Nor the horn nor harp-clang, nor the heroes' singing—
> Not to one of them on earth—nor the organ tone,
> Nor the singing of the sackbut, nor sweet feathers of the swan;
> None of all the other joys that the Eternal shaped
> For the mirthfulness of men in this mournful world.
> So he sings and softly sounds, sweetly blest in joy,
> Till within the southern sky doth the Sun become
> Sunken to its setting. Silent then is he.
> Listening now he lends his ear, then uplifts his head,
> Courage-thrilled, and wise in thought! Thrice he shaketh then
> Feathers whet for flight—so the fowl is still.

Thus lives the Phœnix for a thousand years and then flies far to the Syrian land, where on a high tree he makes his death-nest of odorous leaves; and when at summer time the sun is brightest, the nest is heated, and the fury of fire devours bird and nest. But the ashes, balled together, grow into an apple, and in the apple a wondrous worm waxes till it becomes an eagle, and then a Phœnix as before. Only honey-dew he eats that falls at midnight, and when he has gathered all the relics of his old body he takes them in his claws and, flying back to his paradise, buries them in the earth. All men and all the birds gather to watch his flight, but he outstrips their sight, and once more in his happy isle "dwells in the grove, delighting in its bubbling streams." When Cynewulf has thus brought his bird back, he makes two allegories out of the story—one, of the immortal life of the saints —for Christ after the judgment flies through the air attended by the adoring souls like birds, and each soul becomes a Phœnix and dwells for ever young in the city of life; and the other of Christ himself, who passed through the fire of death to glorious life. "Therefore to Him be praise for ever and ever. Hallelujah!"

It is here, after the *Phœnix*, that we may probably place and date the second part of *St. Guthlac*. Most critics allot it to Cynewulf, and some suggest that if we had its end, it would contain that poet's runic signature. It is preceded by a first part, which is so poor in comparison with the second that, if Cynewulf wrote it, I should place it before the *Juliana*, that is, immediately after his conversion. He would be likely to take, as his first Christian subject, the story of an English saint.

The complete work, first and second parts, follows on the *Crist* in the *Exeter Book*, and Mr. Gollancz has transferred to its beginning a number of lines usually printed as the end of the *Crist*. These form, he says, the true introduction to the *Guthlac*, and he supports his opinion by the fact that there is a blank space in the manuscript before these lines begin. The *Crist* certainly ends better where he now makes it end, at line 1663. But the difficulty of accepting these lines as the beginning of the first part of *Guthlac* is that the quality of their poetry is far superior to anything else in that part. The only way I see out of that difficulty is to hold that Cynewulf placed these lines at the beginning when, several years afterwards, he wrote the second part. He kept then the first as it was, but he remodelled the introduction. That would be natural enough, and would equally suit either the view that Cynewulf wrote the first part in early days, or that he made use of an old poem on *St. Guthlac* written by some other person.

A few pleasing lines of description illuminate the first part, but otherwise it is a hampered and barren piece of work. It rests chiefly on traditions of the Saint. The second part, often differing from the first with regard to the same events, follows closely the *Life of Guthlac* by Felix, written in Latin prose for an East Anglian king between the years 747 and 749. The first part avoids the poetic terms commonly used by heathen poets. In the second, composed when Cynewulf's soul was at peace in forgiveness, he freely uses the old saga expressions.

The death of St. Guthlac is its subject—the last fight of a Christian hero with death and Satan. This is told in almost as heroic a manner as Beowulf's fight with the dragon; and Guthlac's death-praise is sung—not as Beowulf's by his comrades but in as heroic a strain—by the angels who receive him with high pomp of music and lays into the "hereditary seat of the saints."

The scenery, which does not disdain the nature-myths, is carefully painted. The sun plays his part in the contest. Night darkens with her shadowy helm the battle-field; night after night strides like a phantom across the sky. Guthlac stands alone on his hill, as if on Holmgang, and Satan rushes on him with many troops, "smiths of sin, roaring and raging"; but his soul, full of joy, was ready, and the fiend is put to flight. Then death enters the lists, "that warrior greedy of corpses, the stealthy bowman who draws near in the shadow with thievish steps." "How is thine heart, my lord and father," asks his disciple; "Shelter of friends, art thou sore oppressed?" "Death is at hand," Guthlac answers, "the warrior never weary in the fight." Then, "hot and close to Guthlac's heart, the whirring arrow-storm, with showers of war, drove into his body."

But before he dies, he tells his disciple the secret of his converse with an angel who visits him "between the rushing of the dawn and the darkening of the night." My soul, he cries, is struggling forth to reach pure joy. "Then sank his head; but still high-minded, he drew his breath; and it was fragrant as the blowing herbs in summer time, which, each in its own home, drop honey and sweetly smell, winsome on the meadows." The next sixty lines are some of the finest in old English poetry. They begin with the setting of the sun, and the rising of the pillar of light, that common miracle, over the hut where Guthlac lies.

> When the glorious gleaming
> Sought its setting-path, swart the North-sky grew,
> Wan below the welkin; veiled the world in mist,
> Thatched it thick with gloom! Over thronged the night,
> Shrouding the land's loveliness! Then of Lights the greatest
> Holy from the heavens came, shining high, serenely,
> Bright above the Burg-halls!

All the night it blazed, and "the shadows dwindled, loosed and lost in air, till the murmur of the dawn softly drew from the east over the deep ocean." Then Guthlac rose, sent his last message to his dear sister, was "houselled with the food majestic," and the angels bore his soul on high. All heaven bursts into a lay of victory. The ringing sound was heard on earth; "the blessed Burg was filled with bliss, with sweetest scents, with skiey wonders, with the singing of the seraphim, to its innermost recesses, rapture following rapture. And all our island trembled, all its field-floor shook." The messenger, himself shaken by fear, drew out his ship and hurried over seas to Guthlac's sister. This passage brings together so many of the terms by which the Anglo-Saxon poets called the ship that I insert it here. The disciple

> Urged the Stallion of the sea, and the Water-rusher ran
> Snell beneath the sorrow-laden! Shone the blazing sky,
> Blickering o'er the Burg-halls; fled the Billow-wood along,
> Lightly lifting on its way. Laden, to the hithe,
> Flew at speed the Flood-horse, till this Floater of the tide,
> After the sea-playing, scornful surged upon the sea-coast,
> Ground against the shingle-grit.

He gives his message, and the poem, written at the zenith of Cynewulf's power, breaks off suddenly, unfinished.

It is probable that the fragment of a *Descent into Hell* was written about this time, that is, after A.D. 750. Almost every critic gives it to Cynewulf. It has the manner of the first part of the *Crist*, the same trick of dialogue, the same choric outbursts of exalted praise. There is a passage in which the poet apostrophises Gabriel, Mary, Jerusalem and Jordan which almost parallels a passage in the *Crist*, but is better done. For the poem was probably written after the *Crist*. There are traces in it of the use of the pseudo-gospel of Nicodemus, but there are no traces of that gospel in the *Crist*. Moreover, the use of the terms of heroic saga, begun in the *Guthlac*, is here more fully developed. The women who go to the tomb, the disciples, the patriarchs, even the soldiers, are Æthelings. Jesus is the victory-child of God, his death a king's death, his burial the burial of a hero-king. John the Baptist is the greatest of his thegns who welcomes Christ to the doors of Hades, as an English chieftain would welcome his victorious lord. Here is a passage:—

> At the dawning of the day down a troop of angels came,
> And the singing joy of hosts was round the Saviour's burg;
> Open was the earth-house, and the Ætheling's corse
> Took the spirit of life. Shivered all the earth,
> High rejoiced Hell's burghers, for the Hero had awakened,
> Full of courage, from the clay. Conquest-sure, and wise,
> Rose on high his majesty! Then the Hero, John,
> Spoke exulting.

This is the full saga note. It is even fuller when Christ breaks down the gates:—

> On his war-path hastened then the Prince of men,
> Then the Helm of Heaven willed the walls of hell
> To break down and bow to ruin, and the Burg unclothe
> Of its sturdy starkness—He, the strongest of all kings!
> No helm-bearing heroes he would have for battle then;
> None of warriors wearing byrnies did he wish to bring
> To the doors of hell! Down before him fell the bars,
> Down the hinges dashed, inwards drove the king his way!

All the exiles throng to see him, but of the great deeds when the "doors of hell, garmented so long in darkness, gleamed in the glory of the king," John, the great thegn, saw the most. His long speech of welcome breaks off in the midst, and this heroic fragment closes.

If we allow that Cynewulf wrote the *Andreas*,[1] this is the place, before the *Elene*, in which to place it. It is much younger in sentiment, in movement, in fancy than the *Elene*. The heroic strain in it is as full as in the *Descent into Hell*, and fuller than in the *Elene*, or rather, it is used in a ruder way. But the attribution of it to Cynewulf is doubtful. Fritzsche, who started this doubt, gives it to an imitator of Cynewulf, and Wülker agrees with him, though he allows that in the use of words and in the speech of it, as well as in the whole fashion of its representation, there is certainly a great deal which puts one in mind of Cynewulf.

The poem does not possess the personal sentiment so characteristic of Cynewulf, nor his habit of accumulating repetitions of the same thought, nor his slow-moving manner broken by swift and rapturous outbursts of song. On the contrary, it is full of changing incidents, its movement is swift, its pictures are imaginative, and there are few repetitions. Nevertheless, there are many phrases which put us in mind of Cynewulf, but then there are many which recall *Beowulf*. Had Cynewulf read *Beowulf* about this time, he might have been drawn into the manner of the *Andreas*. On the whole it is no wonder that it is attributed to an imitator of Cynewulf, though it is not easy to conceive of an imitator who is as good a poet as his original, who resembles his original at so many different points—in his heroic strain, in the curious badness of his rude humour, in his

[1] "Who wrote the *Andreas*" has been debated over and over again. Ten Brink gives it to Cynewulf, so does Zupitza. Many others agree with this view. Professor Napier emphatically disagrees with them. Sievers, also, holds that *Andreas* cannot possibly be by Cynewulf, and regards this as one of the few certainties of criticism in Old English. Each person seems very sure of his own opinion. But it is plain that the only sure thing is that there is no certainty at all in the matter.

knowledge of a stormy sea and coast. The writer was evidently one who had sailed the seas. It is all these resemblances, combined with the great excellence of the *Andreas*, that makes the difficulty of the imitation theory. In fact, in their anxiety to give nothing to Cynewulf which he has not signed, the critics have pushed their imitation theory too far. It is very difficult to believe that three poets, each of them of a capacity and imagination able to write the *Phœnix*, the *Andreas*, and the *Dream of the Cross*, should have lived at so early a period in the same century, and been companions of a fourth like Cynewulf. Heaven is not usually so gracious. It is possible, as we know from Elizabeth's time and our own, but it is very improbable in the eighth and ninth centuries. The new theory of Mr. Gollancz of the *Fates of the Apostles*, as the epilogue to the *Andreas*, would settle these difficulties, and allot the Andreas to Cynewulf. "The *Fates of the Apostles*," he says, "consists of little more than a hundred lines; it is certainly no meritorious piece of work, and it seems strange that a poet should have been so anxious to attest his authorship thereof by a long runic passage. In the MS. the poem immediately follows the legend of *Andreas*, and I am more and more inclined to regard it as a mere epilogue to this more ambitious epic, standing in the same relation to it that the tenth *passus* of *Elene* does to the whole poem. Its relationship is perhaps even closer, for whereas the ninth *passus* of *Elene* ends with 'finit,' there is no such ending in the case of *Andreas*. At the present moment I see nothing that militates against this view of the Cynewulfian authorship of the *Andreas*, and further investigation will enable us, I think, to claim that Cynewulf inserted his name in his four most important works—the epics on *Christ*, *Elene*, *Juliana*, and *Andreas*." This is a happy suggestion, and we will wish it to be proved true. It adds to the *Andreas* that personal cry the want of which makes us doubt that Cynewulf was its author. It frees us from the difficulty of putting a poem so poor as the *Fates of the Apostles* into Cynewulf's best period, for it is then not a separate poem, but a mere epilogue which we may conceive to have been written carelessly. At any rate its heroic manner is quite in accordance with the *Andreas*. Amid all these conflicting opinions, it is comfortable to be able to turn to something which is certain—to the poem itself. There is very little worth our interest in the question—Who wrote the poem? It is of the greatest interest to us to be able to feel the poem itself.

The *Andreas* is in the *Vercelli Book* along with the *Elene*, and runs to 1724 lines. The source of the legend is the *Acts of Andrew and Matthew*, a Greek MS. discovered in the Royal Library at Paris. There was no doubt a Latin translation of them from which Cynewulf worked. The poet used his original with freedom, and the note of the *Andreas* is fully English— more English than any other Cynewulfian poem. Andrew, Matthew, Christ, the angels, are all English heroes and English sailors, and the scenery is also English.[1]

The poem divides into two parts. The first has an introduction which describes the seizure and imprisonment of Matthew by the cannibal Mermedonians (Æthiopians). This is followed by the vision of Christ to Andrew and his voyage over the sea to deliver Matthew. The second part, which may be called the *Glory of Andrew*, is introduced by another vision of Christ to Andrew, now landed on the Mermedonian coast. This is followed by the delivery of St. Matthew, the martyrdom of Andrew, and the final triumph of the saint in the conversion of the Mermedonians.

The important part of the poem, from the point of view of literature, is the sea-voyage of St. Andrew, and it is so remarkable that I give a full account of it. "When the night-helm had glided

[1] "Lo, from days of old," the poem begins in full English heathenism transferred to Christianity, "we have heard of twelve heroes, famous under the stars, thegns of the Lord! The glory of their warfare failed not when the helms crashed in fight. Far-famed folk-leaders were they, bold on the war-path, when shield and hand guarded the helm upon the battle-field." This preface, speaking of the Twelve, is a sort of prologue which makes it still more probable that the *Fates of the Apostles* is an epilogue to the *Andreas*. Its end is then linked to its beginning.

away, behind it came the light, the trumpet-sound of the dawn." But in the night the Lord appeared to Andrew in a dream, while he dwelt in Achaia, and bade him go to Mermedonia to deliver his brother.

"How can I, Lord, make my voyage so quickly over the paths of the deep. One of thine angels from the high Heaven might more easily do this. He knows the going of the seas, the salt streams, and the road of the swan; the onset of the billows, and the Water-Terror, but not I. The Earls of Elsewhere are unknown to me, and the highways over the cold water."

"'Alas, Andrew!' answered the Lord, 'that thou should'st be so slow of heart to fare upon this path. Nathless, thou must go where the onset of war, through the heathen battle-roar and the war-craft of heroes, is boded for thee. At early dawn, at the marge of the sea, thou shalt step on a keel, and across the cold water break over the bathway.' No skulker in battle was Andrew, but hard and high-hearted and eager for war. Wherefore at opening day he went over the sand-links and to the sea-stead, his thegns with him, trampling over the shingle. The ocean thundered, the billows beat the shore, the resplendent morning came, brightest of beacons, hastening over the deep sea, holy, out of darkness. Heaven's candle shone upon the floods of sea."

This is all in the heroic manner, and more so than in any other Anglo-Saxon poem. Moreover, it is filled with the sea-air and the morning breaking on the deep. The very verse has the dash and salt of the waves in it, and the scenery is more like a Northumbrian than an East Anglian or a Wessex shore. The sand-dunes, the shingle, the thunder of ocean, resemble Bamborough so closely that I have often thought that the writer of the poem may have lived at Holy Island.

Then, as Andrew stood on the beach, he was aware of three shipmasters sitting in a sea-boat, as they had just come over the sea, and these were Almighty God, with His angels twain, "clothed like ship-farers, when, on the breast of the flood, they dance with their keels, far off upon the water cold."

"Whence come ye," said Andrew, "sailing in keels, sea-crafty men, in your water-rusher, lonely floaters o'er the wave? Whence has the ocean stream brought you over the tumbling of the billows?"

"We from Mermedonia are," replied Almighty God. "Our high-stemmed boat, our snell sea-horse, enwreathed with speed, bore us with the tide along the way of the whale, until we sought this people's land; much grieved by the sea, so sorely were we driven of the wind."[1]

"Bring me there," said Andrew; "little gold can I give, but God will grant you meed."—"Strangers go not there," answered the Lord, standing in the ship; "dost thou wish to lose thy life?"—"Desire impels me," said Andrew, and he is answered from the bow of the boat by God, who is, like a sailor of to-day, "sitting on the bulwark above the incoming whirl of the wave," and the extreme naïveté of the demand for payment, and the bargaining on the part of God, belong to the freshness of the morning of poetry; while the whole conversation is a clear picture of the manners and talk of travellers and seamen. We stand among the merchant carriers of the eighth century in England.

"Gladly and freely," the shipman says, "we will ferry thee over the fishes' bath when you have first paid your journey's fare, the scats appointed, as the ship-wards will desire of you." Then answered Andrew, sore in need of friends: "I have no

[1] I give here a small piece of the original, translated by Prof. A. S. Cook, to show how the English writer has worked up the poem with English manners, sea-terms, and natural description.

"Then Andrew arose early and went to the sea with his disciples, and when he had gone down to the sea-shore, he saw a little boat, and in the boat three men sitting. For the Lord had prepared a ship by His power, and He Himself was as a steersman in the ship; and He brought two angels, whom He made to seem as men, and they were seated in the ship. Andrew, therefore, when he saw them rejoiced with very great joy, and coming to them said, 'Whither go ye, brethren, with this little ship?' And the Lord answered, 'We are journeying into the country of the man-eaters.'"

That is enough for comparison with the text above (see Cook's *First Book in Old English*).

beaten gold, nor treasure, nor lands, nor rings, to whet hereto your will."—"How then," said the King, "would'st thou seek the sea-hills and the margin of the deep, over the chilly cliffs, to find a ship? Thou hast nothing for comfort on the street of sea; hard is his way of life and work who long makes trial of the paths of sea."

Andrew tells him he is God's thegn, and on His mission. Ah, answers God the Sailor, if it be so, I will take you. And they embark, but the whale-mere is soon mightily disturbed by a gale:—

> The sword-fish played
> Through ocean gliding, and the gray gull wheeled
> Greedy of prey; dark grew the Weather-torch;
> The winds waxed great, together crashed the waves,
> The stream of ocean stirred, and drenched with spray
> The cordage groaned; then Water-Terror rose
> With all the might of armies from the deep.[1]

And Andrew's thegns were afraid, but as in *Beowulf*, as in the *Fight at Maldon*, they will not leave their lord. "Whither can we go then?" they say; "in every land we should be shamed before the folk, when those known for courage sit to choose who best of them has stood by his lord in war, when hand and shield upon the battle plain, bowed down by grinding swords, bear sharp straits in the play of foes." And Andrew cheers them by telling them of the storm that was calmed by Christ:—

> So happened it of yore when we in ship
> Steered for the sea-fords o'er the foaming bar,
> Riding the waves; and the dread water-roads
> Seemed full of danger, while the ocean-streams
> Beat on the bulwarks; and the seas cried out,
> Answering each other; and at whiles uprose
> Grim Terror from the foaming breast of sea,
> Over our wave-ship, into its deep lap.

---

[1] I translate these passages from the *Andreas* into blank verse, in a different manner from the other passages in this book. Naturally, they are not, like the others, literal. A certain freedom is used in them.

>   . . . And then the crowd
> 'Gan wail within the keel, and lo, the King,
> The Glory-giver of the angels, rose
> And stilled the billows and the weltering waves,
> Rebuked the winds! Then sank the seas, and smooth
> The might of waters lay. Our soul laughed out,
> When we had seen beneath the welkin's path
> The winds and waves and water-dread become
> Fearful themselves for fear of God the Lord.
> Wherefore in very sooth I tell you now
> The living God will never leave unhelped
> An earl on earth if courage fail him not.

The thegns sleep, but Andrew and the steersman renew their talk. "A better seafarer," Andrew says, "I never met. Teach me the art whereby thou steerest the swimming of this horse of the sea, this wave-floater, foamed over by ocean. It was my hap to have been time after time on a sea-boat, sixteen times, pushing the deep, the streamings of Eagor, while froze my hands, and once more is this time—yet never have I seen a hero who like thee could steer o'er the stern. The sea-welter lingers on our sides, the foaming wave strikes the bulwark, the bark is at full speed. Foam-throated it fares; most like to a bird it glides o'er the ocean. More skilful art in any mariner I've never seen. It is as if the ship were standing still on a landstead where nor storm nor wind could move it, nor the water-floods shatter its foaming prow; but over seas it sweeps along, swift under sail. Yet thou art young, O refuge of warriors, not in winters old, and hast the answer of a sea-playing earl, and a wise wit as well."

"Oft it befalleth," answers Almighty God, "that we on ocean's path break over the bath-way with our ocean-stallions; and whiles it happeneth wretchedly to us on the sea, but God's will is more than the flood's rage, and it is plain thou art his man, for the deep sea straightway knew, and ocean's round, that thou hadst grace of the Holy Ghost. The surging waves went back; a fear stilled the deep-bosomed wave."

Andrew, hearing this, broke into a song of praise, and this

part of the poem closes; for now Christ changes the subject, and asks Andrew to tell him of his master Jesus, that is, of Himself—a pleasant motive. They have a long conversation until sleep overtakes Andrew. He wakens on shore in the morning, and sees a landscape which I have also thought might have been drawn direct from Bamborough:—

> Until the Lord had bid in brightness shine
> Day's candle, and the shadows swooned away,
> Wan under clouds; then came the Torch of air,
> And Heaven's clear radiance blickered o'er the halls.
> Then woke the hard in war, and saw wide plains
> Before the burg gates, and precipitous hills,
> And, round the gray rocks and the ledges steep,
> Tile-glittering houses, towers standing high,
> And wind-swept walls.

Then Andrew awakened his comrades. "Twas Christ the Ætheling," he says, "that led us across the realm of the oar."— "We, too," they answer, "have had our adventure"; and this poet, who has a special turn for various incident, develops for them the dream in which they are brought into the heavenly Paradise:—

> Us weary with the sea sleep overtook !
> Then came great earns above the yeasty waves,
> Swift in their flight and prideful of their plumes;
> Who from us sleeping took away our souls,
> And bore them blithely through the lift in flight,
> With joyful clamour. Bright and gentle they
> Caressed our souls with kindness, and they dwelt
> In glory where eternal song was sweet,
> And wheeled the firmament.

And there they saw the thegns of God, the patriarchs and martyrs and prophets, and the apostles and archangels praising the Lord. And Andrew gives thanks to Christ, who now in form of a young Ætheling draws near. "Hail to thee, Andrew," he cries, "the grim snare-smiths shall not overwhelm thy soul."

"How could I not know thee on the journey?" Andrew answers. "That was a sin."

"Not so great," replies Christ, "as when in Achaia thou saidst thou could'st not go over the battling of the waves. But now arise, set Matthew free. Bear many pains, for war is destined to thee. Let no grim spear-battle make thee turn from me. Be ever eager of glory. Remember what pains I bore when the rood was upreared. Then shalt thou turn many in this burgh to the light of Heaven."

Andrew then—and here begins the Delivery of St. Matthew—enters invisibly the town, like a chieftain going to the field of war. Seven watchmen keep the dungeon. As the saint drew near, death swept them all away; hapless they died; the storm of death seized on these warriors all beflecked with blood. The door fell in, and Andrew, the beast of battle, pressed in over the heathen who lay drunken with blood, ensanguining the death-plain. In that murder-coffer, under the locks of gloom, he found Matthew, the high-souled hero, singing the praises of God. They kissed and clipped each other. Holy and bright as heaven a light shone round about them, and their hearts welled with joys. Now when Andrew had delivered Matthew, he went to the city and sat him down by a pillar of brass on the march-path, full of pure love and thoughts of bliss eternal, and waited what would happen. And here begins the story of his suffering. The folk-moot is held, and the Mermedonians send for Matthew to devour him. He is gone, and an agony of hunger falls on them. The council is called, and the burghers, like English folk, "come riding to the Thing-stead on their horses, haughty with their ashen spears," and cast lots whom they shall eat. A youth is given up by his father, but Andrew blunts the knife, at which a devil cries—"It is Andrew, a stranger Ætheling, who has done this. There he stands." He is seized; God cheers him, but he is dragged through gorges and over stony hills, and "over the streets paved with parti-coloured stones," and brought back, his thought still light and his courage unbroken, to his prison. A bitter night of frost is then painted, to frame and enhance the lonely figure of the martyr.

> Then was the Holy One, the stark-souled Earl,
> Beset with wisdom's thoughts the whole night long,
> Under the dungeon gloom.
>   Snow bound the earth
> With whirling flakes of winter, and the storms
> With hard hail-showers grew chill, and Frost and Rime—
> Gray gangers of the heath [1]—locked closely up
> The homes of heroes and the peoples' seats !
> Frozen the lands ; and by keen icicles
> The water's might was shrunken on the streams
> Of every river, and the ice bridged o'er
> The glittering Road of the Sea.

The next day's martyrdom follows, till "the sun, gliding to his tent, went under a headland of clouds, and Night, wan and brown, drew down her helm over the earth and veiled the steep mountains."

A wild scene takes place in the prison when the Devil, with seven shield-companions, attacks and is repulsed by Andrew, and another day of torment closes with the vision of Christ, who tells him he shall no longer suffer; and he looks on the track where his blood has gushed forth, and it is sown with blowing bowers laden with blossoms. On the plain where he has been left for dead are two upright stones, which are the two tables of the Law, and at Andrew's word they send forth a mighty, weltering torrent, and air and earth and fire join in the overwhelming. The yellow waters swell, the wind roars, fire-flakes fall on the town, the earth trembles, and a great angel withstands the warriors. All the wicked ones are swallowed by a cleft in the hills, and the rest, repenting, cry—"Hear Andrew, he is the messenger of the true God." He baptizes them, builds a Church, appoints Plato as Bishop, and the poem closes with the description of his departure, such as the poet may have written when he read in Bæda how Ceolfrid went away from the shores of Tyne.

> Then by the nesses of the sea they brought
> The eager warrior to his wave-wood home,

---

[1] Or (another reading), war-steppers = hild-stapan. I have already given this passage in another connection and in a literal translation.

And weeping after him, stood on the beach,
As long as they could see that Æthelings' joy
Sail o'er the seals'-path, on the tumbling waves.
Then they gave glory to the glorious Lord,
Sang in their hosts, and this it was they sang—
"One only is the eternal God! Of all
Created beings is his might and power
Lauded aloud; and over all, his joy,
On high a holy splendour of the Heavens,
Shines through the everlasting ages far,
In glory beautiful for evermore
With angel hosts—our Ætheling, our King."

The *Dream of the Rood* is in the *Vercelli Book*. There is great discussion concerning its authorship. A large number of critics allot it to Cynewulf, but they lessen the weight of their opinion by giving other poems to Cynewulf which have nothing in them of the artist. Ten Brink and Zupitza both maintained against Wülker the authorship of Cynewulf. No assertion can be made at present on the subject. It is a matter of probabilities.

I not only think it probable that Cynewulf wrote it, but I believe it to be his last poem, his farewell to earth. It seems indeed to be the dirge, as it were, of all Northumbrian poetry. But I do not believe that the whole of the poem was original, but worked up by Cynewulf from that early lay of the Rood, a portion of which we find in the runic verses on the Ruthwell Cross. That poem was written in the "long epic line" used by the Cædmonian school, and I think that when in our *Dream of the Rood* this long line occurs, it belongs to or is altered from the original lay. The portions by Cynewulf are written in the short epic line, his use of which is almost invariable in the *Elene*.

What he did, then, was probably this. Having had a dream of the Cross in his early life which converted him and to which he refers in the *Elene*, he wished to record it fully before he died. But he found a poem already existing, and well known, which in his time was attributed by some to Cædmon, and which described the ascent of Christ upon the Cross, His death and burial. He took this poem and worked it up into a description of the vision in which the Cross appeared to him. Then he wrote to this a beginning and an end of his own, and in the short metre he now used.

This theory, whatever its worth may be, accounts for the double metre of the poem, does away with the strongest argument —that derived from metre—against Cynewulf's authorship, explains the difficulty of the want of unity of feeling which exists between the dream-part and the conclusion, and leaves to Cynewulf a number of passages which are steeped in his peculiar personality, which it would be hazardous to allot to any one but himself.

The introduction is quite in his manner, with the exception of two long lines. The personal cry—"I, stained with sins, wounded with my guilt," is almost a quotation from his phrases in the *Juliana* and *Elene*. The impersonation of the tree, the account of its life in the wood, is like the beginning and the manner of some of the *Riddles*. The subjective, personal element, so strong in his signed poems, is stronger in his parts of this poem. It would naturally be so if the poem were written, when he was very near to death, as his retrospect and his farewell. It is equally natural, if this view of the date of the poem be true, that he would enshrine at the last, by means of his art, the story of the most important hour of his life, and leave it as a legacy to the friends of whom he speaks so tenderly. "Lo," it begins—

> Listen, of all dreams, I'll the dearest tell,
> That at mid of night, met me (while I slept),
> When word-speaking wights, resting, wonned in sleep.
> To the sky up-soaring, then I saw, methought,
> All enwreathed with light, wonderful, a Tree;
> Brightest it of beams! All that beacon was
> Over-gushed with gold; jewels were in it,
> At its foot were fair; five were also there

High upon the shoulder-span, and beheld it there, all the angels of the Lord
Winsome for the world to come! Surely that was not, of a wicked man the
    gallows.

These two last lines may belong to the original poem, which Cynewulf was working on. Now he goes on himself:—

> But the spirits of the saints saw it (shining) there,
> And the men who walk the mould, and this mighty universe!
> Strange that stem of Victory! Then I, spotted o'er with sins,
> Wounded with my woeful guilt, saw the Wood of glory,
> All with joys a-shining, all adorned with weeds,
> Gyred with gold around! And the gems had gloriously
> Wandered in a wreath round this woodland tree.
>
> Nathless could I, through the gold, come to understand
> How these sufferers[1] strove of old—when it first began
> Blood to sweat on its right side. I was all with sorrows vexed,
> Fearful, 'fore that vision fair, for I saw that fleet fire-beacon
> Change in clothing and in colour! Now beclouded 'twas with wet,
> Now with running blood 'twas moist, then again enriched with gems.
> Long the time I lay, lying where I was,
> Looking, heavy hearted, on the Healer's Tree—
> Till at last I heard how it loudly cried!
> These the words the best of woods now began to speak:
> "Long ago it was, yet I ever think of it,
> How that I was hewèd down where the holt had end!
> From my stock I was dissevered; strong the foes that seized me there;
> Made of me a mocking-stage, bade me lift their men outlawed,
> So the men on shoulders moved me, till upon a mount they set me."

These lines seem to me partly Cynewulf's and partly of the old poem. He has introduced personal modifications to fit them into his dream. Now, he scarcely touches the old work: and the lines run on to a length which contrasts strangely with those of the conclusion to the dream itself:—

> "Many were the foemen who did fix me there! Then I saw the Lord, Lord of folk-kin he,
> Hastening, march with mickle power, since he would up-mount on me."

"But I—I dared not, against my Lord's word, bow myself or burst asunder, though I saw all regions of earth trembling; I might have felled His foes, but I stood fast:—

[1] That is, the Rood and the Saviour on it.

Then the Hero young, armed himself for war,—and Almighty God he was;
Strong and staid of mood stepped he on the gallows high,
Brave of soul in sight of many, for he would set free mankind.
Then I shivered there—when the Champion clipped me round;
But I dared not, then, cringe me to the earth.

A Rood was I upreared, rich was the King I lifted up; Lord of all the heavens was he, therefore I dared not fall. With dark nails they pierced me through and through; on me the dagger-strokes are seen; wounds are they of wickedness. Yet I dared not do them scathe; they reviled us both together. Drenched with blood was I, drenched from head to foot—blood poured from the Hero's side when he had given up the ghost. A host of wrathful weirds I bore upon that mount. I saw the Lord of peoples serve a cruel service; thick darkness had enwrapt in clouds the corse of the King. Shadow, wan under the welkin, pressed down the clear shining of the sun. All creation wept, mourned the fall of the King: Christ was on the Rood. I beheld it all, I, crushed with sorrow. . . . Then they took Almighty God: from that sore pain they lifted him; but the warriors left me there streaming with blood; all wounded with shafts was I:—

So they laid him down, limb-wearied; stood beside the head of his lifeless
    corse.
Then they looked upon him, him the Lord of Heaven, and he rested there,
    for a little time.
Sorely weary he, when the mickle strife was done! Then before his Banes,
    in the sight of them,
Did the men begin, here to make a grave for him. And they carved it there
    of a glittering stone,
Laid him low therein, him the Lord of victory. Over him the poor folk
    sang a lay of sorrow
On that eventide!

And there he rested with a little company." Here the old work ends, and Cynewulf, touching in what he had learnt from the Legend of Helena and the Cross, is told by the Rood to tell his dream to men, to warn them of judgment to come, and to bear, if they would be safe, the Cross in their hearts.

Now the Rood ceases to speak, and Cynewulf's personal conclusion follows. Its first lines are retrospective. They tell how he felt in early manhood, immediately after the dream which was the cause of his conversion. He felt "blithe of mood," because he was forgiven, "passionate in prayer, eager for death"—a common mixture of feelings in the hearts of men in the first hours of their new life with God. "Then, pleased in my heart, I prayed to the Tree with great eagerness, there, where I was, with a small company, and my spirit was passionate for departure." But he did not die, forced to out-live many sorrows —"Far too much I endured in long and weary days." Then he turns from the past to the present—"Now I have hope of life to come, since I have a will towards the Tree of Victory. There is my refuge." Then he remembers all the friends who have gone before him, and sings his death-song, waiting in joy and hope to meet those he loved at the evening meal in Heaven. "Few are left me now," he says, "of the men in power I knew":—

> Few of friends on earth; they have fared from hence,
> Far away from worldly joys, wended to the Lord of Glory!
> Now in Heaven they live, near to their High Father,
> In their brightness now abiding! But I bide me here,
> Living on from day to day, till my Lord His Rood,
> Which I erst had looked upon, long ago on earth,
> From this fleeting life of ours fetch my soul away—
> And shall bring me there, where the bliss is mickle,
> Happiness in Heaven! There the High God's folk
> At the evening meal are set; there is everlasting joy!

At last, with a happy reversion to that earlier theme he loved—the deliverance of the Old Testament saints from Hades—he turns from himself, now going home, to the triumphant home-coming of Jesus; soaring, as his custom was, into exultant verse:

> Hope was then renewed,
> With rresh blossoming and bliss, in the souls who'd borne the fire!
> Strong the Son with conquest was, on that (soaring) path,

> Mighty and majestical, when with multitudes he came,
> With the host of holy spirits, to the Home of God—
> And to all the Holy Ones, who in Heaven long before
> Glory had inhabited—So the Omnipotent came home,
> Where his lawful heirship lay, God, the Lord of all.

This is the close of the *Dream of the Rood* and the closing song of the life and work of Cynewulf. We see him pass away, after all storms and sorrows, into peace.

The most vigorous part of the poem is the old work, but its reworking by Cynewulf has broken it up so much that its simplicity is hurt. The image of the towering Tree, now blazing like a Rood at Hexham or Ripon with jewels, now veiled in a crimson mist and streaming with blood, is conceived with power; but, as imaginative work, it is not to be compared with the image of the mighty Rood in the *Crist* which, soaring from Zion to the skies, illuminates with its crimson glow heaven and earth, the angels and the host of mankind summoned to judgment. The invention of the Tree bringing its soul from the far-off wood, alive and suffering with every pang of the great Sufferer, shivering when Christ, the young Hero, clasped it round, longing to crush His foes, weeping when He is taken from it, joining in the wail of burial, conscious that on it, as on a field of battle, death and hell were conquered, is full of that heroic strain with which Cynewulf sympathised, and the subject was his own. It was he, more than any other English poet, who conceived and celebrated Christ as the Saviour of men, as the Hero of the New Testament.

CHAPTER XIII

OTHER POETRY BEFORE ÆLFRED

THE rest of the English poetry, before the revival of learning under Ælfred, is of little value, and consists of a number of small pieces, of varied kinds, of various age, and of various worth. The most remarkable of them are the *Whale*, the *Panther*, and the *Partridge;* *An Address of the Soul to the Body;* a *Warning of a Father to a Son;* the *Fates of Men;* the *Gifts of Men;* a fragment on the *Falsehood of Men;* four collections of *Proverbs* or *Gnomic Verses;* two poems on *Solomon and Saturn*, and the *Rune Song*.

The three first must be taken together, and form part or the whole of an English *Physiologus*. A *Physiologus* in the literature of the Middle Ages was a collection of descriptions of beasts, birds, or fishes, of their life and habits, and each of these was followed by a religious or moral allegory based on the description. We have already seen an example of this in the *Phœnix*. For the most part, the animals are taken as types of Christ or the Devil, and in our poems the *Panther* is the image of Christ and the *Whale* of the Devil. This allegorical treatment of animals is of great antiquity, and came down to us from the East, but the taste for it was established by the Fathers of the Church. It was common in the eighth and ninth centuries, to which these English poems of ours belong. It grew, as time went on, among poets and preachers till it became the source of a widespread mediæval literature. Our Physiologus has this special interest, that it is the oldest in any modern language.

The earliest was in Greek, and from it the Æthiopian as well as the Latin Physiologus were translated. The Latin one is supposed to be the source of these three Anglo-Saxon poems, and also of two Physiologi of the ninth century, B. and C. In B., after twenty-two other animals, the *Panther*, the *Whale*, and the *Partridge* follow one another. In C. the *Panther* and the *Whale* are retained, but the *Partridge* is omitted. It is suggested that the English writer chose these three concluding animals, not at random, but with the intention—since each of them represents one of the three kingdoms—of making a short but complete Physiologus. *Finit* stands in the manuscript after the fragment of the *Partridge*. The *Panther* and the *Whale* have some literary interest.

"In the far lands, in deep hollows, the Panther lives, glittering in a many-coloured coat like Joseph's, a friend to all, save to that envenomed scather, the Dragon. When he has fed, he seeks a hidden place among the mountain dells and slumbers for three nights. On the third day he wakes; a lofty, sweet, ringing sound comes from his mouth, and with the song a most delightful steam of sweet-smelling breath, more grateful than all the blooms of herbs and blossoms of the trees. Then from the burgs, and from the seats of kings, and from castle halls, pour forth the troops of war-men and the swift lance-brandishers and all the animals, to hear the song and meet the perfume. So is the Lord God, the Prince of Joys, and so the hope of salvation which he gives. That is a noble fragrance."

The *Whale*, since it has to do with the sea, is more wrought out by the poet, and more interesting than the *Panther*. The first part of the legend—of the sailors landing on the monster's back as on an island—may come from the East. It is in the story of Sinbad the Sailor, but it continued a long time in English literature, through Middle English to Chaucer, and so on to Milton's simile. Our description here is the first English use of the tale. It is fairly done, and filled in with special sea-phrases. "I will tell of the mickle whale whose name is

> Floater of the Flood-streams old, Fastitocalon !
> Like it is in aspect to the unhewn stone,
> Such as movèd is, at the margent of the sea,
> By sand-hills surrounded, thickly set with sea-weeds;[1]
> So the sailors of the surge in their souls imagine
> That upon some island with their eyes they look.
> Then they hawser fast their high-stemmèd ships
> With the anchored cables on the No-land there;
> Moor their mares of ocean at this margin of the main !
>   . . . Thus the keels are standing
> Close beside that stead, surged around by ocean's stream.[2]

The "players of the sea" climb on the island, waken a fire, and are joyous, but suddenly the Ocean-Guest plunges down with the bark, and in the hall of death prisons fast, with drowning, ship and seamen. So plays the Fiend with the souls of men.

Yet another fashion has this proud "Rusher through the water." When he is hungry, this Ocean-Ward opens his wide lips, and so winsome an odour pours forth that the other fishes stream into his mouth till it is filled; then quick together crash the grim

---

[1] "Thickly set with sea-weeds" is literally "greatest of sea-weeds or sea-reeds." I take it to mean that the stone looks as if it were itself the very greatest of sea-weeds, so thickly is it covered with them.

[2] Compare Milton—

>   Or that sea-beast
> Leviathan, which God of all his works
> Created hugest that swim the ocean-stream,
> Him, haply slumbering on the Norway foam,
> The pilot of some small night-foundered skiff,
> Dreaming some island, oft, as seamen tell,
> With fixed anchor in his scaly rind,
> Moors by his side under the lee, while night
> Invests the sea, and wishèd morn delays.
> So stretched out huge in length the Arch-Fiend lay,
> Chained on the burning lake.—*Par. Lost*, Book I.

It is a whole lesson in art to contrast this with its predecessor of the eighth century. "Ocean-stream" is pure Anglo-Saxon for "stream"—"sea."

gums around his prey. So, too, it is with men and the accursed one. When life is over, he claps his fierce jaws, those gates of hell, behind them. This is the common image of the entrance of hell—as seen, for example, in the rude pictures of the Cædmon manuscript—like the gaping mouth of a monstrous fish.

The next two poems may be called didactic. The *Address of a Father to a Son* is of no literary value. It consists of ten pieces of advice to practise virtues and to avoid vices; but the *Discourse of the Soul to the Body* has some points of interest. It exists in full as a double poem. The first is the speech of a lost soul to its body; the second, of a saved soul to its body. The first is in the *Exeter* and the *Vercelli Books;* the second, a fragment, is only in the *Vercelli Book*. The second is poor work, and may have been written much later than the first, in order to complete the representation of the subject. It has one peculiarity. "No poem of a similar kind," Hammerich says, "in which a saved soul speaks to its body, is found in any other literature."

The other, the *Lost Soul to its Body*, may date back to the year 700, if we take the phrase used in it—"that the spirit shall draw near to its body for three hundred winters, unless God work sooner the end of the world"—to refer to the common belief that the end of the world was to come in the year 1000, but the whole manner of the poem belongs to a later date than this, and we may suppose that this phrase crept in from some earlier poem upon the same subject.

"Cold is the voice of the Spirit, and grimly it calls to the corpse: 'O gory dust, why didst thou vex me? O foulness, all rotted by the earth; O likeness of the clay! Thy sinful lusts pressed me down; it seemed to me thirty thousand winters till thy death-day. Thou wert rich in food, sated with wine, but I was thirsty for God's body, for the drink of the Spirit. Dearer to none than the black raven, thou hast nought but thy naked bones, but by night I must seek thee, and at cock-crowing go away. Better, on the day of doom, hadst thou been beast or bird or the fiercest of snakes. Wroth will then be the Lord; and what shall we two do?'" Then the spirit flies away, and into the silent body the worms make their way to rive asunder and to plunder. One of them is leader: *Gifer* is he named:—

> Sharper than the needle are the jaws of him!
> He, the first of all, drives into the earth-grave
> Tears the tongue asunder; through the teeth he pierces!
> And above, inside the head, he eats into the eyes;
> Works for other worms way unto their food,
> To their wealthy banquet.

This captain of the worms, *Gifer*, venomous Greed, who pierces a path for his warriors into the prey, is almost worthy of Ezekiel.

The *Crafts* or *Gifts of Men*, the *Weirds of Men*, and the *Gnomic Verses* may be taken together. The two first are writings which, in their contemplative view of life, might have been written by some retired and pensive scholar, such as looked from his college windows at York on the changes of the kingdom. They have both been allotted to Cynewulf; but the man who wrote the *Gifts of Men* was not capable of writing the *Weirds of Men*, so much does the latter poem excel the former. The art in both poems is different, the poets are different; and though both of them carry in them the influence of Cynewulf, their work does not resemble his.

The chief interest of the *Gifts of Men* is that it may be a Christian working up of a heathen poem from which Cynewulf in the *Crist* also drew his passage on the Gifts of Men. The subject was common. Homer has used it, and St. Paul enumerates the gifts of the Spirit. Gregory's Homily on Job dwells upon them. Our writer uses St. Paul and Gregory, but, as many of the gifts are frankly profane, he may also have used an English heathen song as well. He celebrates harp-playing, running, archery, steering the war-ship, smithery, skill in dice, in riding, hunting, drinking, in hawking and juggling, among other nobler or more sacred gifts. It is a mere catalogue, however, without any literary quality.

The *Weirds of Men* is different. It has some form; its introduction is good, and in it shines a poet's hand. It begins with the birth of a child, its growth, education, and entrance into the world. What will become of it? God only knows by what death it may die, or if its weird be fatal. The man may die by the wolf, that gray ganger of the heath; by hunger, by blindness, by lameness, by falling from a tree, by the gallows, by fire, by quarrel at the feast; in misery from exile or loss of friends or poverty—and the descriptions of these various kinds of death give us several aspects of English life and scenery. But others, by the might of God, shall win to a happy and prosperous old age, with troops of friends—so manifold are the dooms God gives to men. Then the writer slips into the related subject of the *Gifts of Men;* and the same matter is done over again, but now by a poet, which we have had in the last poem.

The *Gnomic Verses* are in four collections—three in the *Exeter Book*, one in the *Cotton MS.* at Cambridge. They consist of folk-proverbs and maxims, short descriptions of human life and of natural occurrences, thrown together, without any order. They vary in length from half a line to eight lines. Some are of early simplicity, others show knowledge of the world, of war, of courts, of women, of domestic life; some are quotations from the poets. There is one (line 81) which almost reproduces the 1387th line of *Beowulf*. Some have come straight down from ancient heathen times; others, derived from heathenism, have been Christianised; others were written when Christianity was fully established, and others are much later than the eighth century. I think it probable that these collections were originally made in the school at York, and afterwards re-edited in Wessex, when new matter was added, the introduction written, and their ends. The last line of the first collection may be the wish of the editor to be thanked for the trouble he or another has taken—"Let him have thanks who got together for us these pleasures." The last four lines of the third part seem to have been a late addition.

Some one found this ancient folk-saying about weapons, and tagged it on at the end:—

> Yare be the War-board and lance-head on shaft,
> Edge on the sword, and point on the spear,
> Brave heart in warriors; a helm for the keen,
> And the smallest of hoards for the coward in soul.[1]

The *Rune Song* belongs—as well as we can guess—to the eighth or ninth century. Some heathen elements appear in it, but its form is generally Christian. Each of the twenty-nine runes are taken, and a verse made on the meaning of the word which names the rune. It is a poetical alphabet like those in our nursery rhymes. Here is one:—

> ᚱ. Bull is a fierce beast, broad are his horns.
> A full furious deer, and fighteth with horns,
> A mighty moor-stepper—a high-mooded creature.

Most of the verses are of this type; they do not belong to Literature. Two mistakes as to the meaning of the runes *Os* and *Sigel* induce critics to believe that the editor did not understand them, and that this song is a late Christian redaction of an old alphabet. One verse on the 22nd rune [Ing] is clearly ancient, and is explained by Victor Rydberg to enshrine an episode in the first great Northern Epic—broken fragments of which only remain scattered here and there in Sagas, and in *Saxo Grammaticus*—the epic of "the first great war of the world," as it is called by the seeress in Volospa:—

> x. Ing[2] was first seen among the East Danemen;
> Then he betook him, eastward, o'er sea!
> Vagn hastened to follow:
> Thus the Heardings called the hero.

---

[1] I have put in an Appendix the most interesting and oldest of these Gnomic verses.

[2] Ing is, as Tacitus tells us, the Father of all the German tribes dwelling on the sea-board of the *Ingævones*; he is the old German god of the Heavens. According to Rydberg (see *Teutonic Mythology*, Eng. trans. p. 180), the *waen* (= *wain*) of the third line is to be read *Vagn*, the proper name of the giant foster-father of Hadding, whose folk are the *Heardings* of the text.

P

There are two dialogues between *Salomo and Saturn* with which we may close the poetry of the ninth century. They are fragmentary. The oldest is the second in the manuscript [ll. 179-506]. We guess this from the vigorous way in which it begins: "Lo I heard, in the days of old, strive together concerning their wisdom, men cunning of wit, Lords of the World. Solomon was the most far-famed, though Saturn had the keys of many books." Saturn had wandered through all the East, and Solomon asks him about "the land where none may walk." The answer is romantic. "The sailor over the sea, Wandering Wolf was his name, was well known to the tribes of Philistia, and the friend of Nebrond. On the plain he slew at daybreak five-and-twenty dragons, and then fell dead himself. Therefore none may fare to that land nor bird fly over it. Yet shines the hero's sword, mightily sheathed, and over his burial-howe glimmer the hilts." Then Solomon answers, and Saturn begins his questions. Their wits are set over one against the other. Solomon stands as the representative of Christian wisdom, Saturn of the heathen wisdom of the East.[1] I quote a question and answer to show the poet's way:

"What is that wonder that fareth through the world, that goes so fiercely, beating down the under-stones of towns, wakening the droppings of sorrow? Nor star, nor stone, nor the steep gem, nor water, nor wild beast, nor aught can get away from it."

"Age" (the answer) "is on earth, powerful over all things. With its gripping chains of war, with its huge fetters, it reaches far and wide, and halters all it will. It crushes the tree and breaks its twigs ... it overcomes the wolf in fight, it overlives

[1] These Solomon dialogues became common in Western literature, but under the title of *Dialogues between Solomon and Marculf*. In these dialogues Marculf does not play the grave part of Saturn, the Eastern sage, but that of the peasant or mechanic full of uneducated mother-wit and rough humour. This suits the mediæval temper, always a little in rebellion against the predominance of the Church, the Noble, and the King. And again and again Marculf's native wit has the better of Solomon. But in this early Anglo-Saxon dialogue no such levity is allowed.

the rocks, it overtops the mountain path, it eats the iron with rust, it eats us also."

The other poem of *Salomo and Saturn*, though it begins the manuscript, is the later of the two. It has no introduction, and Saturn at once asks Solomon to explain to him the power of the Paternoster. The answer takes up the whole poem, and in the course of it many interesting examples of folk-lore and superstition occur. Every letter, for instance, of the Paternoster has its own special power. "Prologa prima, whose name is P: this warrior has a long rod with a golden goad. Ever he smites fiercely into the grim fiend, on whose track A, with mighty power, follows and beats him also." It continues in this quaint fashion until the couplets cease. Then a prose fragment is inserted full of curious things concerning the shapes which the Devil and the Paternoster will take when they contend together, of how the Paternoster will shoot at the Devil, of what kind of a head and of a heart the Paternoster has, and of all the wonders of his body; wonders so heaped up and amazing that they may have had their origin in Eastern imagination.

CHAPTER XIV

ÆLFRED

ÆLFRED, whom men have called the "Great" and the "Truth-teller"; whom the England of the Middle Ages named "England's Darling"; he who was the Warrior and the Hunter, the Deliverer and the Law-maker, the Singer and the Lover of his people,—"Lord of the harp and liberating spear"—was, above all, for the purposes of this book, the creator and then the father of English prose literature. The learning which had been lost in the North he regained for the South, and York, where the centre of literature had been, was now replaced by Winchester. There, Ælfred in his king's chamber, and filled with longing to educate his people, wrote and translated hour by hour into the English tongue the books he thought useful for that purpose. They are the origins of English prose.

He was born in 849, at Wantage in Berkshire, the youngest son of Æthelwulf and grandson of the great Ecgberht. At the age of four years the boy saw Rome, voyaging with an embassy to the centre of the world of thought and law. Leo IV. ordained and anointed him as king and received him as his adopted son. Two years later he went thither again with his father, who loved him more than his other sons, and stayed in the city until he was seven years old. The long journey through diverse countries, the vast historic town, its noble architecture, the long tradition of its law and story, its early Christian life, the spiritual power of the Roman Church, even the temporal power which flowed from it into Charles the Great of whom Ælfred had heard so much, must have made a profound impression, for inspiration and education, on a boy of genius. We can trace some of the results in his after-life. He was never satisfied till he was able to read Latin literature; he knit the Church of Rome and the crown of Wessex into a close friendship. We know from the *Chronicle* how often he sent embassies and gifts to Rome.

But this was not the only foreign influence which played upon his youth. He lived, on his return from Rome, for three months with Charles the Bald at the Frankish Court. The memory of the intellect and power of Charles the Great still shed, after nearly fifty years, a departing ray over the dying empire, and it shone into the mind of the child. We may be sure that the learned men of the court did not forget to talk with him of the English scholar, Alcuin, who had brought to the kingdoms of Charles the treasures of learning from York. His own country and his own folk had done this great work, and Ælfred never forgot it. When years had passed by, he recalled it in one of his prefaces.

With these new impulses he returned to England, desiring knowledge, but, as afterwards, there was none to teach him. One thing, however, he could do—he could learn the songs and stories of his own people in his own tongue; and the tale, with all its difficulties, which Asser tells, at least embodies his early love of books and of English verse. As he stood with his brothers at his mother's knee, she read to them out of a book of English songs. Æthelstan and Æthelred had no care for book or poetry, but Ælfred, delighted by the beauty of the illuminated letters, eagerly turned over the pages. "Whoever of you first learns the songs," said the Queen, "shall have the book," and Ælfred had no rest till he won the prize. The love of his native literature never left him. Night and day, we are told, he was eager to learn the "Saxon songs," and in after-life one of his chief pleasures was to recite English songs, to hear the singers of the court declaim them, to collect Saxon poems, to teach them to his children, to get his nobles to care for them, and to have them taught in his schools. He knew the English sagas, and the heroic names. He mentions Weland, the mighty smith; he told Asser the story of Offa's daughter Eadburga, a tale which was imported into Mercian history from the legend of Offa of the ancient Engle-land; and he recorded, with added touches of personal interest, the story of the first poet of England.

It may be imagined, then, with what bitter sorrow he heard at the age of eighteen, in 867, that there was not one religious house from the Tyne to the Humber which was not ravaged and burnt by the heathen; that not one trace, save perhaps in York and in a few abbeys north of the Tyne, was left of the learning and libraries of Northumbria. And his sorrow would be still more bitter when in 869 the rich abbeys of East Anglia were destroyed by the pirates Ivar and Hubba, and Wessex, his own land, lay open to the ravager. Guthrum or Gorm led this new attack, and the long-gathered wrath of the patriot and the lover of learning whetted Ælfred's sword when, on the height of Ashdown, around the stunted and lonely thorn-tree, he and his brother Æthelred made their final charge and beat the invaders down the hill with a pitiless slaughter. In the battles that followed Æthelred was wounded to death, and in 871 Alfred, now twenty-two years old, became the king.

The first years of his reign were dark as the night. Wessex barely held to life; Mercia was a desolation; all the seats of learning in Bernicia were now ruined, and at the beginning of 878 the Danes were in the heart of Wessex, apparent conquerors. But Ælfred was greatest when all seemed lost. He refuged himself at Athelney (the Æthelings' isle) a hill, defended by morass and forest, at the confluence of the Parret with the Frome, among the deep-watered marshes of Somersetshire. It is here that legend places the scene of the cowherd's hut and Ælfred watching and forgetting the burning loaves; and it was here that the famous jewel of gold and enamel was found, with the inscription—"Ælfred bade me to be wrought." There he sat for three, perhaps for seven months, gathering a host; and broke forth from his solitudes in the spring of 878, attacked the Danish army at Ethandun, drove them to their camp, forced their surrender in a fortnight, and dragged from them the peace of Wedmore. That peace, in spite of the later struggle of 885-886, settled England. It broke the advance of the Danes and weakened their power in England and abroad. It left Wessex and Kent in the hands of Ælfred; it secured for the English that part of Mercia which was west of Watling Street—from the Ribble to the Severn valley and to the upper valley of the Thames. The rest of England from the Tees to the Thames, including London (which Ælfred, however, got in 886), was in the power of the Danes and is called the Danelaw.

Over the Danelaw—to interrupt for a moment the tale of Ælfred—Danish customs, religion, and commerce prevailed; the Danish sagas were sung, and the Danish spirit grew. One would think that these folk, especially when they became Christian, would have left some traces of their keen individuality on the poetry or prose of the Danelaw. The stories of Horn and Havelok, rooted in Danish and Celtic traditions, were taken up by the Anglo-Norman, and then by Middle-English poets. There are, moreover, a few Danish legends in Layamon's poem. But now, and after the Norman Conquest, there is nothing but place-names and folk-tales to show us that more than half, and in after-years, the whole, of England belonged to Danish kings and to Danish folk. But the Danes who took England were scarcely a nation; when they settled down they became part of the English people and absorbed their ways. And they did this the more easily because they were of the same race and tongue as the men they conquered. Christianity also knit them to the English who made them Christians. With the loss of their wild gods half their individuality fled away. The land also and its scenery had their assimilating power on the new indwellers.

When Ælfred was forced to leave the Danelaw in Danish hands, he little thought that he was making Englishmen.

But at present the English and the Danes were two, not one; and Ælfred had to keep the English elements uppermost. It was well then, having this stern work at hand, that he was not only the student and the singer, but also a great warrior, and active in all bodily exercises. He was a keen hunter, falconer, rider, and slayer of wild beasts. "Every act of Venery," says Asser, "was known and practised by him better than by others." No man was bolder in the fight, none more watchful in the camp or wiser in the council. His people who fought along with him hailed him with joy. His look shone, it is said, like that of a shining angel in the battle. At Ashdown, "he charged again and again like a wild boar," and the slow gathering, knitting together, and inspiration of his men when he lay hid like a lion at Athelney and sprang forth, roaring, to overwhelm his foes, shows that his prudence, skill, and mastery of the art of war were as great as his personal courage.

When Ælfred had thus won peace for his people, he wished to educate them. But he had at first something more needful to do; and he spent the six years of quiet from 878 to 884 in repairing the ruin made by the Danes, in reforming the army, in building a navy, and in establishing just government and law. The peace was broken in 885 by a fresh attack of the Northmen, but was again secured in the following year. Ælfred was now complete master, not only of his kingdom, but also of the national imagination. "In that year," says the *Chronicle*, "all the Angelcyn turned to Ælfred, except those in bondage to Danish men." In the following year he began, with his mingled humility, good sense and self-confidence, that revival of learning which he had so long desired. The foundation for this great purpose had already been partly laid. He had collected, and continued to collect, around him a number of scholars who should be, first, his teachers; and afterwards enable him to teach the English people in the English language what they ought to know as citizens of a great country, and as pilgrims to a heavenly country. He called to this work Werfrith, Bishop of Worcester, who himself presided over the school in that town; Denewulf of Winchester; Plegmund, whom he drew from Mercia to make Archbishop of Canterbury; two Mercian priests, Æthelstan and Werwulf, who were his chaplains and teachers (all three children of the college at Worcester); and these exhausted all that England could do for him. In this penury he turned to foreign lands for help. "Men once came," he said, "from out-land countries to seek instruction in England; now if we need it we can only get it abroad." So he called Grimbald from Flanders and put him over the new abbey rising at Winchester, and John the Old Saxon from the monastery of Corvëi in Westphalia to preside over the religious house his gratitude had dedicated to God at Athelney.

His incessant spirit kept these men up to their work. He translated books such as Gregory's *Pastoral Care* to teach the clergy their duties; he urged the bishops to give their leisure to literature, and urged it as a religious duty. He gave them books to translate and insisted on their being finished. He may be said to have driven them to write, as much as he drove the judges to learn the duties of their office and the Laws of England.

The difficulties he had with the clergy were much greater with the nobles. The English warriors and courtiers of mature age were sorely troubled when the king compelled them to learn to read and write, or if they could not learn, to hire a freeman or slave to recite before them at fixed times the books needful for their duties. When at last he despaired of the elder men, he sent all the young nobility and many who were not noble into the schools where his own children were educated, that they might learn how to read both English and Latin books, and to translate the one language into the other. But this was afterwards. To teach himself now was his first business, and Æthelstan and Werwulf, his daily tutors, were not enough for him. He needed a better scholar and one whom he could love as a friend. So he asked Asser of St. David's, in the farthest border of Wales, to live and study with him. Asser saw the king at Dene, near Chichester, in the early part of the year 884, and stayed three days with him. "Stay with me always," said the king, and when Asser objected his love of Wales and his duties there, the king replied, "Stay with me at least six months in the year." A fever kept Asser away for more than a year, but in July 886 he came to Leonaford, and remained eight months at the court. It is probable that then he went back slowly to Wales, and returned to Ælfred in the middle of the year 887. From that time he seems to have spent six months every year with the king. Then Ælfred's close study began. "I translated and read to him," writes Asser, "whatever books he wished, for it was his custom day and night, amid all his afflictions of mind and body, either to read books or have them read to him." Thus he learned Latin, and the first result of this association with Asser was Ælfred's *Handbook*. One day Asser quoted to him a phrase he liked out of some Latin author. "Write it down for me," said the king, and he pulled out of his breast a little note-book. The book was full, and Asser proposed to begin a new book of quotations, which as the king made he then translated into English. The new book grew till it became almost as large as a Psalter; and he called it his *Handbook*, finding no small comfort therein. This *Handbook* was his first work, and he was thirty-five years old when he began it. It consisted of extracts from the Bible and the Fathers, and of a few scattered illustrations made of these passages by Ælfred or Asser—"divinorum testimoniorum scientiam —multimodos divinae scripturae flosculos... congregavit." "Quos flosculos undecunque collectos," is afterwards said of this book. William of Malmesbury has two extracts from this Manual. Both have to do with the earlier history of England and of Ælfred's own house, but it is exceeding improbable, as some have argued from these quotations, that there was any history of Wessex in the *Handbook*. "These passages are most likely only allusions or illustrations which crept into this book of religious extracts.

Else William of Malmesbury would have used the whole book." This remark of Wülker's seems to settle the matter. This *Handbook*, begun in Nov. 887, was fully set forth in English in 888 for the use of the people. It is a great misfortune that it is lost.

The next piece of writing he did was the *Law-book*. He compiled it out of the existing Codes of Kent, Wessex, and Mercia, that is, out of the laws of Æthelberht, Ine, and Offa. It had an introduction, followed by three parts—(1) Ælfred's Laws; (2) Ine's Laws; (3) Ælfred's and Guthrum's Peace; and it was composed, said William of Malmesbury, "inter fremitus armorum et stridores lituorum." This suggests that the collation of the laws had been begun in 885 or 886. The introduction begins with the Decalogue of the second Nicæan Council and some words on the Mosaic laws. Ælfred adds the letter sent by the Apostles to the Church after the Council at Jerusalem. Then he quotes—"Whatsoever ye would that men should do unto you, do ye even so unto them; for this is the law and the prophets." He tells every judge in the kingdom that "Judge so as ye would be judged" is the foundation of their duty. As to the laws, he did not make many of his own, but kept and rejected out of the above codes those which by the counsel of his Witan he thought best for his kingdom; clinging like an Englishman to precedent. The whole book, since the Scriptural quotations in the preface suggest that it came after the *Handbook*, was probably issued in 888.

By this time he was fairly well acquainted with Latin, and as the most necessary class to benefit were the clergy, the instructors of the people, he chose as the first book to be translated the *Cura Pastoralis*—the "Herdsman's Book"—of Gregory the Great, a kind of manual of the duties of the clergy. It recites in four divisions the ideal of a Christian priest; and the king took care that a copy of it should be sent "to every bishop's seat in my kingdom." A copy was sent, as mentioned specially in Ælfred's preface, to Plegmund, Archbishop of Canterbury. Plegmund was first made Archbishop in 890. The translation then was probably done in 889, and sent to the bishops in 890.[1]

That this was his first book is maintained by some critics, who support their view by arguments drawn from the well-known preface which Ælfred prefixed to it. I do not understand how, after reading that preface, a number of other critics refer the book to a much later period in Ælfred's life. Almost every paragraph suggests the beginning not the end of his translating work. It is also not likely that after the small effort of the *Handbook* he would undertake so long and difficult a business as either the translation of Orosius, or of Bæda's history, or of Boethius. The book is also done with more closeness to his author than any other of his translations, and no clearly original matter is inserted. He certainly paraphrases, omits, expands, explains, and changes the place of his text, where he is anxious to make things clear for his people, but he does this briefly, tentatively, and less than elsewhere. The book is the book of a beginner. In it, however, English literary prose may be said to have made its first step. Bæda's translation of St. John's gospel, that portion also of the English Chronicle which already existed up to the death of Æthelwulf, can scarcely be called literary prose. As we think, then, of the king, seated with Asser or Plegmund in his bower at Winchester or Dene, and bending over the Herdsman's book of Gregory, we think also of all the great prose of England, the fountain of whose stream arose in these quiet hours of more than royal labour. It is well, though the preface is long, to quote it in full. It is the first piece of any importance we possess of English prose. It is redolent of Ælfred's character and spirit. It marks the state of English literature at the time it was written. It makes us realise how great was the work Ælfred did for literature and the difficulties with which he had to contend.[2]

---

[1] There are many different arrangements made by critics of the dates of Ælfred's translations. I have adopted the arrangement I think the best.

[2] For the text of this preface, see Sweet's *Anglo-Saxon Reader*, pp. 4-7.

This Book is for Worcester

King Ælfred biddeth greet Bishop Wærferð with loving and friendly words, and I let it be known to thee that it has come very often into my mind what wise men there formerly were both among the clergy and the laymen, and what happy times there were then throughout England; and how the kings who had rule over the people (in those days) obeyed God and his ministers, and they kept peace, law and order at home, and also spread their lands abroad; and how it was well with them both in war and in wisdom; and also how keen were the clergy about both teaching and learning and all the services they owed to God, and how men from abroad sought wisdom and teaching hither in (our) land, and how we must now get them from without if we would have them. So utterly had it (learning) fallen away in England that there were very few on this side of the Humber who could understand their service-books in English, or even put a letter from Latin into English; and I think there were not many beyond the Humber. So few there were of them that I cannot think of even one when I came to the throne. Thanks be to God Almighty that we now have any supply of teachers. And therefore I bid thee do, as I believe thou art willing to do,—free thyself from the things of this world as often as thou canst that thou mayst put to work the wisdom that God has given thee wherever thou canst. Think what punishments have come upon us in the sight of the world when we neither loved it (wisdom) ourselves, nor let other men have it. We only loved to have the name of Christian, and (to have) very few (Christian) virtues.

When I remembered all this, I remembered also how I saw (before it was all harried and burned), how the churches over all England stood filled with treasures and books, and also a great host of God's servants; and at that time they knew very little use for those books, because they could not understand anything of them, for they were not written in their own language. It was as if they said: "Our forefathers, who held these places before us, loved wisdom, and through it they got wealth and left it to us." Here one can still see their footprints, but we cannot follow them because we have lost both the wealth and the wisdom, since we would not bend our heart to follow their spoor.

When I remembered all this then I wondered exceedingly about the good and wise men who were formerly throughout England, and who had fully learned the books—that they did not not wish to turn any part of them into their own tongue. But I soon answered myself and said: They did not look for it that men would ever be so careless, and that learning would so fall away. For this desire they left it alone:—wishing that there should be the more wisdom here in the land the more we knew of languages.

Then I remembered how the Law was first given in the Hebrew tongue, and again, how when the Greeks learned it, they turned it all into their own tongue, and also all other books. And again, how the Romans did the same. When they had learned it they turned all of it by wise translators into their own tongue. And also all other Christian peoples turned some part of (the old) books into their own tongue. Therefore it seemeth better to me, if it seemeth so to you, that we also turn some books—those which are most needful for men to know—into the tongue which we can all understand, and that ye make means—as we very easily can do, with God's help, if we have stillness—that all the youth now in England of free men who have the wealth to be able to set themselves to it be put to learning while they are not of use for anything else, until the time when they can well read English writing; but those whom one wishes to teach further, and to forward to a higher place—let them afterwards be taught further in the Latin tongue.

When I remembered how the knowledge of the Latin tongue had before this fallen away throughout England, and yet that many could read English writing—then I began amidst other divers and manifold occupations of this kingdom to turn into English the book which in Latin is named *Pastoralis*, and in English *Shepherd's Book*; sometimes word for word, sometimes meaning for meaning, as I had learned it from Plegmund, my archbishop, and Asser, my bishop, and from Grimbold, my mass-priest, and from John, my mass-priest. When I had learned it so that I understood it, and so that I could quite clearly give its meaning, I turned it into English. And to each bishopric in my Kingdom I will send one, and in each there shall be an "æstel" (*indicatorium*) worth fifty mancuses. And I command, in God's name, that no one take the "æstel" from the book nor the book from the minister; it is unknown how long there may be such learned bishops, as now, God be thanked, are nearly everywhere. Therefore I would that they should be always kept in that place, except the bishop wish to have the book with him, or it be lent out anywhere, or any one be making a copy from it.

This ends the Preface. Then, after a short space, some alliterative lines follow. They tell us that "this message (Gregory's treatise) Augustine brought over the salt sea to the island-dwellers, as the Pope of Rome, that warrior of the Lord, had decreed. In many a Right-spell the wise Gregory was versed. . . . Afterwards, King Ælfred turned every word of me into English and sent me south and north to his scribes to be copied that he might send these copies to his Bishops, because some who least knew the Latin tongue were in need of them."

The translation follows, and at the end Ælfred has added some verses of his own. They have a faint touch of imagination; their simplicity reveals his childlikeness; their rudeness of form and phrase belongs to one who had but begun to write, but they mark his interest in English poetry. He who loves poetry will try to write poetry.

These are the waters — I paraphrase the verses — which the God of Hosts promised, for our comfort, to us dwellers on the earth; and His will is that from all who truly believe in Him these ever-living waters should flow into the world; and their well-spring is the Holy Ghost. . . . Some shut up this stream of wisdom in their mind, so that it flows not everywhere in vain; but the well abides in the breast of the man, deep and still. Some let it run away in rills over the land; and it is not wise that such bright water should, noisy and shallow, be flowing over the land till it become a fen.

But now, draw near to drink it, for Gregory has brought to your doors the well of the Lord. Whoever have brought here a water-tight pitcher, let him fill it now; and let him come soon again. Whoever have a leaky pitcher, let him mend it, lest he spill the sheenest of waters, and lose the drink of life.

The second book Ælfred translated (890-91) was Bæda's *Ecclesiastical History of the English*, and this was addressed not only to the clergy but also to the laity, who ought to know the history of their own land. This translation also clings closely to its original, but omits many chapters not likely to interest the ordinary reader— letters from the Pope, theological disquisitions, the account of the Easter controversy, and some purely Northumbrian affairs. But Ælfred takes pains, as if it were a subject of national interest, to translate in full the story of the origin of English poetry. It is a pity, but it is characteristic of his early translating, that he inserts no original matter. No one could have given a better account of the history of the Church in Wessex and of the kingdom; and this is precisely the point where Bæda is weak and less accurate than usual. That Ælfred did not do this is probably owing to the fact that about the year 891 he had begun to work the *Chronicle* up into a national history, and saw no need to put forth two accounts of the same matters. The loss is indeed all but repaired in his editing of the English Chronicle. That this editing came after his translation of Bæda is at least suggested by the repetition in the *Chronicle* of certain mistakes he made in that translation. Moreover, the king might naturally feel that history should follow history.

It was the habit of the monasteries to put down on the *Easter Tables* the briefest and driest records of the events of the year, chiefly the deaths and enthronements of bishops and kings. For Wessex and Kent this would be done at Winchester and Canterbury, but it is plain the Roll would be most carefully kept at Winchester. Professor Earle has skilfully wrought out when the various recensions were made before the reign of Ælfred. It is enough for our purpose to say that at the time of Æthelwulf or shortly after his death, some one man, and probably Bishop Swithun of Winchester, filled up the Winchester Annals from tradition back to Hengest, combined them with the Canterbury Chronicle, made a genealogy of the West Saxon kings from Æthelwulf to Cerdic, from Cerdic to Woden, and from Woden to Adam; and then, having inserted new matter throughout, told at some length the wars and death of Æthelwulf. This part of the *Chronicle*, running to 855, was found by Ælfred on his accession and remained as it was till the days of peace. Then about 891, having conceived the notion of making it a national history, he caused the whole to be gone over, and the part from the accession of his brother Æthelred, with a full account of his own wars with the Danes, to be written in. It is, from its style, the work of one man, and it may be that Ælfred did it himself. As historical prose it is rude, but also condensed and vigorous.[1] In this recension many fresh entries were made from the Latin writers and Bæda's history. This then is the manuscript of the *Annals of*

[1] Some think that the first part, from 60 B.C. to A.D. 755, was not done at Æthelwulf's death, but now.

Winchester which, written by a single hand, was presented by Archbishop Parker to Corpus Christi College at Cambridge; and it is the source of the historical prose of England.[1]

The new book Ælfred now translated,[2] most probably in the years 891 to 893, was the *History of the World* by Orosius, a book written originally in the year 418, at the suggestion of Augustine, and with the purpose of proving, as Augustine himself tried to do in the third book of his *Civitas Dei*, that the wars of the world and the decay of the Roman Empire were not due, as the heathen declared, to Christianity. Though a poor work, it became a standard authority. It was the only book which the Middle Ages read as a universal history. Ælfred, knowing its value in education, and anxious to inform his people not only of the history of England but also of the world beyond, gave them this book in their native tongue. He left out all the controversial part, and all that he thought would be of no use or pleasure to his readers. On the other hand, he inserted a number of new facts, interspersed with original remarks full of his inquiring and eager intelligence. But the chief insertion he made, in a clear and simple style, was a full account of the geography of Germany and of the places where the English tongue had of old been spoken. "It bears traces, in its use, for example, of Ostsä, instead of the Anglo-Saxon Eastsä, of being derived from German sources." Indeed, the king made inquiries of every traveller who came to Wessex, and when he heard of two in particular who had made long sea-voyages, Ohthere and Wulf-

[1] Ælfred's work on the *Chronicle* ceases in 891. In 894 a writer of ability and force took up the task, and carried it on to 897. From that date to 910 the book was neglected. In 910 it was again undertaken by an excellent writer.

[2] Not only does Wm. of Malmesbury mention the book as Ælfred's, but the following allusion can only be to the history by Orosius :—

Il [Ælfred] fist escrivere un livre Engleis	E des reis ki firent la guere
Des aventures e des leis	E maint livre fist il escrivere
E de batailles de la terre	U li bon clerc vont sovent lire.

Geffrey Gaimar's Trans. of the *Estorie des Engles*, ll. 3451-56.

stan, he had them up to his house, and while he sat at his desk, made them dictate to him their travels along the coasts of Norway and the German shores of the Baltic. "Ohthere," it begins, "said to his Lord King Ælfred, that of all the Northmen he dwelt the farthest north," and he told how he had sailed along the coast of Norway till he reached the White Sea and the mouth of the Dwina; and then of another voyage past Denmark and the islands till he saw the Baltic running many hundred miles up into the land. "He had passed by," says the king, "before he came to Haithaby, Jutland, Zealand, and other islands on his right, where the Engle dwelt before they came hither." Wulfstan then told his tale—how he had sailed from Haithaby along the northern shores of Germany for seven days and nights until he reached the mouths of the Vistula and the land of the Esthonians, of whose country and customs he gives an account which must have delighted the keen curiosity of the king. I give a short extract from Ohthere's voyage in order to show Ælfred's hand.

Ohthere told his lord, King Ælfred, that he, of all northmen, dwelt the farthest north. He said that he dwelt in that northward land by the West Sea. That land, he said, is very long from there to the north, but it is all waste except in a few places. Here and there the Finns dwell in it, hunting in winter and fishing in summer, along the sea. He said that once he longed to try how far that land stretched to the north, or whether any one dwelt north of the waste. So he went due north along the land, the waste land on the starboard, the open sea on the larboard, for three days. Then the land bent right to the east, or the sea in on the land, he knew not which, but he knew that he awaited there a north-west wind and sailed then east, along by the land, as far as he could sail in four days. Then he had to wait for a wind right from the north, because the land bent due south. Then he sailed thence due south along the land as far as he could sail in five days. Then there flowed a great stream up into the land, and they turned up into the stream, because they durst not sail past it because of foes, for on the other side of the stream the land was all inhabited. Nor had he before met any inhabited land since he had set out from his own home. . . . Chiefly he went thither, in addition to the viewing of the land, for the horse-whales (walrus), because they had very excellent bone in their teeth,—some of their teeth they brought to the king—and their hide is very good for ship-ropes. That whale is much smaller than other whales; it is not longer than seven ells. But in his own land is the best whale-hunting. They are forty-eight ells long, and the greatest fifty. Of those, he said, he was one of six who slew sixty (?) in two days.

There is a freshness as of a sea-voyage, a personal breath in the simple writing which makes us realise how closely Ælfred listened to these rough seafarers, and how much he sympathised with their spirit of discovery. This is the first record in English of the mighty roll of great adventurers upon the ocean, and Ælfred was as eager to secure the geographical and national knowledge of these men as the Geographical Society would be to-day.

These translations were the work of about five years, from 888 to 893, years of the "stillness" that Ælfred loved, years when he nourished in the arts of peace and literature, as he had done in wars and government, that "desire I have to leave to men who should live after me a memory of me in good deeds." I have said that it is probable that during this time he received and collected the Northumbrian poetry. Bæda's account of Cædmon would have set him to inquire about it. Its translation into the West Saxon dialect would follow, and I should like to have seen Ælfred reading *Beowulf* for the first time, or Asser and Ælfred reading together the *Crist* of Cynewulf. Nor did literature alone engage him. He still sang and listened to English song, but he cared also for things and men beyond England. He kept open house for all who brought him outlanders' tales; he received pagan Danes, Britons from Wales, Scots, Armoricans, voyagers from Gaul and Germany and Rome, messengers from Jerusalem and the far East. Irish scholars came to confer with him,[1]

---

[1] We find in the *English Chronicle*, under the year 891-892, the following romantic entry, part of which reads like a myth—like the voyage of St. Brandan—but which is in full accordance with Celtic love of adventure:—
"And three Scots came to King Ælfred in a boat without oars from Hibernia" (Yrlande in another MS.), "whence they had stolen away, because, for the love of God, they would be on pilgrimage—they recked not where. The boat in which they fared was wrought of three hides and a half, and they took with them enough meat for seven nights. Then after seven nights they

and we hear that he sent a messenger to visit the Christian Churches in India. The arts also were not neglected. He restored and developed the art of shipbuilding. He fetched many architects from the continent, and was himself an architect. He rebuilt the fortresses; he rebuilt London into a goodly city. He made new roads and repaired the old. He adorned and laid with fair stone his royal country-houses. In his reign enamel work, gold-weaving and gold-smithery flourished, and certain mechanical inventions were his amusement. He still hunted; it is a tradition that he wrote a book on falconry; and the forest and the pools saw the king flying his royal birds and chasing the boar and the stag with the eagerness but not the strength of a young man. Through all this lighter work he pursued the heavier work of ruling his kingdom and preparing it for war, and in his translation of Boethius there is a statement inserted of the powers and means of Government, of the division into classes a great king makes of his people for the sake of the kingdom, of the necessity laid upon him to use this material nobly. It is worth reading, not only for the insight it gives into his kingship, but for the personal touches of sentiment which give it a literary charm.

Reason! indeed thou knowest that neither greed nor the power of this earthly kingdom was ever very pleasing to me, neither yearned I at all exceedingly after this earthly kingdom. But yet indeed I wished for material for the work which it was bidden me to do, so that I might guide and order with honour and fitness the power with which I was trusted. Indeed thou knowest that no man can show forth any craft; can order, or guide any power, without tools or material—material, that is, for each craft, without which a man cannot work at that craft. This is then the material of a king and his tools, wherewith to rule—That he have his land fully manned, that he have prayermen, and army-men, and workmen. Indeed, thou knowest that without these tools no king can show forth his craft. This also is his material—That he have, with the tools, means of living for the three classes

---

came to land in Cornwall and went then straightway to King Ælfred. Thus were they named—Dubslane, Maccbethu, and Maelinmum. And Swifneh, the best teacher that was among the Scots, died."

—land to dwell upon, and gifts, and weapons, and meat, and ale, and clothes, and what else the three classes need. . . .

And this is the reason I wished for material wherewith to order (my) power, in order that my skill and power should not be forgotten and hidden away, for every work and every power shall soon grow very old and be passed over silently, if it be without wisdom; because whatsoever is done through foolishness no one can ever call work. Now would I say briefly that I have wished to live worthily while I lived, and after my life to leave to men who should come after me my memory in good deeds.

These were his happiest days, but he lived, as he said, "with a naked sword always hanging over his head by a single thread," and his quiet was destroyed when the sword fell in 893. "Hardship and sorrow a king would wish to be without, but this is not a king's doom"; and the sorrow came when the pirates from Boulogne, with 250 vessels in their train, seized on the forest of Andred, and Hasting, with 80 vessels, pushed his way up the Thames. In 894 Hasting got into Hampshire, and shortly after the whole of the Danelaw rose and joined the invaders. It was their dying effort. Ælfred was well prepared, and the war, though carried to Chester in the North and to Exeter in the South, was victoriously finished by the capture of the Danish fleet in 897. From that date till his death in 901 Ælfred had peace; and he returned, worn out but a conqueror, to his literary work.

The book he now undertook was Boethius' *De Consolatione Philosophiae*. The translation, with its original handling of the material, points to one who now had become an expert in translation, who boldly transferred himself into the soul of his author. This self-confidence is that of a long practice in translating, and places the book at the end of Ælfred's life in the years 897 and 898. His choice this time was directed not so much by a desire to teach his people as by personal feeling. The philosophic consolation of the book, to which Ælfred added his own profound Christianity, was in harmony with the temper of a man who had seen how fleeting were wealth and power, bodily strength and fame; and who needed and loved to have a deep religious foundation in the soul. He had known sore trouble, his life had been a long battle with foes, with national ignorance and stupidity, and with bodily disease; and now, in this book which he made his own, he mused, full of courage and of weariness, from his watch-tower of quiet, on the tragic and changing world, on the rest of the world to come, and on the power God had given him to act for his kingdom and endure for his people. The preface which I here give may have been dictated by Ælfred himself.

King Ælfred was the translator of this book, and turned it from Latin into English as it is now done. Sometimes he set down word for word, sometimes meaning for meaning, as he could translate most plainly and clearly, in spite of the various and manifold worldly cares which often occupied him in mind and body. These cares, which in his days came on the kingship he had undertaken, are very hard for us to number. And yet, when he had learned this book and turned it from Latin into the English tongue, he then wrought it afterwards into verse, as it is now done. And now he begs, and for God's sake prays every one whom it may please to read the book, that he pray for him, and that he blame him not if he understood it more rightly than he (the king) could. For every one, according to the measure of his understanding and leisure, must speak what he speaketh and do what he doeth.

The *De Consolatione* was written by Boethius in the prison where Theodoric, King of the East Goths, had laid him on a charge of conspiracy. Composed to comfort his heart in trouble, it is a dialogue between him and Philosophy, who consoles him for the evil changes of fortune by proving that the only lasting happiness is in the soul. Inward virtue is all; everything else is indifferent. The wise and virtuous man is master of himself and of events. The book is the last effort of the heathen philosophy, and so near to a part of the spirit of Christianity that it may be called the bridge between dying paganism and living Christianity. And so much was this the case that the Middle Ages believed Boethius to be a Christian, and his book was translated into the main European languages. Ælfred made it popular in England, Chaucer got it into prose in the fourteenth century; in the fifteenth it was put into English verse; under Elizabeth it was again put into English prose.

Its serious and sorrowful note harmonised well with the spiritual life of Ælfred. He expands, but does not improve, the grave ethical paragraphs. He does not wear the stoic robes with grace. Sometimes, leaving his original aside, he writes out of his own heart, and these passages are for the most part engaged with that contempt of wealth and luxury and power which the long harassment of his life had bred in him. He claims adversity as his friend, not his foe; and he speaks of wisdom and friendship with an equal love. He adds to Boethius a deep religious fervour. The prayers are the writings where he reaches most beauty of expression. The sentences on the Divine nature, steeped in reverence, awe and love, soar with ease into that solemn thought and adoration which we may well believe filled the silent hours of the king's meditation on his own stormy life and on the peace of God. It is a contrast, as we have seen in Cynewulf, which was dear to the English writers. Sometimes he yields himself to the charm of metaphysics, and discusses free will and the Divine preordination. In the fifth book, where these excursions come, he puts his own work almost entirely in place of his original, and explains the problems of Boethius from the Christian point of view. Nowhere does Ælfred stand more clearly before us, and the clearer he is the nobler he seems. As we read, our admiration of him as king and warrior and law-giver is mingled with our pity and reverence. And the pity is that tender pity which men feel for the veteran who has laid by, sore wounded, sword and shield; and for whom pity is another word for love. It is now that the phrase—England's Shepherd, England's Darling—may most justly be on our lips. The prayer at the end of the book fitly closes a work he loved to do, and reveals so intimately the man's heart, that we feel he could never have published anything so personal had he not felt that his people loved him dearly and were at one with him.

I have said that we get close to Ælfred's inner life in the additions he makes, with great freedom, to this translation of the *De Consolatione*. It seems worth our while to isolate a few of these additions. They reveal him as man and king, but chiefly as one who had thought all his life long on the temper of mind and spirit which should rule over the doings of a king. In the passage already quoted concerning the organisation of the kingdom, he speaks directly to his subject. In these that follow, on wealth and power and wisdom, there is no direct reference to his kingship, but we feel that he is thinking while he writes of his high place and its temptations; and his nobleness and humility, his deep sense of duty, his apartness from the baser elements of the world, appear in every line.

Riches are better given than withheld. No man can have them without making his fellowmen poorer. A good name is better than wealth. It opens the hollow of the heart; it pierces through hearts that are closed. It is not lessened as it goes from heart to heart among men. No sword can slay it, no rope can bind it.

The goods of life are good through the goodness of the man who has them, and he is good through God. The goods of life are bad through the badness of the man who has them.

True friends are, of all the goods in this world, the most precious. It is God who unites friends. Indeed they are not of this world, but divine. Evil fortune cannot bring them nor take them away.

Wisdom hath four virtues — prudence, temperance, courage, and righteousness. If thou wouldst build Wisdom, set it not up on covetousness. No man builds his house on sandhills. As the drinking sand swallows the river, so covetousness swallows the frail bliss of this world, because it will always be thirsty.

He that will have eternal riches, let him build the house of his mind on the footstone of lowliness. Not on the highest hill where the raging wind of trouble blows or the rain of measureless anxiety.

Power is never a good unless he be good who has it. No one need care for power or strive for it. If you be wise and good, it will follow you, though you may not desire it. Thou shalt not obtain [*and here he thinks of all he has borne as king*] power free from sorrow from other peoples, nor yet from thine own people and kindred.

Never without fear, difficulties, and sorrows, has a king wealth and power. To be without them, and yet have them, were happy. But I know that cannot be.

But whatsoever trouble beset a king, he would care only to rule over a free people. [*In a discussion on Free Will, Reason says:*] "How would it look to you if there were any powerful king and he had no free men in his kingdom, but that all were slaves?"

Ælfred: "It would not be thought by me right or reasonable if enslaved men should only attend on him."

"Then," quoth Reason, "it would be more unnatural if God, in all His kingdom, had no free creature under His power."

Proud and unrighteous kings are adorned with gold and swords and thegns; but strip them of their trappings, and they are no more, even worse, than many of their thegns. Let them fall from power, and their past luxury makes them angry with their present, weak through sadness, useless for getting back what they have lost.

This sentence, shortened from the original, reads as if he were thinking of Athelney. Then, having disposed of wealth and power as making a man, he passes on to rank.

"Art thou," he says, "more fair for other men's fairness? A man will not be the better because he had a well-born father, if he himself is nought. The only thing which is good in noble descent is this—That it makes men ashamed of being worse than their elders, and strive to do better than they."

Two more phrases mark the man—

We underworth ourselves when we love that which is lower than ourselves.

For me, I dread no ill weirds. They can neither help nor harm a man. Ill luck is even happiness, though we do not think it is. One can trust it; what it promises is true.

What a pathetic note sounds through all these sentences! It is the note of one who is almost overpowered by difficulty, alone within, with few friends, sore troubled with disease—of one who works for justice and peace in his kingdom with inadequate helpers, but who at every point just conquers life; having his ideal aims and faithful always to them; and having, beyond the storms of the world, a sure faith in the greater King. We do not dwell in a history of literature on the religion of a man, but no account of Ælfred could be true which did not say that he rested on God for his support and inspiration, that his incessant work in this world was combined at every point with the life of his spirit in the diviner world. I quote one passage out of many to emphasise this, and in itself it is a piece of literature. It is the prayer at the end of the *Boethius*:—

> Lord God Almighty, shaper and ruler of all creatures, I pray thee for thy great mercy, and for the token of the holy rood, and for the maidenhood of St. Mary, and for the obedience of St. Michael, and for all the love of thy holy saints and their worthiness, that thou guide me better than I have done towards thee. And guide me to thy will to the need of my soul better than I can myself. And stedfast my mind towards thy will and to my soul's need. And strengthen me against the temptations of the devil, and put far from me foul lust and every unrighteousness. And shield me against my foes, seen and unseen. And teach me to do thy will, that I may inwardly love thee before all things with a clean mind and clean body. For thou art my maker and my redeemer, my help, my comfort, my trust, and my hope. Praise and glory be to thee now, ever and ever, world without end. Amen.

In the *De Consolatione*, Boethius interspersed his prose with verses, with *Metra*. The prefaces of our two English manuscripts tell us that the king, having translated the *Metra* in prose, put them afterwards into poetry, and the oldest of the manuscripts has this poetical version of the *Metra*. Some think we have here the king's work. If we take the short poetical prologue to be a true statement[1]—and indeed it might be the king's own writing—the English versification of the *Metra* is his own. If so he was only a poor versifier. But others say that these verses were done from Ælfred's prose by a writer of the age of the manuscript, that is, of the tenth century. The question has been argued at great length by a crowd of critics, and remains as yet undecided. The argument does not seem worth the trouble. The *Metra* in English verse are not good poetry. It is a pity, if Ælfred wrote them, to connect them with his name. If he did

---

[1] Here are the first verses of the prologue—
      Thus Ælfred us an old-spell told,
      Set forth his song-craft, used a maker's skill,
      King of West Saxons he! And mickle lust he had
      For this his folk to sing his song,
      And mirth for men and sayings manifold!
A fragment of a third MS. has been lately found by Prof. Napier.

not write them, it would be well if they could be forgotten. Yet the personal touches in them, if we could be sure of Ælfred's authorship, are interesting; moreover, though one does not care for the poetry, yet, were it Ælfred's, it would illustrate his intellectual activity that he should attempt verse as well as prose.

What else the king did before his death is not quite clear. A translation of the *Soliloquia* of St. Augustine has been imputed to him, and is very probably his. There is a preface, which, if this book belong to the end of Ælfred's life, is a pathetic farewell to all that he has done as a translator of good books for his people, and a call to his fellow-workers to continue his labours for the sake of their English brethren. This is put in the form of a parable;[1] and its personal feeling and imaginative form—the first so common, the second so rare in Ælfred's writing—make it worth quoting.

> Then I gathered me darts[2] and pillar-shafts and stead-shafts, and handles for each of the tools which I was able to work with, and "bay timbers" and "bolt timbers," and for each of the works which I knew how to work, the most beautiful wood, which, felling, I could bear away. Neither came I home with an overweight; it pleased me not to bring all the wood home, (even) if I could carry it all. On each tree I saw somewhat of that which I needed at home. Therefore I advise every one who may be strong enough and have many a wain, that he go to the same wood where I cut these pillar-shafts, and there fetch himself more, and load his wains with branches, so that he may make many a trim wall and many a beautiful house, and build a fair town of them, and there may dwell joyfully and peacefully both winter and summer as I (till) now have not yet done. But he who taught me, to whom the wood was pleasant, he can make me dwell more peacefully, both in this passing dwelling on this wayfaring, while I am in this world; and also in the

---

[1] The suggestion of the parable is Wülker's. The houses Ælfred mentions as built by him are the books he has translated, fetching his materials from the wood (of Literature). But much more material remains behind. Let others, his friends, go and fetch it in, and build with it, as he has done. Yet here, in St. Augustine and others, there is the material for another house, eternal in the Heavens.

[2] "Darts," "javelins," must mean here poles sharpened at one end like spears, for driving into the ground.

eternal home which he hath bid us hope for through St. Augustine, St. Gregory, and St. Jerome, and many of the holy fathers; even so I believe also that he will make (for the worthiness of them all) both this wayfaring better than it was ere this time; and especially enlighten the eyes of my mind, to this end, that I may find the way to the everlasting home, and everlasting honour and everlasting rest which is promised to us through the holy fathers. . . . May God grant that I have power for both—to be useful here, and surely to go thither.

The translation is made up from Augustine's Latin into two English books; and a letter of Augustine's *De Videndo Deo* is added. The letter is thrown into a dialogue, and this is done in order to harmonise it with the *Soliloquia* which are couched in the form of a dialogue between Augustine and his Reason. The first book is called by the editor a collection of flowers. "Here end the blossoms of this book"; and this flower-title is given also to the second book. The third book (that derived from Augustine's *Letter*) closes with the words: "Here end the sayings of King Ælfred," etc. The date is probably 900.

But his eager spirit, even when tamed by the approach of death, would have desired to do something new. And William of Malmesbury tells us that he translated part of the *Psalms of David*. "Psalterium transferre aggressus, vix prima parte explicata vivendi finem fecit." It is supposed that we have in the first fifty Psalms in prose of a Psalter called the *Paris Psalter*, this last piece of Ælfred's literary labour;[1] and it is a work we may well imagine his spiritual intellect would do with comfort before he died. He did not live to finish it. In 901, "the unshakeable pillar of the West Saxons, a man full of justice, bold in arms, learned in speech, and above all, filled with the knowledge which flows from God," passed away and was buried at Winchester.

[1] This is a suggestion, merely a suggestion, of Wülker's. Wichmann has endeavoured to prove Ælfred's authorship of these fifty Psalms. But Dr. Douglas Bruce of Pennsylvania, in an elaborate dissertation on the Anglo-Saxon version of the Psalms, commonly called the *Paris Psalter*, has, I think with good reason, shown that Ælfred's authorship of these Psalms is open to the gravest doubt. But this doubt does not deny that Ælfred did translate some of the Psalms—only that the *Paris Psalter* Psalms are his work.

Only two books not done by himself appeared, as far as we know, in his reign. The first was the *Dialogues of Gregory*, translated at Ælfred's instance by Werfrith of Worcester, and with a preface written by the king. Werfrith is not mentioned in the preface, but both Asser and William of Malmesbury speak of him as the translator. These *Dialogues* are divided into four books, and contain the conversation of Gregory with his deacon Peter. Their subject is the lives and miracles of the Italian saints, and in the fourth book the life of the soul after death. The doctrine of Purgatory, as held in the Middle Ages, may be said to have been settled in this fourth book. Ælfred's preface, given in full by Earle in his *Anglo-Saxon Literature*, brings us, as usual, close to his character.

I, Ælfred, have clearly known that it is specially asked of those to whom God has given high rank on this earth, that they should bend their minds to the divine law, in the midst of earthly carefulness; therefore I sought of trusty friends that they would translate the following dialogues, that I, being strengthened through their warning and love, may at whiles think on heavenly things amid the troubles of this world.

The other is the *Book of Martyrs*. This is allowed, after Cockayne's arguments, to date from Ælfred's time, and was probably compiled at his desire. It begins with the 31st of December, with St. Columba; and ends with the 21st of December, with St. Thomas. Of course, the fewness of these remains does not assert that no other books were made in English. But the silence is expressive. And Ælfred's loneliness and sadness, as he drew to the close of life, makes all the more impression on us, when we think that his effort to make a literary class was a failure, and that he himself was the only important English writer in his kingdom. Asser's *Life* of the King[1] was written in Latin. Plegmund and John the Old Saxon seem to have been quite

[1] That Asser wrote this book has been questioned again and again. But we have little reason to doubt that the bulk of the book is by the man whose name it bears. Additions have probably been made to it, legends inserted, events coloured and heightened to glorify the King, but on the whole its record is historical, and contemporary with Ælfred.

silent. The writer of the king's wars with the Danes in the *English Chronicle* was probably Ælfred himself. Werfrith appears to have been forced into translating the *Dialogues of Gregory*, and to have done no more. The king really stands by himself; and yet he had far heavier work to do than any of his friends. No figure is lonelier and nobler in the long gallery of the literary men of England.

The character of Ælfred as warrior, ruler, and statesman has been sufficiently displayed by historians old and new, but of that part of his character which appears in his literary work we may here say a few words before we bid him farewell. The more intimate personality of the king, that tender, naïf, simple, humble, self-forgetful nature, which played like a child with the toys of knowledge, with the Greek and the Roman tales; which would have been weak through sensitiveness were it not for the resolute will to attain the full height of his royal duties, would have remained unknown to us, had he not been a writer as well as a king. What that inner personality was is sufficiently clear from the extracts I have given, and those who read them will, each in his own way, feel the man.

There are, however, points belonging to the intellectual character of Ælfred which have a remarkable interest. He was the only man in his kingdom who was filled with so great a curiosity for knowledge, and whose range of interests was so wide, that his spirit might justly be compared with that of the men of the Renaissance. In this he stood far above mere scholars like Asser or Werfrith, who were probably more than content with what they knew. Ælfred was never satisfied. This was the peculiar grace in him, that he would not only live well as king, but learn the life beyond a king's, know as well as act, belong to the world where pursuit and its object had no end. No limit lay to learning.

It may be that the first seeds of this unquenchable curiosity were sown in Rome, where he lived among the records and ruins of the past, where every stone still awakens the desire to know. It is more than probable that at the Frankish court he heard

the story of the love of learning which was so strong in Charles
the Great, and that, even as a boy, he urged himself to imitate
the Emperor. It is certainly true that when he came to the
throne, he acted precisely as Charles had acted. He sent for
foreigners to help him in educating his people, as Charles had
sent for Alcuin and others. He tried, as Charles had done, to
get a nest of learned men in his court. He made, like Charles,
schools for his nobles, and forced them, like Charles, to learn.
He set up schools and monasteries, without the success of Charles.
Asser and Werfrith and other men had the same friendly relation
with him that Einhard and Alcuin, Peter of Pisa, and Paul the
Lombard had with Charles. And he collected the old songs of
his English people, as Charles had reduced to writing and learnt
by heart the old Teutonic sagas—"those most ancient songs of
the barbarians, in which the actions of the kings of old and their
wars were chanted." Indeed, in this collecting of his country's
songs, Ælfred began to feed his curiosity; and his main curiosity
was to find out everything he could about his own land. Nothing
lay deeper in his heart than love of England, even though he ruled
over so small a part of it. English songs, as we have seen,
engaged his boyhood; English poetry his manhood. He sought
from Bæda's history to know the foundations of English policy
and English religion. He sought from sailors who had seen the
Baltic to know what manner of land it was where the English
lived before they came to his own England. He mastered the
existing English laws; he set on foot a national history; he
recorded what he himself had done for England in war and peace.
He determined to learn Latin, because knowledge was hidden in
that tongue; and when he had gained it, he made all he read into
English that his own people might know all that he knew. It was
a misery to him that England was not as athirst for knowledge as
himself. The words in which he expresses his pity for England's
loss of learning in the past, and his hope for all she might gain
in the future, are such as a Roman scholar of the early Renaissance
might have used concerning his own country.

But his curiosity was not satisfied with the knowledge of England. He desired to know the world beyond; not only what he could learn from the men he fetched from the Continent, not only the courts and nations with which he was politically connected—this might be the desire of any king—but also the past history of great peoples, their manners, their ways in war and peace, the stories of their poets, the theories of their philosophers, the course of religious life among them, the geography of ancient lands, and the discoveries of new lands. He sent messengers even to the East. It is strange, in the midst of an England dead to pleasure of this kind, to suddenly meet with this eager personage. It is not strange to find, when he lives in this sphere, that he then forgot his kingship and only remembered the new worlds of learning which he had to conquer. When he is talking to Asser or Ohthere, when he is writing to Werfrith or to his people about literature, kinghood slips off him. When he is speaking of Greece or Rome or the Germans, he writes without a trace of insularity. Hence in all his work, even in his policy to the Danes, there is an extraordinary absence in Ælfred of any national feeling as against other nations. His patriotism, his sense of kingship, were strong, but they were modified by a clear recognition that all men who loved knowledge were of the same country and of the same rank—one in the commonalty of literature. This also is characteristic of a man of the Renaissance. Along with this eagerness to learn there was the same eagerness to teach which marked the men of the New Learning. He risked his popularity as a king by his endeavour to make his people study. He seems to think that his nobles, clergy, and people must feel on this matter as intensely as himself. To educate became a part even of his religion. To give money for a school was to give to God.

But that which, even more than a passion for knowledge and for teaching, brings him into line with the scholars and artists of the New Learning is his individuality. The personal element stands forth clear in all his literary work. It is this which takes even translations out of the region of the commonplace, and which lifts his prefaces into literature. In war, and as a king, he had genius; but in literature he is either a plodder or a child. He never rises into any original power, not even in the *Chronicle*, or in the additions to the *De Consolatione Philosophiae*. But the aspiring personality of the man animates and pervades the poverty of the work with a humanity which pleases us more even than good writing. He has all the gracious naïveté of a child. He plays with the Greek stories like those of Orpheus and of Ulysses and Circe, with the same kind of natural simplicity with which Turner treated them in painting; and this naturalness has so much charm that we should regret to lose it in finish of style and in art of words. In all that is personal he belongs to literature. He creates his character in his subjects, and the impression he made upon the future writing of England is owing to that, and not to his literary ability. It was a great thing to do.

What, then, is his place? He has no originality as a worker in literature, no creative power. He was a good receiver and a good reproducer of knowledge. Even where he seems to be original, he may not be so. We do not know how much of the additions to the Boethius may be derived from Asser's conversation. But the style is his own; its simplicity is as effective in prayer and philosophy as it is in the *Chronicle*, and very pleasant coming from a great king. It is also pervaded by a strong desire for clearness and for use, and by a love of his people. It succeeds in being clear and useful, and it pleases by the force of these elements; but most of all, perhaps, by the deep feeling for his people which animates and warms it. We might also say that his long intercourse with public affairs and with the management of wars adds a weight to the style, of which, as we read, we are vaguely conscious. But even when all this has been said, the king, in literature, is but a learner, not, in any sense of the word, a master.

CHAPTER XV

THE OLD ENGLISH POETRY IN AND AFTER ÆLFRED'S TIME

I HAVE said that the remains of the English poetry of Northumbria were most probably collected by Ælfred; and were translated into the Wessex dialect, partly in the later years of his peace, and partly in the first twenty years of the tenth century. Among the poems translated in his reign we may surely count those of Cædmon, one fragment of which Ælfred himself put into English in his translation of the *Ecclesiastical History*. *Genesis A* also, whether attributed then to Cædmon or not, appeared now in West-Saxon. The gap in its manuscript caused the insertion of *Genesis B;* and this set of poems may have kindled some poet of this time into the composition of the cantatas which once bore the title of *Christ and Satan*, and which are contained in the second half of the manuscript of the "Junian Cædmon." These new poems with *Genesis B* are now believed to be the property of Wessex, and to have been written at the end of the ninth or the beginning of the tenth century.

The *Later Genesis* (*Genesis B*) belongs in its original form to the last years of the ninth century—and what follows is conjectured to be its history. There was an Old Saxon poem written on the book of Genesis (a few fragments of which have lately been discovered), either by the author of the *Heliand* himself, or more probably by some imitator of the *Heliand*.[1] Some English scholar (an Old

---

[1] The *Heliand* is an almost heroic poem of the ninth century on the life of the Healer, the Saviour; and *Genesis B* closely resembles it in language

Saxon by birth and perhaps, as Ten Brink suggests, John of Athelney) translated this poem, word for word, during Ælfred's life, into West Saxon. In the tenth century a copyist of the *Elder Genesis* (*Genesis A*), finding a great gap in this poem after the line 234, inserted, in order to fill up the space and out of this West Saxon translation of an Old Saxon poem, the lines 235 to 851; and we call them the *Later Genesis*. This theory is held to account for the difficulties of language, of metre, of manner, of sentiment and of intellect which make this insertion so different from the rest of the *Genesis* in the Junian manuscript. It is true, it still remains only a theory, but philological investigation, and the discovery of new evidence—such as the identity of the fragments of an Old Saxon poem, line for line, with the corresponding lines in the *Later Genesis*—tend year by year to confirm the theory.

The insertion opens with a repetition of the subject of the beginning of *Genesis A*. The fall of the rebel angels is told over again. God returns to heaven after the creation of man, and Lucifer's pride is hurt. His glory is described, "so mighty in intelligence, so beauteous in body, like to the brilliant stars," that he seemed to himself to be equal with God. And he breaks forth into a fierce soliloquy, which follows here, literally translated, and showing the long epic line which this writer used:—

Why then should I toil, quoth he. Not a shred of need there is
Now for *me* to have a master! With these hands of mine I may
Work as many wonders! Mickle force to wield have I
For the setting up of a goodlier stool than He,
And a higher in the Heaven! For His favour why should I be of Him the slave,
To Him bow in such a bondage? I can God become, like Him!
With me stand strong-hearted comrades, who will not in struggle fail me,
Heroes hard in spirit! They have for their Lord chosen me and hailed me;

---

and in diction, while both writers have used a Latin poem by Avitus, Bishop of Vienne.

Far-famed fighters they ! Any one can plan a rede with such followers as
  these,
With such folk companions frame it ! They are ready friends of mine,
True in all their thoughts to me ! . . .
                    . . . So it is not right, methinks,
That for any favour I should need to fawn on God,
Or for any good. I'll no longer be His vassal.

This is the bold Teutonic earl, whose pride in his manliness, whose insolence of individuality bids him stand alone, even against the gods. In his claim to build a kingdom for himself, to be God if he please; in his sense of the close comradeship between his brothers in arms and himself, and in his praise of good rede, the speech belongs to a heathen Viking, and there are many just as bold in the Norse sagas. Then hell is drawn with northern imagination—the abyss of pain, swart, deep-valleyed, swept at dawning by the north-east wind and frost, then by leaping blaze and bitter smoke through darkness and vapour dun; where Satan lies on his bed of death, hafted down with heat-smitten fetters over neck and breast, but unconquered still; his thought as hot about his heart as the hell that clasps him. "O, how most unlike," he cries, "is this narrow stead to that other home which we knew of old in the high realm of heaven!"[1]

[1] This also, like some passages in *Genesis A*, has a far-off likeness to Milton—
    O how unlike the place from which they fell.

So also Satan's address to his thegns is similar to the argument of Beelzebub in *Paradise Lost*, Book II. It is a question whether Milton ever saw the *Genesis*. He could not have read it, but Junius was his friend, and it is not improbable that he translated part of the poem to Milton. Milton would naturally like to hear what Cædmon was supposed to have said on *Paradise Lost;* and if so, he would retain some of the vivid expressions, and use them. But a great deal too much has been made of the resemblances. They are slight, and Milton, who read widely on his subject, could have found similar phrases in the multitudinous representations of the Fall of the Angels and of Man which had been made before he claimed the subject. Many of these he certainly used.

> This is my greatest sorrow—that a man,[1]
> Adam, made out of clay, should hold my seat,
> My mighty stool, and be in bliss, while we
> This bale must bear, this bitter harm in hell.
> Ai, Ai! but had my hands their rightful craft,
> Could I break out of this for one short hour,
> One winter hour, then with this host would I—
> But, braced around me, lie the iron bands,
> A rope of chains engirths me, realmless me!
> And o'er and under me is mickle fire,
> Immitigable flame. More hateful land,
> Ne'er known till now. . . . Full well God knew my heart,
> And forged these gratings of the hardened steel,
> To haft my throat; else, had my arms their force,
> An evil work should be 'twixt man and me!
> But God has swept us into swarthy mists,
> Into this fierce and fathomless abyss!
> O shall we not have vengeance, and pay back
> Our debt to Him who robbed us of the light?

So, since he cannot free himself, he appeals to his thegns to slake his vengeance by turning man to evil. Bring him also down to this grim abyss. "If I ever gave you the treasures of a king in days gone by, repay me now; fly, one of you, with your feathered garment, to the place where Adam and Eve, wrapt in their weal, are on the earth; make them break God's bidding; make them loathed by Him; overcraft them; then—in these chains softly at last I shall rest myself. Whosoever does this shall sit by me on my high seat." At this cry for the comfort of vengeance, one of his thegns springs to his feet:—

> Then 'gan to gird himself God's grim-set foe,
> Artful, and eagerly equipped himself.
> Above, he set a hollow helm, and hard
> He spanned it down with spangs. Much speech he knew,
> But all of words awry! And then he wheeled

---

[1] I have put the rest of the quotations in this chapter into blank verse for the sake of variety. They do not pretend to a literal rendering of the original, such as I have already given in my *History of Early English Literature*, but they are not far from it.

> His flight, uplifted, through the doors of hell;
> Beating the (murky) air. Strong was his heart,
> And foully bent his mind, as swinging back
> On either side the flame, he found at last
> Adam, in wisdom wrought, upon the earth,
> And with him Eve, the winsomest of wives!

"And a twain of trees stood beside them; one was gentle and lovely, but the other swart above and dusky below, the tree of death that bore the bitter fruit."

The temptation follows: the dialogue has invention and is subtly borne, and the presentation of the subject imaginative—too subtly imaginative for the ancient Cædmon to have written. "I have sat with God of late," speaks the Worm, "and He bade me tell thee to eat this fruit, to learn knowledge. Taste and thy mind shall be mightier, thy heart expanded, and thy form fairer." "God told me," Adam replies, "that to eat this fruit should bring me hell. I know not if thou be a liar, or a messenger from heaven; I know naught of thy ways, but I do know what He bade me. Take thee hence! God can give me all good things, even though He send no vassal here." So the fiend left Adam, and went to Eve: "God will be wrath, Eve, with thee, when He hears Adam's message; but listen to me and His wrath will be turned away. And thine eyes shall be so clear, sheenest of women, that thou shalt see the whole world and God Himself; and more, thou shalt turn Adam round thy will, if thou wouldest that." At which she took the fruit, and all the sky and earth were lovelier to her, for the great Scather moved about her mind. "See, Eve the good, how thy beauty and breast are enlarged. Light itself is gladly breaking on thee. I brought it from heaven; look, thy hand may touch it? Tell Adam what a sight thou hast seen; what powers thou hast now." Then to Adam went the winsomest of women, and of the unblest fruit part she bore in her hand and part was hid in her heart. "Adam, she cried, "this apple is sweet, and comes from God. I can see Him now, throned in the south-east, sitting by Himself, wrapt in His own weal, He who wrought the world; and, wheeling round Him, His angels in their feathered vesture, of all war-hosts the fairest; and all the music-mirth of the whole heavens I hear. Look, I have the apple here; gladly I give it, take it, my lord, I know it is from God."

It is characteristic of English feeling, though curiously unlike Milton whose Adam yields at once to Eve, that Eve, whose motives are all good, takes the whole day in this poem to persuade Adam. At last he took from the woman "Hell and Hither-going, heroes' overthrow, murder of men, the Dream of Death, though it was only named a fruit"; and Satan's thegn bursts into triumphant mockery. Revenge is the finest play a Teutonic fiend can have who clings fast as a war-comrade to his captive lord. He "has won his high seat"—that is a personal pleasure; but it is nothing to his pleasure in thinking that now his lord will be blithe and comforted, forgetting his pain in the thought that he has paid out God and man for all his direful woes. "My heart is enlarged," he cries, "I have never bowed the knee to God"; and refusing to stay in Paradise, he takes his flight straight to the flaming fire to tell his lord the good tidings. But before he leaves the garden, his rapture in vengeance makes him speak as if he were face to face with Satan, though Satan is far away in the deepest cone of hell.

> See, Lord! thy favour now is won, thy will
> Accomplished! Man is now befooled. No more
> Shall heaven, but the swart descent to hell,
> Be now their weird! O Thou, who liest in sorrows,
> Rejoice, thou needst no mourning now. Be blithe,
> Laugh in thy heart. All is paid back again!
> For me, my heart is healed, my thought enlarged,
> Our harms are well avenged! In swarthy Hell
> Satan is clasped, my captive Lord, and there
> In flame I seek him.

Adam and Eve are left conscious of their fall. In Milton lust follows, and then mutual horror and mutual blame, and then repentance. Here Eve loses the vision of clear heaven, and, in dread contrast, Adam sees black hell; then, with northern quickness of conscience, immediately repents. There is no recrimination between them, as in Milton. All is tenderness. Adam makes but one reproach, not in bitterness, but sadness, and Eve's answer is loving and quiet: "Thou mayst reproach me, Adam, my beloved, yet it may not worse repent thee in thy mind than it rueth me in heart." And Adam replies by a broken and impassioned outburst of desire at all risks to know God's will and bear His punishment: "Were the All-Wielder to bid me wade in the vast sea—not so fearfully deep were the flood of ocean that my mind should ever waver—into the abyss I would plunge, if only I might work the will of God. But naked like this we may not stay. Let us seek the covert of the holt. So they went mourning into the greenwood," and there they fell to prayer. Here ends, at line 851, the *Later Genesis*, and the earlier poem, after this insertion, takes up the story.[1]

The second part of the poems which pass under the name of Cædmon, and which are in a handwriting different from and later than the first part, were given the name of *Christ and Satan*. They are now divided into three poems or fragments of poems—the first called the *Fallen Angels*, the second the *Harrowing of Hell*, and the third the *Temptation*. I have elsewhere said that they were probably composed in the eighth century, and by a follower of Cynewulf in Northumbria, and on the whole, till further evidence, I cling to that opinion; but as the majority of critics, and among them such men as Ten Brink and Wülker, allot them to the tenth century, and, I suppose, to Wessex, I place them here, along with the *Later Genesis*, and as written some time after the insertion of that poem into *Genesis A*. They are simple, direct, and passionate; dialogue enlivens them; their human interest is thus made greater, nor are the characters ill sustained. This is especially true of Satan, who differs at many points—in his variety, in the form of his regret for his loss and for that of his followers, in his sudden aspiration after heaven, and

[1] See p. 138.

in this writer's half-pity for him—from the Satan of the *Later Genesis*. The poetry has a rugged power of description, and its outbursts of praise closely resemble the passionate hymns of Cynewulf.

The three divisions of the *Fallen Angels* end each with a psalm of praise, as if they were three lays sung on three different evenings on the same subject. The poem begins with a sketch of the fall of Satan into hell, and of the fiery ruin in which he lives. He wanders in a hall, brooded over by abysmal cloud, cold and dark, where serpents and black-faced demons run to and fro. Outside the hall, sunk deep in the core of space, a weltering sea of fire mingled with venom breaks on high cliffs, at whose base on the fiery marge the fiends meet and mourn. Flame-breathing dragons are at its gates; but twelve miles beyond them, the gnashing of the demons' teeth is heard in the vast of space. When Satan speaks, fire and poison flicker from his lips, and he wails for the home he has lost. His companions, quite unlike Satan's thegns in the *Later Genesis* who love their lord, scorn and reproach him here. He is a liar, a deceiver, a wretched robber. Again and again he cries his sorrow, and then breaks out into this strange agony of repentance:—

> O Helm of banded hosts! O glorious Lord!
> O Might of the Great Maker! O Mid-Earth!
> O dazzling daylight! O Delight of God!
> O angel hosts, and O, thou upper Heaven!
> O me! bereft of everlasting joy!
> Never again to reach my hands to Heaven,
> Nor with these eyes of mine look up again,
> Nor ever hear once more with happy ears
> Clash clear the clanging clarions of God!

The second song of the poem and the third repeat the motives of the first, and end as the first ends, with psalms that celebrate the bliss of heaven.

The *Harrowing of Hell* begins at line 366: "Anguish came on hell and thundercrash at dawn of day, before the Judge when he shattered the gates of hell. 'Terrible is this,' cry the fiends, wailing far and wide through the windy hall, 'since this storm has come on us, the Hero with his following, the Lord of Angels. Before Him shines a lovelier light, never seen since we were on high among the heavenly host. So our pains will be the keener.'" Then the good spirits in prison gather round Christ, and Eve tells their story, and that three nights ago Judas came and told them the King was coming; and how the Old Testament saints "lifted themselves, leaning on their hands, midst all their pain delighted," to hear the happy tidings. "Take us forth, O my beloved Lord," and Christ, driving the devils deeper into hell, bore the redeemed on high. "That was fair indeed when they came to their fatherland, and with them the Eternal into His glorious burg." Christ sits with them at the feast, and speaks to them like an English king to the assembly of his Wise-men. And the poem turns to tell of the Resurrection and Ascension, of Pentecost and the Last Judgment, and each fragment ends with a hymn of praise.

At line 665 another fragment of a separate poem begins, a part of the story of the *Temptation*. It is only remarkable for the mocking speech of Christ, such as an English victor might make to his foe. "Go, accursed, to the den of punishment; take no jot of hope to the burghers of hell; promise them the deepest sorrows. Go, and know how far and wide away is dreary hell! Measure with thine hands and grip against its bottom. Go, till thou knowest all the round of it, from above to the abyss; mete out how broad is the black mist of it. Then wilt thou understand that thou fightest against God."

"So he fell to dreadful pains"—and the stages of his fall are vividly marked out—for first, "he measured in thought the torment and the woe; and then as he descended the lurid flame smote upwards against him; and then he saw the captives on the floor of hell; and then their howl, when they saw him, reached his ears; and then he on the bottom stood. And it seemed to him then that to hell-door from the mount where he had been was 100,000 miles by measure." This is as accurate and close as

Dante. And he looked round on the ghastly place, and there rose a shriek from all the lost, and they cried to their Lord :—

> There! be ever in thine evil, erst thou would'st not good.

With this fine passage close the last poems which have borne the name of Cædmon. Though he was not their writer, though perhaps more than two hundred years separate them from him, yet they are fitly gathered under the name of the man who first sang of God and man in England, who began the illustrious roll of the religious poets of England, whose subject Milton took, and who made the path by which the poetry of heathenism carried its matter and manner into Christian song.

These are the last religious poems before the Conquest which show any trace of imagination or of original power. The rest of which we know seem to be the dry and lifeless production of cloistered persons who, not being able to write in prose, chose to write in poor and broken rhythm. Religious poetry became mere alliterative versing, and was finally altogether replaced by prose. Then prose—and this is common when poetry decays—tended, in order to satisfy man's desire for musical movement, to become rhythmical. Ælfric, in the tenth and eleventh centuries, wrote much of his prose in a jingle of alliteration. The versing, then, of the eleventh century was often bad prose. About 1010, a homily attributed to Wulfstan contains 200 lines out of a poem of the tenth century, which are deliberately used as prose. Even in the tenth century the religious poems were few. There are a small crowd of expanded versions of the Creeds, the Lord's Prayer, and the Canticles in the Roman service. Of longer poems, there is a Saints' Kalendar entitled the *Menologium*, which we may date after the middle of the tenth century. It is quite plain that when this poem was written the earlier English poets were known and studied, for many passages are taken from them by this versifier. But this we may say for him, that the Northumbrian love of nature had filtered down into his soul. He speaks with a true feeling for May and Summer, and of the charm of their happy world. The *Last Judgment*, which had vogue enough to reach Northumbria, for this is the poem that Wulfstan quotes, belongs also to the middle of the tenth century, and is a Wessex translation of a Latin poem, perhaps by Alcuin. To the same date is allotted a metrical translation of fifty psalms which is found scattered through a Benedictine Service-Book. Then there is a poem advising a gray-haired warrior to a Christian life, which is dated before the year 1000, since it warns the old man that the end of the world is near; and another poem urging its readers to prayer, in which Latin and English, as in the *Phœnix*, are mingled in the same lines. We must also remember, if we do not give the metrical translation of the *Metra* of Boethius to Ælfred, that it was written somewhere at the beginning of the tenth century. These exhaust the poetic efforts of religion, and mark the swift degeneration of imagination. They were followed by the death of this kind of poetry. During the Danish Conquest and the reigns of the last two English kings, religious song of any literary value in our tongue may be said to be silent.

CHAPTER XVI

SECULAR POETRY AFTER ÆLFRED TO THE CONQUEST

SECULAR poetry among the English after the time of Ælfred was chiefly in the form of ballads or of war-songs. The ballads seem to have been made on any striking story in the lives of the kings and of the chief men of the nation, and there were probably ballads made in every village on the traditions of their families. We seem to understand from the biographies of Dunstan that there were songs belonging to Glastonbury and Athelney and to his own family history, which he was accustomed to sing. Moreover, it was the custom to put into the *Chronicle* accounts of the coronations and deaths of kings, in verse. These, which are only annals versified, suggest the belief that there were songs or ballads on these events written at a much greater length, and this is a general opinion. It has been conjectured also that we find in the *Chronicle* brief fragments of songs embedded in its prose. Names have even been given to these supposed songs—"the *Sack of Canterbury*, 1011 ; the *Wooing of Margaret*, 1067 ; the *Baleful Bride-Ale*, 1076 ; and the *High-handed Conqueror*, 1086." The actual verses in the *Chronicle* are the *Battle of Brunanburh*, 937 ; the *Overcoming of the Five Towns*,[1] 942 ; the *Coronation of Eadgar at Bath*, 973 ; *Eadgar's Death and his Good Times*, 975 ; the *Slaying at Corfe*, 979 ; *Ælfred the Ætheling's Slaughter*, 1036 ; the *Son of Ironside*, 1057 ; and the *Dirge of King Eadward the Confessor*, 1065.

[1] These were the Danish boroughs in Mercia—Leicester, Lincoln, Nottingham, Stamford, and Derby.

All these, with the exception of the *Battle of Brunanburh*, which stands alone, cannot be called songs. One of them, however, has some importance—that on the death and good deeds of Eadgar. The way in which it is expressed recalls the heroic poetry, and proves that it had not been neglected or forgotten.

All these abrupt verses may represent the subjects on which the ballad poetry of England exercised itself. We find further proof of this continuance of song in the stories told of this period by the Norman Chroniclers, by William of Malmesbury, and Henry of Huntingdon. It is plain that they put into their Latin prose English songs concerning early English history which were still sung in the country at the date at which they wrote; and we shall see of what kind they were. But before we speak of them and of the two long war-poems we possess, there is one secular poem to be mentioned. This is the so-called *Rhyme Poem* in the *Exeter Book*. It belongs to the tenth century, and probably to the years between 940 and 950. The reason for that date is this. The poem is the only one in the English tongue which is written in the form called in Scandinavian *Runhenda*. It adds to the usual alliteration the rhyming of the last word of the first half of the verse with the last word of the second half. This is the form used by Egill Skallagrimsson, the Icelandic skald and warrior, in the poem *Höfuð-lausn*, by which he saved his life in Northumbria from Erik Blood-Axe in the year 938. Egill was twice in England, and was a favourite for a time at the court of Æthelstan. It is supposed then that Egill made known to the writer of the *Rhyme Song* this form of poetry, and the poverty of the poem and the clumsiness with which the form is used suggest a first and solitary experiment. Its subject, one common to English poetry—is the contrast between a rich and happy past and a sorrowful present, and may be, as Ettmüller conjectured, the complaint of a soul in purgatory, or even in hell, as he thinks of all that he enjoyed on earth. If so, the poem would belong to the religious poems, but I prefer to think of it as secular

Its suggested resemblance to the epilogue of the *Elene* has no weight.

We turn now to the ballads and war-poems from the *Song of Brunanburh* to the *Song of Maldon*. In the years between Ælfred's death and the accession of Æthelred the Unwise, from 901 to 979, England grew into a great and united kingdom under famous kings. Eadward the Elder was the first of these, and with the help of his sister Æthelflæd, the Lady of Mercia, became overlord of the whole of Britain and king of a great part of it. His glory (he was called the Unconquered) spread over the continent. His daughters were married to the Emperor Otto, to Charles the Simple, King of the East Franks, to the King of Arles, and to the Count of Paris. A united England, and an England in full relation with the great courts abroad, ought, with Ælfred's work behind it, to have had more literature than we find in it. And Eadward, though unable to push literature himself, may have been interested in it. He had learned with care, when young, "English books, and chiefly English songs." No doubt then his victories were sung in battle-ballads, but none of these have come down to us.

Æthelstan the Steadfast succeeded him in 925. He was the son of a lovely peasant girl, whom Eadward had met at his old nurse's home, and, like King Cophetua, wooed and married; and a ballad was made out of this romantic thing. His grandfather, Ælfred, loved the handsome boy to whom his mother's beauty had descended; and it is told in a story, which may have been derived from a song, that Ælfred gave him a purple cloak, over which Æthelstan's long hair fell like a river of gold; and girt him as a soldier, when he was only six years old, with a noble sword in a golden sheath, hung from a belt studded with gems; and prayed him to grow up into a good and glorious king. And the prayer was answered. England, under Æthelstan's chieftainship, vindicated her unity against the Danes, the Welsh, and the Scots at Brunanburh, and two war-ballads tell the story of the fierce battle. The first is preserved in Latin prose by William of Malmesbury. It tells how Anlaf, one of the Danish kings, went in the disguise of a gleeman to spy out the camp of Æthelstan on the night before the battle. The firelight flashed on his face as he sang to his harp, and a soldier who had fought under him in other days seemed to know him, and watched him; and when he saw that Anlaf buried the money his foes had given him, made sure he was the king. But he would not tell Æthelstan till Anlaf had gone. "Why didst thou let him go free?" said Æthelstan. "Had I betrayed," answered the soldier, "him whose man I once was, wouldst thou, whose man I am now, have trusted me?" And the king praised the answer and the man. The next day the battle was fought, and we possess in the *Chronicle* the song which recorded its triumph. It does not seem to have been written by an onlooker. It is without any of those personal touches which we find in the Battle of Maldon. We miss in it the naturalness, invention, and simplicity of the ballad of battle, as it would spring out of the heart of the people. It is a composition, and the verse and style are both unimpeachable. Yet it is worthy of the hero-poetry of England; full of patriot exultation and heathen wrath. It recalls in its abrupt and clashing lines the "Battle of Agincourt," the "Battle of the Baltic," and the "Charge of the Light Brigade." Tennyson's translation of it is so fine an example of the way genius transfers itself with creative energy into another atmosphere than that of its own age that I am grateful for the permission to insert it here.

BATTLE OF BRUNANBURH

Constantinus, King of the Scots, after having sworn allegiance to Athelstan, allied himself with the Danes of Ireland under Anlaf, and invading England, was defeated by Athelstan and his brother Edmund with great slaughter at Brunanburh in the year 937.

I.

[1] ATHELSTAN King,
Lord among Earls,

---

[1] I have more or less availed myself of my son's prose translation of this poem in the *Contemporary Review* (November 1876).

Bracelet-bestower and
Baron of Barons,
He with his brother,
Edmund Atheling,
Gaining a lifelong
Glory in battle,
Slew with the sword-edge
There by Brunanburh,
Brake the shield-wall,
Hew'd the lindenwood,[1]
Hack'd the battleshield,
Sons of Edward with hammer'd brands.

II.

Theirs was a greatness
Got from their Grandsires—
Theirs that so often in
Strife with their enemies
Struck for their hoards and their hearths and their homes.

III.

Bow'd the spoiler,
Bent the Scotsman,
Fell the ship-crews
Doom'd to the death.
All the field with blood of the fighters
Flow'd, from when first the great
Sun-star of morningtide,
Lamp of the Lord God
Lord everlasting,
Glode over earth till the glorious creature
Sank to his setting.

IV.

There lay many a man
Marr'd by the javelin,
Men of the Northland
Shot over shield.
There was the Scotsman
Weary of war.

---

[1] Shields of lindenwood.

V.

 We the West-Saxons,
 Long as the daylight
 Lasted, in companies
Troubled the track of the host that we hated,
Grimly with swords that were sharp from the grindstone,
Fiercely we hack'd at the flyers before us.

VI.

 Mighty the Mercian,
 Hard was his hand-play,
 Sparing not any of
 Those that with Anlaf,
 Warriors over the
 Weltering waters
 Borne in the bark's-bosom,
 Drew to this island :
 Doom'd to the death.

VII.

Five young kings put asleep by the sword-stroke,
Seven strong Earls of the army of Anlaf
Fell on the war-field, numberless numbers,
Shipmen and Scotsmen.

VIII.

 Then the Norse leader,
 Dire was his need of it,
 Few were his following,
 Fled to his warship :
Fleeted his vessel to sea with the king in it,
Saving his life on the fallow flood.

IX.

 Also the crafty one,
 Constantinus,
 Crept to his North again,
 Hoar-headed hero !

X.

Slender warrant had
He to be proud of
The welcome of war-knives—
He that was reft of his
Folk and his friends that had
Fallen in conflict,
Leaving his son too
Lost in the carnage,
Mangled to morsels,
A youngster in war!

XI.

Slender reason had
He to be glad of
The clash of the war-glaive—
Traitor and trickster
And spurner of treaties—
He nor had Anlaf
With armies so broken
A reason for bragging
That they had the better
In perils of battle
On places of slaughter—
The struggle of standards,
The rush of the javelins,
The crash of the charges,[1]
The wielding of weapons—
The play that they play'd with
The children of Edward.

XII.

Then with their nail'd prows
Parted the Norsemen, a
Blood-redden'd relic of
Javelins over
The jarring breaker, the deep-sea billow,

---

[1] Lit. "the gathering of men."

Shaping their way toward Dyflen[1] again,
Shamed in their souls.

XIII.

Also the brethren,
King and Atheling,
Each in his glory,
Went to his own in his own West-Saxonland,
Glad of the war.

XIV.

Many a carcase they left to be carrion,
Many a livid one, many a sallow-skin—
Left for the white-tail'd eagle to tear it, and
Left for the horny-nibb'd raven to rend it, and
Gave to the garbaging war-hawk to gorge it, and
That gray beast, the wolf of the weald.

XV.

Never had huger
Slaughter of heroes
Slain by the sword-edge—
Such as old writers
Have writ of in histories—
Hapt in this isle, since
Up from the East hither
Saxon and Angle from
Over the broad billow
Broke into Britain with
Haughty war-workers who
Harried the Welshman, when
Earls that were lured by the
Hunger of glory gat
Hold of the land.

The unity of England which this battle vindicated, and which was a necessity for a national literature, was not established by it. The country was as yet too heterogeneous to be ruled by one man, and the system, which now began, of the great Ealdormanries,

[1] Dublin.

divided England again, and lasted even through the Danish kings until the Norman Conquest. That conquest did finally for England what Eadward and Æthelstan had temporarily done. It made one kingdom, and in doing so made a national literature possible.

Eadmund succeeded Æthelstan in 940, and this "Doer of Deeds" did one thing of which a song was written. It recorded his retaking of the *Five Towns* in the northern Marchland, and a small portion of it was placed in the *Chronicle*. There may also have been a song made of his murder by Leofa and of the bitter mourning of Dunstan over him when he was laid in Glastonbury. In 946, Eadred the Excellent came to the throne, and then Eadwig in 955; and on his death Eadgar, the Winner of Peace, was King of all England from 959 to 975. There are three stories about him, one belonging to his wilder youth, which were probably in the form of ballads and which William of Malmesbury put into prose. The first of these is the ballad of *Ælfthryth and Æthelwold and of the King*, and it has many relations in the folk-tales of all countries. Ælfthryth was so fair a woman that the king heard of her loveliness and sent his friend Æthelwold to her father, saying, "Give me thy daughter to wife." But Æthelwold, made foolish by her fairness, told the king that she was unworthy of her fame, and married her himself. When the king heard the truth, his anger was deep, but hiding his heart he played the friend with Æthelwold, and said, "I will come and see thee and thy wife." Æthelwold told his wife what he had done, and said, "Make thyself unbeautiful, put on thy most common clothes, and we may yet deceive the king." But the woman, wroth with his fraud and longing to be a queen, clothed herself in glorious garments and made her beauty greater, and smiled upon the king. Then Eadgar, hunting with Æthelwold next day, slew him with his spear and avenged the lie. "What thinkest thou of this hunting?" he said, turning in his fierceness to Æthelwold's son by another wife. "My lord," said the young man, "what is pleasing to thee cannot be displeasing to me"; and Eadgar gave him gifts in atonement; but he married Ælfthryth, and the woman had her way. Afterwards she feared for herself, and founded a nunnery.

In later days Eadgar, leaving his wild passions, was a strong and wise king, who loved honour and was ready with his hands. Another ballad, made into Latin prose by William of Malmesbury, is of him and the Scot-king Kenneth. For Kenneth, one day feasting with his men, said of Eadgar, who was little of stature, "'Tis wonderful to me that so many folk should do the will of so small a man." And Eadgar, hearing this, bid Kenneth meet him in a lonely glade, and brought with him two swords. "Take a sword," he said, "let us see which is the best man, and whether I am not fit to have bigger men than I to do my will; nor shalt thou go till we have proved this, for it is not meet for a king to say at the drink what he will not stand to in battle." But when Kenneth heard that, he asked forgiveness. "'Twas but a jest," he said.

There is yet another song, or what seems to have been one, which proves how proud and famous a king Eadgar was thought to be. When he came to Chester to be crowned, seven years after his coming to the throne, and steered his long barge on the river, eight kings, of whom he was the overlord, were his rowers—five Welsh kings, and Kenneth, and the Danish king of the Southern Isles, and the King of Cumberland; so he had great state; and even the kings of Dublin obeyed him. He died in 975 and was succeeded by Eadward the Martyr, of whose death also a song was made. Coming back from the chase one day, he stayed at his stepmother's, for he was thirsty; and while he drank she caused him to be stabbed in the back, and he fell from his horse and was dragged through the woods till he died. "There was never so evil a deed done among the English since first they came to Britain." And he was buried in Ælfred's minster of Shaftesbury.

These were the great kings of England, and these the songs which were made of them, and many more were doubtless made which have been forgotten, for singing and making of ballads never ceased in England. Even in the next reign, of Æthelred the Unwise[1] (979-1016), during which the Danish conquest of England by Swein Forkbeard and Cnut was begun, there is one fine battle-poem, the Death of Byrhtnoth, the alderman of Essex, who fought in 991 with the Danes at Maldon.

The poem runs to 300 lines, and is unfortunately without a beginning or an end. The manuscript in which it was found was burnt among others in the Cottonian library, and we only possess it in the copy which Hearne printed. The oldest manuscript of the *Chronicle* and four later ones record the battle and death of Byrhtnoth. The first makes it happen in 993, but the other four and the history of the Church of Ely place it in 991. That is, then, the chosen date. Some suppose it was written by a monk of Ely, because Byrhtnoth was a rich benefactor of that Abbey. If so, he either saw the battle or spoke with one who had been in the van of it.

Its historical interest is great. It tells of the first outbreaking of the tempest which, long accumulating in the North, was to end in the Danish conquest of England. One of the roving Viking bands which had gathered some years before round Swein of Denmark, but which his expulsion from Denmark had let loose, landed on the east coast of England, plundered Ipswich, and, sailing up the river Panta, landed on the long spit of ground which divides the stream into two branches. Opposite to them, on the northern shore, was Mældun (Maldon), and Earl Byrhtnoth came down from the town to meet the pirates. The tide was in, and the stream flowed deep between the two armies. They challenged one another, and shot their arrows to and fro till the ebb came. Then they dashed into the ford and came to blows in the water. Long and well they fought, but the Danes had the better, and the earl died on the bank of the stream. I have put into a rough metrical movement part of the poem.[2]

---

[1] I take the word "Unready," the uncounselled, to mean one who would not take good rede, that is, who was unwise.

[2] A literal translation of the whole is placed in the Appendix.

The earl gathers his men. One lets his hawk fly away, another grasps his arms, and Byrhtnoth puts his men in array; riding and giving rede among them, till all were ready. Then he lighted from his horse and stood among his hearth-men. On the other side of the stream, now full of the flood-tide, the herald of the Vikings shouted mightily the threat of the sea-thieves—

    Hail! the swift sea-farers send me;
    Bid me tell you—" Send them rings,
    Better send them to defend you
    From the rushing of our battle
    Than that we should deal you slaughter!
    If thou givest to the Vikings,
    At their dooming, gold for friendship—
    We betake us to our shipping
    With the scats, and o'er the waters
    Fare away in peace with you."
    Byrhtnoth spake, and raised his shield,
    Shook his tapering ashen-spear,
    Steadfastly and fierce he answered—
    Hear, thou Seaman, what this folk say—
    " Spear-points they will give for tribute,
    Swords of old time, venomed edges,
    Battle-gear that brings no gaining!
    Seamen's herald, take the message!
    Here stand I, an Earl, and warding
    With my host our fatherland.

    .   .   .   .

    Fall, ye heathen, in the war!
    Shameful would it seem to me
    Should ye fare to ship unfoughten,
    With our scats, when ye have hither
    Marched so far into our country.
    Is't so easy to get treasure?—
    First shall spear and sword encounter,
    And the play of war be grim,
    Ere we give a scat of tribute."
    Then he bade them bear the shield,
    Till they stood along the stream-edge.

Each the other could not meet
For the flood-tide followed now
On the ebb, and stream and tide
Mixed their waters—Long it seemed
Till they bore their spears together.
So about the Panta's stream
Stood arrayed the Saxon line,
And the army of the ships;
None of them could harm the other
Save by flying of the arrows!
Ready, eager for the battle
Were the Vikings, when the flood
Ebbed at last—and Byrhtnoth cried
"Wulfstan, kinsman, hard-in-war,
Hold the passage, Son of Ceola!"
Then the first who strode the ford[1]
Wulfstan smote him with his spear.
Fearless warriors were with Wulfstan,
Maccus, Ælfere, high-hearted,
Who would never fly the pathway.
Firm they held it 'gainst the foemen.
When the Vikings saw how fell
Were these warders of the ford,
Hateful, they began to feign—
"Give us passage o'er the ford."
And the Earl, in scornfulness,
Let too many foemen land.
O'er the cold stream Byrhthelm's son
'Gan to call the Vikings—"Come!
Quickly come, for here is room
For the battle. God alone
Knoweth who the field shall win!"
Then the slaughter-wolves, the Vikings,
Reckless of the water, went
Over Panta; bore their shields,
O'er the gleaming water bore,
All their linden-shields to land.
Byrhtnoth 'gainst the bloody foe
With his men stood ready there.
"Make the war-hedge," then he cried,

---

[1] The word is bridge—but there was no bridge in our sense of the word.

" Steady stand, for now the battle
Draws anigh, and now must fall
All the weirded."—Then the shouting
Rose on high ; the ravens wheeled ;
Carrion-greedy, barked the eagle ;—
Then they let the sharp-set darts
Fly their fingers, and the spears
Edged to keenness. Busy now
Were the bows, and now the shield
Stopped the spear-head ; bitter then
Charged the battle : on each side
Fell the warriors, youths and men,
Dead upon the slaughter-field.
Wounded was Wulfmær ; he chose
Death to sleep in, Byrhtnoth's kinsman ;
Sorely was he hewn with swords.
But a vengeance met the Vikings ;
One was slain by Edward, he
Smote him with a mighty stroke ;
At his feet the fated fell.
And his Lord gave thanks to him ;
Edward was his bower-thegn.

Byrhtnoth whetted them to battle ;
He, the Hard-in war, strode forward,
Shook his spear on high, and holding
Shield aloft for shelter, stepped
Firm against a Viking ! Each
Thought on death to each. The Seaman
Sent a southern dart, and wounded
Byrhtnoth, lord of fighters, who
Thrusting downwards with his shield
Broke the shaft, and loosed the spear.
Fierce was Byrhtnoth then, and pierced
With his spear the boasting Viking,
Skilful sent it through his throat.
Quickly then he flung another,
Cleft the byrnie's woven rings ;
In the Viking's heart the venom
Stood—and blither was the Earl ;
Laughed, and gave the Maker thanks,
For the work the Lord had given.

> Then another Viking sent
> Flying from his hands a spear,
> And it pierced the Ætheling,
> Byrhtnoth, thegn of Æthelred!
> There beside him stood a youth,
> Yet a boy, who forth withdrew
> From his Lord the bloody spear,
> Son of Wulfstan, young Wulfmær!
> And he sent that very spear
> Sharp and keen against the Viking;
> In the point went, and he lay
> Dead who erst had struck his Lord.
> Then a fighter sought the Earl,
> All to seize his rings and armour,
> And the armlets and the sword;
> But the Earl unsheathed his bill,
> Broad and edged with brown, and smote
> At the byrnie of this foe.
> Ere he struck, the Viking marred
> Byrhtnoth's blow, and sliced his arm;
> And his fallow-hilted sword
> Fell to earth, and never more
> Could he hold or wield the blade.
>
> Yet the hoary fighter spoke,
> Heartened up his men, and bade them
> Be good comrades; then he looked
> Up to Heaven, and spoke this word—
> "Thanks I give Thee, King of peoples,
> For the joys I found on earth!
> I have need, O Lord of Mercy,
> That Thou grant my ghost Thy kindness;
> That my soul to Thee may wend;
> To Thy keeping, Lord of Angels,
> Fare in peace: of Thee I pray
> That hell-scathers may not hurt it."
> Then the heathen hewed him down;
> And the men who stood by him,
> Ælfnoth and Wulmær, lay dead;
> Life they yielded with their Lord.

Thus ends the first part of the battle with the great earl's cry to God, the mighty Lord of all folk. He does not sing the tale of his famous deeds, as Beowulf would have done; he sings thanksgiving for the joy he had in this world, and prayer that his soul may fare forth in peace and forgiveness. It is the first time in English war-song that the dying warrior ends his life, not with the boast of the hero or his farewell to his folk, but with the prayer of a Christian man. It brings us near to that poetry of Romance in which the knight dies with the name of Christ upon his lips. Yet, though *Byrhtnoth's Death* has thus varied from the ancient traditions of English song, the poem is as heroic and northern in feeling as *Beowulf*. It uses the old motives, words, and urgings. Its challenges sound like those in the *Fight at Finnsburg*. And courage and honour before all things else, and faithfulness to the oath of service, and the closeness of the tie between the thegn and his lord, and the shame of cowardice, and death better than a shamed life—these, with which English saga begins, are vital in the last song it sings before the Conquest.

CHAPTER XVII

ENGLISH PROSE FROM ÆLFRED TO THE CONQUEST

ENGLISH prose-writing all but died with the death of Ælfred, and ninety years had passed away before the impulse he gave it bore its full fruit in the work of Ælfric whose first homilies appeared in 991. But its blossoms began to appear more than thirty years earlier in the founding of the school of Glastonbury by Dunstan, and of Abingdon and Winchester by Æthelwold, the scholar of Dunstan and the master of Ælfric.

It is not difficult to say why Ælfred failed to make England learned, or even to make a literary class. He tried at first to influence the parish clergy, who had now to do the work formerly done by the mission preachers of the monasteries, and who did not do it. The appeal he made to them by his *Pastoral Care* fell dead. They were ignorant and demoralised, save the few whom Ælfred praises. They drank heavily, they hunted, they sang rude songs and made them, they married (in the Danelaw the marriage of the clergy was legalised), and they did worse than marry. Their hungry sheep looked up and were not fed, and if a few were bettered by Ælfred, they fell back after his death into their sturdy ignorance and ill-living. No literary work was done by the secular clergy.

Nor can we say that the influence he brought to bear on the bishops and higher clergy produced any lasting result. He seems to have found only one man among them whom he thought capable of good prose. He urged them to write, but Werfrith's translation of *Gregory's Dialogues* was the only book he dragged out of his bishops. In fact, they had but little leisure, and were inevitably drawn into political life. When the king pressed them, they tried to do some learned business, but when Ælfred's successors urged them no more, Church and State were much more interesting occupations. No great ecclesiastic, till Dunstan came, did any work for literature in England; and even Dunstan, when he left Glastonbury, was soon completely involved in the labours of the State.

Ælfred's effort to make a cultivated laity also failed. He tried to interest them in the history of their own country and in the history of the world, but the interest he did awake was not enough to induce any of them to leave their hunting and war for literature. Even his own sons and grandson failed him in this respect. They attended his schools along with the nobles, but when they came to reign, they had far too much to do against a host of foes to give any time to learning. They had to make history, not literature; to unite, not to educate England. They listened to the bards who made poems on their great doings, and gave them "rings," and in that lame conclusion ended Ælfred's hope to make a learned laity. Not till nearly a century afterwards do we meet with educated nobles like Æthelweard and his son, and they were more interested in, than capable of, literature.

So, in the end, Ælfred took to writing English for his own pleasure, and for the sake of the future England. His translation of the *De Consolatione* may record not only his longing to comfort himself for the troubles of the world, but for his failure to make a learned class in England. However, his experience had taught him, long before the date of this last translation, that at first there was only one way to re-create literature in England. This was to re-establish monasticism. What was left of the monasteries in Wessex had become unmonastic. Malmesbury and Glastonbury were still abbeys, but were served by secular priests. A few monks may have lived there under rule, but the rule was inoperative. Ælfred endeavoured to reorganise these abbeys, but in vain. He established nunneries at Hyde and Shaftesbury, and succeeded, with his own daughter as abbess, in getting Shaftesbury into some working order, but the place decayed. He set up Athelney for monks, but the sturdy objection of English folk to the monastic habit forced him to make a foreigner its abbot, and to fill it with priests and deacons from beyond sea, with young Gauls and Danes, even with children to be trained into monks; but before very long the abbey broke up in disorder. In this attempt to revive monasticism for the sake of literature he also failed. And the failure lasted a long time. Even in 955-959, during Eadwig's reign, monasticism was still at a low ebb. "Sad and pitiable," says William of Malmesbury, "was the face of monachism. Even the monastery of Malmesbury, which had been dwelt in by monks for 270 years, the king made a sty for secular canons." Yet in monastic leisure alone, while the country was harassed by wars and invaders, could any learned work be done. The tendency of monasteries was to do that work in Latin. But when it was started by Dunstan and carried on by Æthelwold and Ælfric, a great deal of it was done in the English tongue, and in honest English prose. In Ælfric's resolute use of the vernacular, ninety years after Ælfred's death, we find the resurrection of Ælfred's influence and of his principle—"Teach the people in their own tongue; make the English language the language of literature." This is the story of Ælfred's failure, of that apparent failure which befalls a genius who is before his time.

Only one man seems to have carried on after Ælfred's death the tradition of his work. Ælfred's prose was chiefly secular, and we might expect, at a time when the glory of the country grew, that the impulse he gave to the history of that glory would continue in one at least of his band of scholars. We find him in the writer who composed the narrative in the *Chronicle* of the wars and work of Eadweard from 910 to 924. From 901, when Ælfred died, to 910, the story is but poorly recorded, but in 910 the pen is taken up by probably the same hand which wrote the account of the years from 894 to 897 with so much breadth, earnestness, and power.[1] Of course we cannot be sure of this, but from 910 to 924 we have the narrative of one who at least rivals the previous writer. It is well composed, clear, individual in style, brief, but not too brief to be effective. This is the sole piece of secular prose of this date. From 925 to 940, during the reign of Æthelstan, the meagreness of the *Chronicle* is only broken once by the song of Brunanburh. From 940 to 946, during the reign of Eadmund; from 946, when Eadred came to the throne, to the death of Eadgar in 975, the *Chronicle* ceases altogether to be literary. Three short poems of no value only make the thinness of its entries more remarkable. Secular prose, then, had died in Winchester. But religious prose had begun to move again into life with the restoration by Dunstan and Eadgar of the monastic life of England.

Dunstan, "the chief of monks," was born in the reign of Eadward, Ælfred's son,[2] and died when Æthelred the Unwise had been ten years on the throne, in 988. He lived, then, through all the glorious reigns of the House of Ælfred, and saw the beginning of its decay. He played a great part in politics and in the Church. But our chief interest is in what he did for learning and literature when he came to man's estate. Even in his boyhood and youth he was a good example of how far culture and

[1] Ælfred's work, or his seeming work, on the *Chronicle* ended in 891.
[2] The usual date is that of Æthelstan's accession, 924 or 925. But critics have agreed to put it back a little. There are several biographies of Dunstan. There is one, about 1000, by a Saxon priest whom Stubbs thinks was a scholar from Liège, living under Dunstan's protection at the time of his death. Another is by Adelard, a monk of Blandinium, about the same date. Osbern wrote another after the Conquest, shortly before Anselm's archbishopric. Eadmer, Anselm's biographer and writer of the *Historia Novorum*, composed another, deriving his information from St. Wulfstan of Worcester, and from Nicholas, a learned monk of the same town, who treasured up and cared for the English traditions. Both these biographers were precentors of Christ Church, Canterbury. The next life of Dunstan was written by William of Malmesbury, and Capgrave made a compilation from all of them in the early part of the fifteenth century.—See Stubbs's *Memorials of Dunstan*.

the arts had under Ælfred's House penetrated into the south of
England. Born in the fenland of Somersetshire, close by Athelney
and Wedmore whence the glory of Ælfred shone into his eyes,
he grew up to boyhood in his father Heorstan's hall, under the
hill of the ancient Church of Glastonbury. His mother's name
was Cynethrythis, and she was connected with the royal house.
He went to school to the Irish pilgrims who, gathering round
the tomb of the younger Patrick, had set up something like a
colony at Glastonbury. The abbey, if it can be called such, for
its monastic life was now extinct, was served by secular priests
and clerks. They were ignorant men. Dunstan's real teachers
were the Irish scholars. The Celtic legends of Glastonbury were
no doubt instilled into his mind,[1] and held an equal place therein
with the memories of Ine and Ealdhelm, and with the later
memories of Ælfred. These traditions were likely to kindle the
imagination of a sensitive and ardent youth; and how great his
imagination was we can clearly trace in the legends which cluster
round his youth at Glastonbury. They were his own record
of the visions he saw and the voices he heard, taken down
from his own lips; told, when he was an old man, to ·his
friends, to the children that stood at his knees—and they
reveal the noble and beautiful temper of his soul. And he continued, all his life long, to see and hear these immortal sights
and sounds. Once, when his friend Æthelfleda was dying, he
saw a fair white dove descend from heaven, and heard of a spirit
who talked with her; again, when he was designing a stole for
a certain matron, Æthelwynn, his. harp, hanging on the wall,
began to play the sweetest music, and Dunstan, turning his eyes
to it, said: "The souls of the saints are now rejoicing in heaven."
When Eadred died, he heard a voice thundering over his head:
"Now King Eadred sleeps in the Lord"; and on a day when he
fell asleep in the church while waiting for Eadgar who had gone

[1] A trace of these legends lingers in a Dunstan-story of a dish which fed
all those who dipped into it, like that Irish chaldron whose powers were afterwards transferred to the Holy Grail.

out hunting, he heard in a dream a solemn service performed in heaven, and waking, remembered the music, which he set to the Cantus — "*Kyrie rex splendens*," long time sung in England. These are a few of the visions which his poetic spirit made, and of which he told the tale. Bæda saw no such visions, though he loved to hear of similar stories. But Dunstan lived in a world of religious faerie all his life, even to old age. And yet, with another side of his nature, he was the safeguard of the realm of England, managing with keen business capacity its affairs for thirty years. Indeed, he sometimes mingled both these powers, for many of his visions have directly to do with state affairs.

But when he was young, he did not think much, though always devout, of the graver things of life. He let the variety and brightness of his nature have full play. The "vain ballads" of the history of his own family, the gay songs and the "foolish dirges" of the people were his delight; he sang them to the harp which he always carried on his journeys. He was passionately fond of music. He is said to have himself invented a new instrument for Church melody which seems to have had some resemblance to the virginals. He learned how to paint and illuminate, and two manuscripts, one at Oxford and another in London, contain pictures, in the first of which he has painted himself adoring Christ, in the second Gregory the Great sending to England two missionaries, Augustine and Mellitus, while he kneels between both in the lower centre of the illuminated page. As Abbot of Glastonbury he collected precious crosses, crucifixes, cups and jewelled books, and practised himself in fine gold-working and engraving. He designed embroideries for noble ladies when he was still young, and he drew to his charm the women of the valley. Fair-haired, not tall, but with brilliant eyes, he rode well and hunted boldly. But his chief love was learning, and his natural wit and clinging memory and hot pursuit of books made him the marvel of the neighbourhood, and all the more, because he was of a quick and ready speech, ornate, inventive, and gay; swift to put all he had read into attractive form. His fame grew till Æthelstan called him to the court; but the jealousy of his rivals expelled him. He took refuge at Winchester and there he became a monk. Thence, full of eagerness for learning, he went back to Glastonbury, where for some years he read and studied, and was well loved by Æthelfleda, a woman of high rank, whom in all honour he clave to and loved in a marvellous fashion. Again called to court at the close of Eadmund's reign, he fell again into disfavour, but Eadmund, chasing the stag one day near the Cheddar cliffs, all but followed his quarry over a precipice, and the king imputed his near approach to death to his injustice to Dunstan. "Saddle your horse," he said to Dunstan, "and ride with me." And he rode to Dunstan's home, kissed him with the kiss of peace, and set him in the chair, Abbot of Glastonbury (946).[1] Eadred, Eadmund's successor, kept Dunstan constantly by his side, but the Abbot found time, during the nine years of the king's reign, to make the school at Glastonbury the first in England. He taught his young pupils himself; he sang Psalms with them; he developed Church music; he drew fresh Irish scholars to his house; he established a good library, books of which still existed at the time of the Reformation; he trained his studious monks to be scholars in philosophy, in the Scriptures, and in the writings of the Fathers; and then he sent them out to be centres of learning in other parts of England. His first effort was the refounding of the Abbey of Abingdon, and King Eadred gave it to Dunstan's best scholar, Æthelwold. Æthelwold (who died in 984) soon made Abingdon as good a school as Glastonbury. Then Oswald, at Ramsey and afterwards as Bishop of Worcester, and Odo the Archbishop of Canterbury assisted Dunstan's early effort to establish monastic schools.

It was not, however, till Eadgar's reign of peace, 959-975, that the monastic revival was fully developed. Dunstan himself

[1] See for a fuller account Stubbs's *Memorials of Dunstan* and Green's *Conquest of England*.

was not much of a monk till he had seen the Benedictine rule at work during his exile in Flanders. Oswald owed his monasticism to his study of the Benedictine rule at Fleury. Æthelwold, anxious to get his monasteries into good order, sent Osgar from Abingdon to Fleury to instruct himself fully in the Rule. But Eadgar himself was the real founder of the new monasticism. Dunstan suggested and advised it, Eadgar made it. He is said to have founded forty monasteries. We may doubt the number, but we may not doubt the great influence the king had in this way on education and on literature.

Dunstan, after Eadgar had made him Bishop of Worcester, then of London, and then Archbishop of Canterbury, seems to have taken little personal interest in the movement. He was probably too busy. But Æthelwold, now Bishop of Winchester, 963, threw himself eagerly into the work. He re-established the monastic rule in Chertsey and Milton. He acted with vigour in Winchester. The cathedral was served by secular canons, who disgraced their clerical profession. Frequently warned, they were still bold and resolute in wrong. Then one Sunday in Lent Æthelwold entered the choir, and sternly looking on them, threw on the floor a bundle of cowls: "The time has come," he said, "when you must make up your minds. Put on the monastic habit, or go. There is no other choice for you." Thus he cleared Winchester, and then turned his energy to other places. Having money from the king, he rebuilt or repaired many ruined monasteries. He restored the glories of Ely; and the ruins of Peterborough, overgrown with forest, were replaced by a new abbey. He bid another rise on the ancient site of Thorney.

Oswald, nephew of Archbishop Odo of Canterbury, and Bishop of Worcester, helped Æthelwold in this revival, but he did little more than establish monasticism in the city of Worcester. He did nothing for it in his diocese, and when he became Archbishop of York he founded no monasteries in the North. The king, in fact, was the head, the heart, and the hands of the movement, and English monasticism looks back to Eadgar as its patron.

The short poem in the *Chronicle* shows how the monks revered him; and there is a manuscript of the tenth century in the British Museum, made by one of the monks, in which a portrait of Eadgar has been drawn with enthusiasm by the illuminator of the monastery. It is the only picture we possess of an early English king. Eadgar stands in the midst with both his arms extended on high, and makes an offering to Christ, who is upheld by angels at the top of the picture. Mary stands on one side of the king and Peter on the other.

William of Malmesbury makes Eadgar himself record how he felt and what he did. "In aid of my pious devotion, heavenly love stole into my watchful care and urged me to rebuild all the holy monasteries of my kingdom, which ruinous outwardly, with mouldering shingles and worm-eaten beams, even to the rafters, were, worse still, inwardly neglected, almost without any service of God; wherefore turning out the illiterate clerks, of no regular order or discipline, I appointed pastors of a holier race, that is, of the monastic order, supplying them with ample means out of my royal revenues to repair their ruined churches."

This royal work was at this time the best thing that could be done for literature. Where the monasteries were, learning grew; where they were not, learning and literature were silent. Art also flourished where the minster rose. Architecture took fresh forms; sculpture, still rude, became more individual; painted glass and mosaic lived again; music sought new expression. The treasuries of the abbeys were filled with goldsmith's work on cross and chalice, with richly illuminated missals, with elaborate embroideries, with jewelled bindings, and every abbot knew where to find in England skilled workmen. We find Æthelwold charging Godeman, perhaps the Abbot of Thorney, to write and illuminate with miniatures a Benedictionale which we still possess.

Not only art, but science, the science of medicine, awakened to a fresher life. The monks were good gardeners and herbalists, and most monasteries had a room, where medicines and spices and perfumes were prepared, to which the sick folk of the village or the city came to be cured. Collections of recipes were made, and we probably owe the various Anglo-Saxon *Leech Books* to the monks who presided over these early laboratories. We have a medicine book—*Læce Bôc*—of the last half of the tenth century. The first two parts of the book are taken from Greek and Latin recipes. Two Englishmen, Oxa and Dun, are mentioned in the third part as medical authorities; Danish and even Gaelic sources are used, and some prescriptions are derived from Helias, patriarch of Jerusalem, who, we are told, "caused them to be sent to King Ælfred." A number of other books of the same character, gathered together by Cockayne in his *Leechdoms*, belong to this and the following century. They are full of strange and interesting folk-superstitions, and contain the ancient English *Charms* of which we have already written.

Winchester, under Æthelwold, soon excelled Glastonbury and Abingdon; and English, in King Ælfred's books, was as keenly studied as Latin. Æthelwold taught his scholars to translate Latin books into English; he "loved his native tongue," and wrote in it a translation of the *Rule of St. Benedict* which Eadgar asked of him; and, in an appendix to it, a treatise on the history of the English Church. This was less a translation than an epitome of the *Rule*, and was made for the nunnery he set up at Winchester. His Latin book on the *Offices of the Church* was sent by Eadgar all over England. An eager, eloquent and attractive man, he sent the love of education and learning with his pupils into the monasteries, and from them to the people. And he combined it with a love of English writing. But the best thing he did for English prose was his education of Ælfric.

But before Ælfric created the new school of English prose the *Blickling Homilies* were brought together; and prove into what active work Dunstan, Æthelwold, and Oswald had awakened the study of English prose. Wülker thinks that the style of these homilies belongs to the elder prose, their substance to the younger. They represent, then, the transition between the prose of Ælfred and the prose of Ælfric. There are nineteen of these homilies, and we may add to them, as probably of the same time, the homilies in the *Vercelli Book.* Some are early in date, and others later. One of them is dated 971, and all appear to be well before the year 990. About the same time as these *Homilies*, and before 990, other books seem to have existed in English, of which Ælfric says, in the preface to his *Homilies*, that "they were full of errors, though unlearned men, being simple, thought them to be full of wisdom." He probably refers in this to books of Ælfred's time, or even before Ælfred. He mentions "Ælfred's translations." He might even refer to poems like *Beowulf* and other sagas then in existence. But he certainly refers to books of his own time when he says— "How can any one read the misrepresentations which they call the *Vision of Paul*, since he himself says that he heard unspeakable words, not lawful for a man to utter?" When we think, however, that this book must have been largely invented from a Latin original, we feel with Ten Brink that its loss is far more to be regretted than that of many homilies. Ælfric also alludes to a book on the *Sufferings of St. Peter and St. Paul.* To this period may belong the Anglo-Saxon version of the *Life of St. Guthlac* written by Felix of Crowland in Latin about the middle of the eighth century, a little book in a better and more natural style than its original. From these scattered things we pass to the steady work of Ælfric which begins with the last decade of the tenth century. The first of his writings is dated 990-994.

What Bæda was to England in the eighth, Ælfric was to the eleventh century. He had no creative power; nothing imaginative comes from his hand, but he had an affection for imaginative work. Some have traced in his work that he had read the poets, and he was always playing at poetry in his prose. Not original in thought, he had a gentle eagerness in writing; he had warmth and moral dignity. His charity, his affectionate friendship, his tact, his practised skill in the affairs of men, appear in all his books and letters. He possessed the excellent power of putting into popular form the thoughts of other men, and of epitomising good books. He gathered together, absorbed and well expressed the learning of his time; he had a strong sense of the duty of communicating it in English to the people, and he passed all the years of his manhood in teaching and writing. And as Ælfred was the creator of the elder, so Ælfric was of the younger Anglo-Saxon prose.

He was a scholar from his earliest years. Born about 955, he was educated under Æthelwold at Winchester. He soon became a monk, and was sent by Ælfheah, Æthelwold's successor, to teach and govern the new monastery of Cernel (Cerne Abbas in Dorsetshire), built near Dorchester by the thegn Æthelmær. While at Cernel, from 987 to 989, he began his work of translating Latin books into English for the use of the people. Following in this the plan of King Ælfred, he addressed the laity as well as the clergy, and at first he imitated the style of Ælfred, whose books were his daily companions. In later years he developed his own easier and more modern style, and he then turned his attention chiefly to religious books for the use of monks and pupils in the monasteries.

His first work, *Homiliae Catholicae*, issued after he had returned to Winchester, consists of two collections of homilies, each forty in number. These are dedicated to Archbishop Sigeric, 990-994, and are on the Sundays and Feast-days of the year. They borrow most of their stuff from Augustine, Jerome, Gregory, and Bæda. A small number of them are in alliterative verse, written as prose. All of them have alliterative passages; and this practice was almost new in English prose. His next works were the *Grammar* and *Glossary*, which he made up out of extracts from Donatus and the *Institutiones Grammaticae* of the Priscians. It is most likely that these were followed by the *Colloquium* (we cannot precisely date it), and that it was written to help the pupils in the school at Winchester. It is a discourse on the occupations of the monks, and on various other conditions of life ; and as the Latin text of one of the manuscripts has an English translation over it, it becomes a kind of vocabulary. We possess it in another manuscript as it was redone by Ælfric Bata, one of Ælfric's scholars—"Hanc sententiam latini sermonis olim Ælfricus Abbas composuit, qui meus fuit magister, sed tamen ego, Ælfric Bata, multas postea huic addidi appendices." This is the only work we have from Ælfric Bata's hand.

The lives of the Saints—*Passiones Sanctorum*—another set of homilies, followed in 996 the *Grammar* and *Colloquium*. They were dedicated, not to Sigeric, who died in 995, but to Æthelweard, the great thegn, at whose desire they were undertaken. Two of them contain in alliterative prose the pith of the books of *Kings* and of *Maccabees*. But they are chiefly on special saints venerated at separate monasteries; and those on English saints not far from Ælfric's own time—on Swithun, Oswald, and Æthelthrith, Virgin; and one on the false gods worshipped by the English, are of greater interest than the rest. The others are in alliterative prose, and so are the homilies which follow them. Only the first of the whole forty is in pure prose. I place here a part of the translation of the Latin preface Ælfric wrote to this book of *Homilies*. It will serve to illustrate his style outside of mere preaching. It does illustrate his character, and it is equally curious to see the monk in it rebelling against English prose and preferring Latin; and the friend somewhat weary with the urgency of his friends, and the conviction, so early in our literary history and so uncommon, that English was a more concise vehicle of thought than Latin. Here is the passage [1]:—

This Book have I also translated from the Latin into the usual English speech. . . . For I call to mind that in two former books I have set forth the Passions or Lives of those saints whom that illustrious nation celebrates by honouring their festivals, and it has (now) pleased me to set forth in this book the Passions as well as the Lives of those saints whom not the vulgar but the monks honour by special services. I do not promise, however, to write very

---

[1] It is taken from Skeat's edition of the *Passiones Sanctorum*

many in this tongue, because it is not fitting that many should be put into our tongue, lest peradventure the pearls of Christ be had in disrespect.

And therefore I hold my peace as to the book called *Vitae Patrum*, wherein are contained many subtle points which ought not to be laid open to the laity, nor indeed are we ourselves quite able to fathom them. . . . Nor am I able in this translation to render everything word for word; but I have, at any rate, carefully endeavoured to give exact sense for sense, just as I find it in the Holy Writing by means of such simple and obvious language as may profit them that hear it. . . .

I abridge the longer narratives of the Passions, not as regards the sense, but in the language, in order that no tediousness may be inflicted on the fastidious, as might be the case if as much prolixity were used in our language as occurs in the Latin. And we know that brevity does not always deprave speech, but oftentimes makes it more charming. Let it not be considered as a fault in me that I turn sacred narrative into our own tongue, since the request of many of the faithful shall clear me in this matter, particularly that of the governor Æthelwerd and of my friend Æthelmer (*Æthelmeri nostri*), who most highly honour my translations by their perusal of them; nevertheless, I have resolved at last to desist from such labours after completing the fourth book, that I may not be regarded as too tedious.

An Anglo-Saxon preface follows, addressed directly to Æthelweard, and beginning—

Ælfric humbly greeteth Æthelwerd, and I tell thee, beloved, that I have now brought together in this book such Passions of the Saints as I have had leisure to put into English, because that thou, beloved, and Æthelmær earnestly prayed me for such writings, and took them from my hands, for the strengthening of your faith by means of this history, which ye never had in your tongue before.

This set of homilies was probably followed by Ælfric's English version of a part (69 out of the 280 questions) of the *Questions of Sigewulf, presbyter, on Genesis*, which Alcuin at Sigewulf's wish had written in Latin. Then came a translation, freely wrought, of the *Hexameron of St. Basil;* then a homily *On the Creation*, with other homilies more or less alliterative. At last, he left this scattered work for a worthier task,—the translation of the Bible; but he was somewhat driven to this by thegn Æthelweard, who begged him to undertake *Genesis*, and who, when Ælfric objected, said "that he only wanted the first part done as far as Isaac, for the rest of the book, already translated by another hand, was now in his possession." Ælfric, thus urged, translated *Genesis* up to chap. xxiv. The rest, as far as the end of *Leviticus*, was not his doing. He also translated *Numbers*, *Deuteronomy*, *Joshua*, the book of *Judges* (but that may be a later insertion), and the books of *Esther*, of *Job*, and of *Judith*. All of them, except the *Genesis*, are not literal translations. Difficult passages, and others not likely to interest the English people, are omitted. Some books, like *Judges*, are put into an homiletic form. Others might be described as heroic sketches of the lives of the heroes and kings of Israel. Ælfric strives to paint them in vivid colours, to sharpen their individuality; it was an effort he made to interest the people in Jewish history; and it was this popular direction of his homilies which drove him, I think, into his poetical prose. Certainly, the rhythmical form of alliterative prose which he had already used in the *Homilies* is fully wrought out in this book. It closes with a hymn of praise to God for all the great chiefs and heroes in Roman, Byzantine, and English history, whom God had made victorious over the enemies of the faith. And it is with some patriotic pride that we read of the English kings so long ago who fought and worked so well—"Ælfred, who brought safety to his people from the Danes; Æthelstan, who fought with Anlaf; Eadgar, the noble king who most of all English kings established the praise of God, whom all kings and chieftains round about him served for the sake of his peace"— phrases which almost repeat the words which describe Eadgar in the *Chronicle*. It brings Ælfric more clearly before us that he gave to these translations a patriotic touch of his own. "I have set *Judith*," he says, "forth in English for an example to you men that ye may defend your country against your foes." For now the Danes were in the land. He used the *Maccabees* for the same purpose.

These books may be said to belong to the laity as well as the clergy. But the *Canones Ælfrici* which followed them were chiefly addressed to the needs of the clergy. His *Grammar* had been made for the pupils in the monastic schools; the *Canones* were a pastoral letter in Latin for the instruction of priests, and, in their two parts, dwelt on the clerical life and its duties, especially on the celibacy of the clergy; on ritual and vestments, on Baptism and the Eucharist and on some Feast Days. A Latin preface dedicates the book to Bishop Wulfsige of Sherborne, who had asked Ælfric to write it. This dates the book. Wulfsige was Bishop of Sherborne from about 998 to 1001.

Shortly after he had finished this book at Winchester, Æthelmær, son of Æthelweard, who had founded a monastery for Benedictines at Egnesham (Eynsham), near Oxford, called Ælfric to take charge of it as its abbot, in 1005. In this quiet office he lived, always working and learning, till he died about 1020-25. His first book from Eynsham was a series of extracts from his master Æthelwold's *De Consuetudine Monachorum*. He calls himself Abbot of Egnesham in the preface. The book was written, then, after 1005. The next year he sent an epistle in the form of a homily to Wulfgeat of Ilmandune (Ilmington), a royal thegn who had suffered the loss of his property under process. The letter has as text—"Esto consentiens adversario," and it is chiefly on the duty of forgiveness. His English treatise *Concerning the Old and New Testament* was composed somewhat later, about 1008, and is written for Sigweard at East Healon in Mercia, a thegn who had often asked Ælfric to tell him about these writings. The book is, then, addressed to the laity. Both parts have prefaces addressed to Sigweard. It is practically an introduction to the study of the Bible; it tells us what books of the Bible had already been translated into English; and though it uses a book of Isidore's on the Bible, is an original work of much interest. The three *Appendices* and an introduction *On the Creation* are worthy of study. About the same date as this book, he sent his letter to thegn Sigeferth on the necessity of the chastity of the clergy—*Emb Clænnysse*. We know it was written after he became abbot. "Ælfric, Abbot," it begins, "greets Sigeferth with friendship."

He turned now from these English books to write again in Latin, and produced an affectionate Life of his master, full of gratitude, the *Vita Æthelwoldi*, about 1008. It was written for and dedicated to Bishop Kenulf of Winchester, who died in 1007 or 1008. It was followed by his *Sermo ad Sacerdotes*, a pastoral letter written for Wulfstan as Bishop of Winchester, between 1014 and 1016. Wulfstan, when he stayed at Worcester and not at York,[1] lived not far from Eynsham, and when he received this Latin letter made Ælfric turn it into English. The book repeats the matter of his *Canones*.

These are the books which internal evidence enables us to date. We have other homilies from his hand; a compilation from Bæda's *De Temporum Ratione*, his *De Temporibus*, and his *De Natura Rerum;* a sermon on the *Sevenfold Gifts of the Holy Ghost*, and an *Admonition by a Spiritual Father to a Son entering the Religious Life*. The writer of this admonition calls himself a Benedictine monk, and says that he has written on St. Basilius. There is a homily on Basil by Ælfric, and it is the only Anglo-Saxon homily on this saint. The style, the alliteration of the preface, and the work are plainly Ælfric's. He died at Eynsham some time between 1020 and 1025.

Wulfstan, who called himself *Lupus*, and to whom Ælfric addressed his *Sermo ad Sacerdotes*, was Archbishop of York from 1002 to 1023, and is most known as an English prose writer by his *Sermo Lupi ad Anglos quando Dani maxime persecuti sunt eos*, which was written in 1012. He had heard of and perhaps seen the results of the terrible raids which Thurkill in 1010 began to make into East Anglia, which he soon extended to Oxfordshire and Buckinghamshire, to Bedford, Northampton, and through Wiltshire and Wessex—ravaging, slaying, and plundering; till, at last, "every English leader fled, and shire would not help shire"— and King Æthelred, having no money to buy off Thurkill, left Canterbury to be sacked, and Archbishop Ælfheah to be murdered

[1] Wulfstan was Archbishop of York from 1002 to 1023, and at the same time Bishop of Worcester from 1002 to 1016.

by the drunken pirates in 1011. As usual, Wulfstan imputes the miseries of England to the sins of her people, and they are bid, a strange consolation, to look forward to the greater punishment which the reign of Antichrist and the Last Judgment will bring upon them. The prose of this piece is not as smooth and cultivated as Ælfric's, but the patriotic passion of the writer gives it weight and vigour. Many other homilies, as many as fifty-three, are allotted to him, but of these fifty-three, Professor Napier has selected only four as the work of Wulfstan. I give here a short passage out of the *Address to the English* :—

> For a long time now there has been no goodness among us, either at home or abroad, but there has been ravaging and onset on onset on every side again and again. The English have now for long been always beaten in battle, and made great cowards, through God's wrath; and the sea robbers so strong by God's allowance, that often in a fight one of them will put to flight ten of the English, sometimes less, sometimes more, all for our sins. A thrall often binds fast the thegn who was his lord and makes him a thrall, through the wrath of God. "Wálá" for the wretchedness, and "wálá" for the world-shame which now the English have, all through God's wrath! Often two or three pirates drive a drove of Christian men huddled together, from sea to sea, out through the people, to the world-shame of us all, if we could in good sooth know any shame at all, or if we would (ever) understand aright. But all the disgrace we are always bearing we dutifully pay for to those who shame us. We are for ever paying them, and they ill-use us daily. They harry and they burn, they plunder and rob and carry off to ships; and, lo, what is there any other in all these happenings save the wrath of God clear and plain upon this people?

Another prose writer of this time, that is, up to the death of Æthelred in 1016, was Byrchtfercth, who had been an acquaintance of Dunstan's, a scholar of Abbo of Fleury, and who now lived in the monastery of Ramsey. A well-known mathematician as well as scholar, he wrote in Latin several commentaries on Bæda's scientific works; a book of his own, *De principiis mathematicis*, and a *Life of Dunstan*. The extensive and varied knowledge he shows in these books makes it all but certain that he was the author of a contemporary *Handboc* or *Manual*, which treats of a number of subjects pertaining to natural philosophy—on the Alphabet, on Weights, on Numbers; on the Alphabets of the Anglo-Saxons, of the Latins, Greeks, and Hebrews; on the divisions of the year, and on some religious subjects. They are in English, but to some of them a Latin gloss is added.

These three persons to whom we can give names—Ælfric, Wulfstan, and Byrchtfercth—are the chief writers in that revival of learning, which, begun by Dunstan at Glastonbury, continued by Æthelwold at Abingdon and Winchester, was raised to its height by Ælfric at Winchester and Eynsham. They carry us forward to a few years after the death of Æthelred the Unwise, for Ælfric died in 1020-25. The result of Ælfric's work, for he was indeed the source of all that followed, was first the creation of a new, clear, flexible, and popular prose, more fitted than Ælfred's to express for the people the number of new subjects of a varied character which not only arose in England, but which now began to enter England from the Continent, especially with the influx of Normans before the Conquest. The fault of this prose, that use of the alliterative rhythm which turns so much of it into a semblance of bad poetry, may have had its good in its attractiveness to the people. Congregations, falling asleep while listening to prose, might well listen to a homily in the alliterative metre they were accustomed to in the tales sung on the village green. And Ælfric, who was a very practical person, may have purposely poetised his prose for educational ends.

The second result of Ælfric's work was the extension of education and learning. The bishops, as we see from the demands made on Ælfric by the Archbishops Sigeric and Wulfstan, by the Bishops Wulfsige and Kenulf, desired to better the condition of their clergy, and to instil into them at least the rudiments of learning. And the impulse thus given by Ælfric to the heads of the Church did extend to the clergy. They were no longer quite ignorant, as in Ælfred's time. They gained and continued to support a higher ideal of their duty; they strove to know something of their Bible and their service books; they lived a cleanlier life; and so many small books on the lives of saints, on Church music, chronology, and various ritual matters, were set forth in the eleventh century, that Ten Brink has good reason to say that the English clergy at the Conquest were not so lazy and illiterate as the Normans represented them to be.

It is also plain that in this revival of learning the class which Ælfred had striven in vain to reach—the class of the nobles—had now been reached, and that a certain number of them were eager recipients and patrons of learning. We have seen that Æthelweard, a royal thegn, and son-in-law of Byrhtnoth who died at Maldon, not only read what Ælfric wrote, but urged him into further writing, and had other writers than Ælfric under his patronage. It was he that projected the translation of the Bible. He was probably himself the writer of the *Chronicle* which goes under his name. His son, Æthelmær, another royal thegn, and a student of learning, almost lived with his friend Ælfric when he was at Eynsham, and brought him into contact with the thegns Wulfgeat of Ilmandune between Warwickshire and Gloucestershire, with Sigeferth, and with Sigweard of Oxfordshire. These nobles can scarcely be said to stand alone. They were probably representatives of a small body of cultivated laymen, who, under Ælfric's impulse, attached themselves to the society of the monastic scholars.

The people, as well as the clergy and nobles, shared in the impulse which Ælfric gave to England. He made for them a history of the Church in the host of homilies, more than 150, which he wrote on the Sunday services, on occasional subjects, on the lives of the saints and martyrs of their own and foreign lands. These, to which he sometimes imparted a national direction, were read to the people; and instructed, entertained, and warmed their minds. Sermons, especially those on the legends of the Saints, were the companions of the saga and the ballad and did the same kind of educating and kindling work.

Lastly, we know that the monasteries, under Ælfric's impulse, again began to be the home of learned men—studious monks, like Byrchtfercht, who wrote on science as well as theology. A whole set of medical books were set forth in the eleventh century, *The Herbarium Apuleii*, a Latin herbal, containing, under the name of Apuleius, the doctrines supposed to be taught by Chiron to Achilles, tracts on the virtues of the herb Betony and on Medicina Animalium, and a continuation from a translation of Dioskorides, was put into English and became a "popular Anglo-Saxon text-book among physicians." Another English book, *Medicina de Quadrupedibus*, gives the use to which the thirteen beasts it mentions may be put for medicinal purposes. *The Læce Bôc*, already mentioned, belongs to the tenth century, but others— *A Catalogue of Prescriptions*, *The School of Medicine*, and some collections of observations on the best times to take medicine, or to undertake businesses, on dreams and their interpretation, on the origin of diseases, on pregnant women, on spells and charms— full of strange and attractive superstitions, belong to this eleventh century. Another set of books—a prose *Dialogue between Salomo and Saturnus*, quite distinct from the prose pieces in the elder *Salomo and Saturnus*; another prose *Dialogue between Adrianus* (the Emperor Hadrian) *and Ritheus*; a translation of a selection from the *Disticha of Cato*—are examples of the ethical tendency which, even before Ælfred, had taken root in England. Among the religious books there is a *Translation of the Four Gospels* about the year 1000, a *Translation of Psalms* and of the *Pseudo-Gospels of Nicodemus* and *of Matthew*; some biographies, some translations from the *Lives of the Fathers*, certain legends of the saints, as, for example, of *Veronica* and *Margaret*, and a number of sermons. On the whole, these belong to the first half of the eleventh century. The *Glossaries* which appeared in this century, and in which the Latin is explained by English words, illustrate the new activity which Ælfric had infused into learning. Among these is the *Ritual of Durham*, with a Northumbrian gloss, a book precious to philologists. The magnificent MS. of the Gospels, the *Evangelium* adorned at Lindisfarne in honour of St. Cuthbert with pictures and illuminations by Eadfrith about the year 700, was now added to by an interlinear version, and the *Rushworth* Gospels were also interlineated. In this century also Leofric, Bishop of Exeter, gave to his cathedral library the *Leofric Missal*, now in the Bodleian. It is "one of the three surviving Missals known to have been used in the English Church during the Anglo-Saxon period."[1]

In this century the Danes had conquered England. Æthelred had died in 1016. With the battle of Assandun, where the golden dragon of Edmund Ironside met the magic raven of Cnut, Cnut finished what Swein had begun, and Edmund's death shortly afterwards left Cnut king of all England. His conquest settled rather than disturbed England. The land, from the Border to the south, was now under one king, and that king more an Englishman than a Dane. He ruled his other possessions from England; he actually sent English bishops and preachers to civilise his northern realms. He established Englishmen in all places of authority in England. The official language of England was the West Saxon. He renewed, confirmed, and publicly swore to Eadgar's laws. He protected and enriched the Church. Hence, during his reign, the new life of learning and literature in the monasteries and elsewhere went on undisturbed, and though Godwine, whom we find Ealdorman of Wessex in 1020, was always in opposition to the monks and never founded an abbey, this was not the temper of Leofric, Ealdorman of Mercia, or of the king, both of whom loved to see the abbeys flourish. The pleasant story which tells how Cnut, boating on the marshes near the knoll of Ely, heard the song of the monks and was charmed with it, shows at least how kindly he felt to those who made sweet music. And the lines he is said to have made are the only scrap of poetry which has come down to us from the traditions of his reign:[2]—

[1] *Leofric Missal*, edited by F. E. Warren, Clar. Press.
[2] Professor Stephens, however, assigns to the reign of Cnut the Lay of Abgar, King of Edessa, an Anglo-Saxon fragment taken from the legend of Abgar's letter to Christ praying the Healer to cure him of his illness.

>Merrily sing the monks of Ely
>When Cnut the King comes rowing by;
>Row nearer to the land, my men,
>That we may hear the good monks' song.

We must not omit in a history of literature the long and noble letter Cnut wrote from Rome to his people, in which, speaking as gravely and worthily as Ælfred of the duties of a king, he reveals the greatness of his character. He had begun his kingship with some of the savagery of his pirate ancestors, but he had now grown into a wise, careful, generous, godly prince and law-giver, open to strangers, just and kind to his people, a giver of gifts to knowledge and religion. He died in November 1035, and eight years after, Eadweard the Confessor came to the throne of England. He had been in Normandy, under the protection of its dukes, ever since 1014; and when he came to England he was Norman rather than English. He spoke the Norman tongue. His Norman kinsmen accompanied him; Norman knights crowded his court; Norman chaplains looked after his religious life. He made a Norman Archbishop of Canterbury, and set Normans up as bishops and rulers in many places.

The first result of this foreign invasion was the strengthening of Latin as the vehicle of learned writings in place of English. Ælfric, with all his kindness for his own tongue, had done with greater pleasure his Latin books. The *Chronicle* of Æthelweard was in Latin. Wulfstan, a pupil of Æthelwold and monk of Winchester, wrote his book *De tonorum harmonia* in Latin; and, to show his skill, translated into Latin hexameters a book which had been written by Lanferht, another Latin scholar — the *Miracula sancti Swithuni*. Thus in the first half of the eleventh century many Latin books were written, and the use of this tongue in monastic writings steadily increased. It is true that in Eadweard's reign, the national feeling which resented an alien king in Cnut grew stronger under the influence of Godwine and his family against the Norman foreigners, but the only English writings that this patriotic feeling produced were the *Annals of*

Worcester, afterwards carried on to 1079; and the new edition of the *Chronicle*, which, begun in 1046 at Abingdon, was continued to 1056; and which, after a few years of meagre reports, was taken up by one who wrote with warmth, vigour, even with passion, of the great deeds of Harold up to his victory at Stamford Bridge. The Worcester annals then resumed the tale and told of William and of Senlac. In this historical department English did not cease to maintain its lead. But elsewhere it decayed. Religious and scientific prose tended more and more to Latin, and the disuse of the English language as the vehicle of learning preluded that swiftly-coming time when the scholars who accompanied the Normans made Latin alone the tongue in which prose on any worthy subject was written.

The second result was that some of the elements out of which the romantic tale was to emerge came for the first time into England out of France. England had had her own sagas, but she had as yet known nothing of that new and chivalrous romance whose original basis was the delight in story-telling, but which built on that foundation a poetry and tales in which the leading conceptions of the Middle Ages were embodied, together with its arts, its science, its theology, its allegory, its love of women, of adventure, and of war. Already the Normans had begun to throw the stories of the East into new forms; already, following the great Frank sagas, they had made a new type of poetry in songs of Roland and of Charlemagne; but nothing of this could as yet take root in England; and it is a curious question whether, had the Normans been driven back by Harold, England would ever have taken to her heart the purely romantic ideas. She could not, however, have remained uninfluenced by France, and she was so influenced before the Conquest. The story of *Apollonius of Tyre*, the story Shakespeare used in the play of Pericles, had been translated into Latin from the late Greek romance, and the Latin translation was now rendered, sometimes word for word, sometimes freely, into the easy and lissome English which Ælfric had bequeathed to his countrymen. Our sole manuscript of this is unfortunately a fragment. But it must have awakened a new sense of pleasure in some English readers, so different it was in spirit, colour, and atmosphere from the Old English poetry and prose. It was followed by two other translations from the Latin which introduced for the first time the wonders of the Alexander romance to Englishmen. They were the *Letters of Alexander to Aristotle from India* and the *Wonders of the East*. Both are accurate translations, and done in excellent English. They are the last books, save the *Worcester Annals*, which were written in the literary language of Wessex. The breath of a new world was in them, new thought, new manners, a new way of living, a new imaginative range. I doubt whether the English priest or layman of Eadward's reign, whether even an educated warrior and king like Harold, would have read them without scorn. Before the English could accept, as long afterwards they did with eagerness, the romantic elements, all that made up their national life needed to undergo the weary education in learning, thought, literary form, love of poetic melody, in religion, in chivalric ideas, in the manners of war and peace, which the presence, influence, and pressure of the Norman drove into their national character. And the work took nearly two centuries to accomplish.

When it was finished England had become a nation, and a national literature was possible. Four national characters (the Anglo-Saxon, the Celt, the Dane, and the Norman with his French amalgam) mixed to make the beginnings, and to continue the life of that literature.

In the making and science of government, in establishing law and organising order; in consolidating a village, a town, a state; in the creation of freedom, in love of it, and in its development; in the founding of national life on the life of home; in the sense of duty; in the capacity of obedience to a leader; in holding together in unity; in the power and desire to sacrifice individual aims to a collective cause; in perseverance combined with endurance; in the splendid conduct of war; in a grim love of adventure; in constant and even passionate desire to discover new worlds, to seize them, develop them, and to extend itself over the world—the English national spirit excelled that of either the Celt or the Dane. These are powers which make, keep, and expand a vast and noble nation. But they do not of themselves make a great and varied literature such as England made at last. The Anglo-Saxon was capable, and alone, of good prose on all practical subjects, of excellent and accurate history, of practical works on science; of close criticism; of religious, moral, or philosophical discourse, touched often with a mystical, even an ideal quality; of a tender, deeply-felt religious poetry; of narrative poetry at disproportionate length; and he had a most natural and happy turn for popular love-songs. But alone, the Anglo-Saxon was quite incapable of producing the literature of England, and the excited persons who proclaim that he has done so cannot have looked into the facts of the matter. But two great and important things he did secure for us. By his dominance in all the qualities which make a free and settled national life, he secured, as a vehicle of literature, the English language—the most capable and flexible instrument for all kinds of literature which exists in the modern world. After a long struggle against French, during which it absorbed and made its own a large French vocabulary; after putting under contribution both the Dane and the Celt; the English tongue, enriched from many quarters, established itself as the most fitting means of representing the thoughts, emotions, and imaginative work of the mixed people of England.

But the greatest thing the Anglo-Saxon did for literature was a result of all those strong national powers of which we have spoken. They made a sure and steadfast foundation for all thought; they laid on all emotion a restraining, powerful, and directing hand, under which its fires ceased to blaze, but grew white-hot; they acted on all the work of the imagination so as to purify, chasten, educate, and guard it from extravagance. They did for English literature what training does for the runner. Again and again it ran wild, or ran into the exuberant weakness of luxury. Again and again the English national powers brought it back to the dignity, simplicity, and temperance of great Art. They have, from the beginning, passed through our literature as strength, penetrated it with the power of continuance, and, by their mastery, enabled it to assimilate and transmute within itself the excellences of other literatures into excellences of its own. It is quite fair, then, to call the literary result, not Celtic or Danish, French or Italian, but English. The dominant note in the literature of these islands is the English note.

There are other persons, not less excited than those who think English literature a purely Anglo-Saxon product, who derive all its excellences from the Celt; and this is as far apart from the truth as the opposite opinion. The Celt, by himself, is as incapable as the Anglo-Saxon of producing that magnificent and varied literature. But he brought to the growth of that great creation a number of elements without which it would never have become what it is. The spirit of the Celt was intimately mingled for long centuries with the spirit of the English, from home to home, from town to town, from county to county, over the north, west, and south-west of England, over the whole of the lowlands of Scotland; and even, by its admixture with the Danes, it influenced the eastern and midland counties of England. It brought with it into the English people, and wove into their nature and literature, a sad ideality; a penetrative and mystic imagination, especially pleased with, and naturally abiding in worlds beyond the senses; copious inventiveness; great love of melody and of its most subtle changes both in music and poetry; a fiery impulsiveness attended by a swift reaction into depression; a root of cherished and romantic melancholy; a passionate love of women; a fury of adventure in war and love; a dreamy union with the life of nature; a love of nature for her own sake; a great power of animating inanimate things, of filling the whole world with life, and of quick-shaping into form what was felt and thought; a satiric vein which tended to be savage in expression and reckless of fact; a capacity for self-mockery;

a recklessness all round of the present and especially of the future; a complete carelessness of the conventional; a fierce and claiming individuality which in politics disliked law, and in literature became a creative but far too great a self-consciousness; a general inattentiveness to criticism, whether good or bad; a feeling as of one belonging to another world and half lost in this, that there was nothing in this earth worth much trouble, much work, or much intensity. Certain of these elements, and especially the two last mentioned, kept the Celt from that close study of the great models, that hard work and perseverance, that boundless humility before the ideal of beauty, that rigid rejection of the unnecessary, that resolution to possess, in whatever is done, great matter of thought as well as depth of emotion—which are necessary for the attainment of perfect form in artistic work. It was not till his powers were mixed with those of the English that this was attained. Unmixed, they have not produced work of the finest kind in either prose or poetry. The Celtic literature, alone, weakened down into poverty-stricken or over-luxuriant expression. Alone, the Celt would have been as incapable, as the Anglo-Saxon was alone, of producing the English literature. But the powers the Celtic nature brought to mingle with the Anglo-Saxon nature were of the highest value for every class of poetry, for the melody of poetry, for its lyric changes, and for its inventive and subtle rhythms. A host of our rhythms are derived from Irish metres, sometimes directly, sometimes passed through France, sometimes through Italy, sometimes through Latin hymns. To these powers our literature owes also much of its fanciful charm, its love of adventurous life, legend and faery, its quaint or magical surprises; its self-conscious melancholy, its satiric laughter; its lavish use at times of colour; its love of nature and of lonely life with nature; its impersonation, with inventive detail, of both the monstrous and the graceful powers of nature.

The Celtic elements did nearly as much for prose. They gave to English prose its natural movement, its subtlety, its mystery, sadness, mockery, and colour. Stealing down, from generation to generation, into the Anglo-Saxon people, these powers made their way, till they were intimately inwoven into the Anglo-Saxon powers; and these in turn gave the Celtic powers the force, the intensity, the tenderness, the moral energy, the perseverance, the solemnity, the serious humanity they needed for permanent and finished art. Separately, the Celtic or the Anglo-Saxon powers would have been inadequate to create English literature. Together they made it, and together they were adequate for its creation. There is no mixture in the world so good for the best work in poetry and in prose as the mixture of the Celtic and the Teutonic spirit. And the mixture, slowly made, like all natural mixtures destined for fine and lasting use, was complete. The attempts made by English and Irish nationalists who are literary critics to seclude what is Celtic or what is Anglo-Saxon in English literature, are curiously futile. There is no product of English poetry or prose in which Anglo-Saxon and Celtic elements are not closely and fervently mixed, and the proportions of each series of elements in any literary work vary indefinitely. Those books are best in which the admixture is most equalised throughout; and when the admixture is most unequal the book is, as literature, not so good as it might otherwise have been. And this is as true of phases and transient outbursts, as it is of periods, in English literature. At no time was early English literature freed from Celtic influence except perhaps during its revival in Wessex under Ælfred, Ælfric, and the rest, a revival marked by absence of imaginative work and by a swift decay. The Northumbrian literature before Ælfred arose in lands deeply imbued with Celtic thought and feeling. When the Danes settled in England, their literature, both of saga and of religious myth, had been strongly influenced and changed by the Celtic. When the Normans came, the lays of Roland and Charlemagne did not enter with any energy into the literature of England. Of all the romantic cycles it least interested England. The cycle which emerged first, and was most developed in England, and which has clung to the heart of English literature up to the present day is of Celtic origin; and steeped, through all its French, German, and English developments, in the Celtic spirit. It was brought by the Normans from Brittany, ministered to from its source when the Normans conquered South Wales; and finally, in the resurrection of English literature at the beginning of the thirteenth century, established a Celtic tale at the head of the literature of England.

But English literature is not the result only of the Anglo-Saxon and the Celtic spirit. Like those atomic compounds which are formed by the addition to their two main elements of a number of other elements in much smaller proportions, English literature added to itself Danish, Norse, Norman, French, Italian, Spanish, Hebrew, and Oriental elements; and owing to its incessant and adventurous pushing into all parts of the world, took into itself a host of heterogeneous matters which mixed with it from time to time, and then ceased their slight and transient impulse.

The Dane and Norseman, both of whom made and cherished a well-ordered literary class, brought to English literature their sagas, both mythical and historical, and a passionate love for recording in long stories the mighty deeds of war-leaders who grew into mythical heroes. They not only told the tales of their own folk, but their energy revivified, by absorbing them, the stories of the countries they invaded. Where the Viking came, life came; and this intensity of life not only animated the folk-tales of their conquered lands into resurrection, but added them to its own, and then changed and developed them into a varied host of adventurous narratives.

We cannot trace before the Norman conquest this influence of the Norseman and the Dane on English literature. But no one can doubt that the vital strength added to the large portion of England occupied by the Danes had its potent influence on the growth and work of English literature. But I have already said—and it shows how complicated is the inquiry here sketched—that by the time the Danes had settled in England the elements in their literary production had been closely mingled with Celtic elements. The Danish contribution to the soil of English literature was therefore almost as much a mixture of Celtic and Teutonic matter as English literature itself became.

Into this river of varied waters flowed the Norman stream. That literary stream itself was mingled of three other streams—of the original Norse; of the French (partly Gaulish and partly Latin); and of the Celt. All these, together with an Eastern strain, make up romance; and this, vitalised through every vein by the Norman energy, and enchanted by all the Celtic legend and spirit of Armorica and Wales, poured in full stream into the Anglo-Saxon and Celtic admixture, and for a century and a half dominated English literature. Along with it, the new Latin learning came into England with the Norman and added a great body of fine historical and theological thought to the soil in which English prose was afterwards to grow. Moreover, certain purely French elements—the *esprit Gaulois*, the audacious gaiety; the loose and lively tale of love; a gross wit; a strange mingling of sexual love with the love of Christ and the Virgin; a logical persistence, especially in theological argument; an additional affection for allegory, and a Latin love of philosophy, entered English literature, but took no deep root therein.

What other influences added themselves afterwards to the stream of English literature; how the Italian waters poured into it; how other and varied streams came from France; how Spain, Italy, Germany, and France again and again brought novel and animating impulses into its ever-increasing river, but were in all cases not reproduced in English literature, till they had been digested, absorbed and changed into individual English waters, is not the work of this book; but whatever changes took place, whatever new stuff was added to the river, the main mass of it, out of which English literature grew, both poetry and prose, was the Anglo-Saxon and the Celtic admixture which began to be made in the sixth century, and which has never ceased to swell in volume and mingle its waters more and more up to the present day.

CHAPTER XVIII

THE PASSING OF OLD ENGLISH

THE Norman conquest put to the sword what was left in Wessex of English literature. What was left was not indeed worth preserving. It was as barren and unimaginative as a desert. But though sorely wounded, English literature was not slain. It rested, retired from the world, in country villages, in secluded monasteries, slowly gathering strength, assimilating fresh influences, until Norman and English were woven politically into one people; and then it raised its comely head, and stepped forth into activity again. The Norman accepted it as his own, and chose its language for his literary work. But when English became again the tongue of literature, it was no longer the same in form as it had been when the *Song of Maldon* and the *Homilies* of Ælfric were written. It was so changed that we call it by the new term of Middle English. It was even more changed in thought and feeling, in the direction and form of the subjects of its literature. Its prose, which was almost entirely religious, had been transfigured by the Norman theology and religious enthusiasm. The romantic impulse, bringing with it new melodies, new metres, new grace and sweetness, had mastered and changed its poetry. The Teutonic elements remained as its foundation, but they were chiefly elements of national character. They coloured with a manly roughness, a passion for freedom and home, and a moral intensity, the translations of French romances. They produced also in the middle of the fourteenth century a reversion to the old English forms of poetical expression. As to the Celtic elements, they passed through the Norman romance and were dominant in the first literary effort of Middle English —in the *Brut* of Layamon, with which, about 1205, the new English story-telling begins.

There was then a transition period during which some English prose and verse existed; but none of its work, with the exception perhaps of the continuation of the *Chronicle*, can be given the name of literature. A brief account of this transition will fitly close this book.

The most important remnant of Old English prose after the Conquest is the *English Chronicle*. The *Winchester Annals*, which form the Parker manuscript of the *Chronicle*, cease to be written in English in the year 1070. They had been preserved in Canterbury since 1005, but the entries between 1005 and 1070 only number eleven, and are short statements of local events. They were made at the election of Lanfranc to the Archbishopric. The rest of these annals is written in Latin, and they close with the consecration of Anselm.

The *Worcester Annals*, on the contrary, were carefully kept up in English to the year 1079. They were probably continued up to 1107, but this continuation was merged, it is supposed, in the *Annals of Peterborough*. Their English is still the English of Ælfric, the standard English of Wessex. Their concluding portion was most likely written by Wulfstan, who held the See of Worcester from 1062 to 1095. His chaplain, Colman, assisted him in this work. Wulfstan, a man of learning, wisdom, and fine character, held fast, amid the scoffing Normans, to his own people and his own tongue; and Colman, called to write his patron's biography, wrote it in a fine English, which it is interesting to know was praised by William of Malmesbury.

The *Peterborough Annals*, which completed the work of Worcester, were of little worth until after the burning of the monastery in 1116. When the minster was rebuilt in 1121 a full edition of them was undertaken. The Annals of

Winchester, Worcester, and Abingdon were used in this edition, A full *English Chronicle* was thus put together, and continued, probably by one hand, to the year 1131. Another hand, using a more modern English, carried on the record from 1132 to 1154, when, with the accession of Henry II., the *English Chronicle* ceased to exist. It began at Winchester; it ended at Peterborough. Nor is its latest work at Worcester and Peterborough unworthy of its royal beginning. The hand that wrote the wars of Harold and the fight at Stamford Bridge is not so bold nor so versed in public affairs as his who pictured the wars of Ælfred with the Danes, or his who with a more practised and sturdier pen recorded from 910 to 924 the mighty doings of King Eadweard. But a breath of the ancient and steadfast power of writing still inhabits it. After the Conquest the stark force of William seems to drive the writer into abundant and picturesque records; he paints with sympathy the miseries of the land, and he draws the aspect and character of William—for he had known him and lived at his court—with a mastery and an absence of prejudice which has been justly praised. It is plain that this writer has studied the Norman historians, for his work is fuller of detail, more varied in the subjects chosen, more interspersed with illustrative anecdote, more fluent, than that grave, dignified, condensed writing of the *Chronicle* of the ninth and tenth centuries, which was disdainful of ornament, concerned about fact, but not about form and style. This writer shapes each reign into a whole, the centre light of which is the King and the condition of England under his government. He is followed by the first Peterborough writer, who, though he tells the story of the land and people, is rather a romantic than a national historian. His interest in the Church is greater than his interest in the nation; his interest in his own monastery greater than his interest in the Church. We may think of him as living in retirement from the world, and gathering from visitors and travellers the stories which enliven his pages. At no time does he write so well as when he tells, with sincere and pleasant affection and pity, the history and misfortunes of his own monastery.

The second writer of Peterborough, writing most probably in 1150-54, begins his work from the year 1132. His vigorous and compassionate account of the lawlessness and cruelty of the nobles and of the dreadful misery of England under the rule of Stephen is lifted into a semblance at least of fine literature by the pathetic passion of an oppressed people which breathes and burns in its pitiful sentences. The story of Stephen is the last which the *Chronicle* tells. This ancient and venerable monument of English prose gave way to the Norman historians, who had now begun to take a vital, even an English, interest in the country their Dukes had conquered.

In other monasteries than Worcester and Peterborough English prose was written during the twelfth century, but it was not original work. Invention, creation of any kind whatever, has passed away from English prose. The old books, chiefly those of Ælfric and Ælfred, were read, copied and reverenced. There was re-editing, but no making of books. The *Homilies* of Ælfric were frequently copied, and the people still heard from them in their own tongue the tales of the English saints and martyrs and the praise of their great kings in a prose which kept the rhythm and the manner of their old poetry alive. The *Hatton Gospels* of this century are a new setting forth in modernised language of the *Translation of the Gospels* made in the eleventh century. The *Rule of St. Benedict* was rewritten in the monastery of Wiveney. The *Herbarium Apuleii*, with illustrations, was recopied, with new English explanations of the words. The English *Herbarium*, whose appearance in the last century has been mentioned, was re-edited with several changes. A *Leech Book*, which opens with a preface—"Concerning the Schools of Medicine"—was made out of the older books of the same kind, and closes the prose activity of the twelfth century. All we can then say is that the monks, in those monasteries which were not Normanised, were the preservers of the old tongue, and continued its use in their annals, their religious and their medical manuals. Moreover, the monasteries kept their titles and charters in Anglo-Saxon, and were obliged during this century to recopy them and modernise their language. Earle speaks of the fresh importance given to these charters under the strict Norman law which rested its decisions so much on documentary evidence, and he quotes from Matthew Parker's edition of *Asser*, 1574, to prove that even in Elizabeth's time it was the habit of the monastic fraternities for some of their number to master Old English, that they might understand the legal documents, the venerable memorials, and the royal charters of their several monasteries. Thus English prose was kept alive, but its life resembled the life of those legendary men who are buried, having eaten a root which suspends life, in the hope of a far-off revival. It did revive, but even after its resurrection it was long before it reached an active or a creative life. And when it revived, it spoke no longer in the way it spoke of old. Its language was not that which Ælfred and Ælfric wrote. It was Middle English.

These remnants of prose, together with a little poetry of which we are now to speak, prove that after 1066 and during the twelfth century, English, in spite of the tyranny of the French tongue, continued its struggle for the victory which it finally won. Like the troops at Waterloo, it did not know when it was beaten. An onlooker, in the last years of the eleventh century, would have thought that English was doomed as a literary language. The court knew no tongue but French. In the castles, in the rich monasteries, the nobles and the learned ecclesiastics spoke only French. Their songs, their romances, their religious books were in French. What was written in theology, in history, in science, was in Latin. But the people of the towns, the villagers round the castles, the parish priest, the wandering minstrel, the monks in those remoter and poorer houses of God which did not engage the greed of the invader; a few learned ecclesiastics like Wulfstan of Worcester who loved the old times; the outlaw in the forest land, and bands of men like Hereward's troop; all men who still hoped to free their country—held fast not only to the old English hand-books of religion in prose, but even more closely to the ancient songs and sagas of England.

The songs which enshrined the glories of the past of England, from the time of Ealdhelm down to the Confessor, were sung openly and commonly in the streets of the towns, in the village fairs, in the English franklin's hall, at the bivouac in the wood or in the fen. William of Malmesbury speaks of those that were common in his time. Henry of Huntingdon used them in his *Chronicle*. Layamon embodied some of them in his *Brut*. Then, too, new songs were made in English whenever a battle was fought, and many belong to the rebellion of the North against the Conqueror. The great deeds of Hereward in the eleventh century were the subject of popular lays. The Latin book—*Gesta Herewardi Saxonis*—which probably dates from the twelfth century, claims as its authority a history of Hereward's youth written by Leofric, his priest. This book is partly made up out of heroic songs, some of which may have been composed by Hereward himself.

The ancient sagas also survived. *Beowulf* may still have been sung from hall to hall. The saga of Weland, always a native English saga, never died out of memory. The local tradition concerning Wayland's smithy in Berkshire shows—since it has no connection with anything in Anglo-Saxon poetry—that many English legends collected round this famous smith, and were continuous in the folk-songs of England. And we need not doubt that other lays and sagas belonging to the Teutonic heroes of myth and legend were kept in the mouths of the people, even in the twelfth century. The Middle English poem of Wada, Weland's father, which Chaucer mentions, and a few lines of which have been lately found quoted in a homily, was based, Ten Brink thinks, on songs which were in existence in the twelfth century. The ancient *Charms and Spells*, sung like nursery rhymes in every English home, retained in memory the character of the old English gods, even the names of some of them; and it is quite possible that the change of Woden into Robin Goodfellow began in folk-ballads of the twelfth century. The same may be said of the creation, out of the deeds of the many leaders of outlaw bands whom popular wrath with the Norman nobles and the dreadful game-laws made into heroic characters, of that one representative of what was best in them all, which has come down to us in the saga, as we may fairly call it, of Robin Hood. It is also probable that stories arising out of English and Danish connections, such as those sagas of *Horn* and *Havelok* which took an original English form in the thirteenth century, existed as popular lays in the eleventh and twelfth centuries, and were sung by the gleemen over England wherever the Danish colonists were thickly clustered. And the distinctly English sagas of *Bevis of Hampton*, *Guy of Warwick* and *Waltheof*, popular local heroes whose stories the Anglo-Normans put into French verse, may also have been well known in English lays of the twelfth century.

Of the existence of these English lays we may fairly conjecture, but we know nothing of those which must have been sung in the North, over the wide hill-lands where English was spoken, between Yorkshire and the Clyde and the Forth by a people partly English in descent, partly Danish, partly Celtic, with intermixtures of Pictish and other unknown elements. From this country came in after-centuries the greater number of the ballads which add so passionate, so archaic, so weird, so tender and so savage an element to English poetry. They began, I believe, in ancient days; they retain Neolithic, Celtic, Scandinavian remnants of thought and feeling, but they took their happy form in the English language, spoken all over this trackless waste of mountain and of moor.

Amid all these heroic phantoms, dimly seen through the mist, one figure shines clear; and his image is handed down to us in an ethical poem, varying forms of which arose in the twelfth century. We possess it in a manuscript of the thirteenth. This is a collection of sententious sayings attributed to King Ælfred, the *Proverbs of Ælfred*, and the introduction to the poem takes a form which is almost legendary. "Thegns, bishops and wise book-men sat at Seaford, proud earls and warriors. Earl Ælfrich was there, who well knew the laws, and Ælfred, shepherd of the English, Englishmen's darling, King in England. And he began to teach, as ye may hear, how they should lead their life. He was a strong king, and clerk, and he loved well the work of God; wise in word and far-seeing in deed; the wisest man in England." The verses which follow record in separate divisions the sage sayings of the King, and each division begins with the words—"Thus quoth Ælfred." The things spoken of suit the character of Ælfred, and may well have been compiled from his works and from traditions concerning him. They have no literary value, but they illustrate the transition from the old alliterative metre to the short line, which was so soon to invade English poetry from France. Rhyme, even the rhyming couplet, has stolen in. We are on the verge of a new world.

In the *Poema Morale*, which, with two *Discourses of the soul to the body*, forms the beginning of English religious poetry in the twelfth century, the change has made further progress, and, indeed, has gone so far in rhythm, in alteration of accent, in the use of the end-rhyme, in the new form the writer gives to old English religious matter, that we can scarcely say that it belongs to Old English poetry. This, and another twelfth-century poem, the *Paternoster*—a poetical expansion of the Lord's Prayer, written in a short rhyming couplet, less English and more French in form than the *Poema Morale*—are the prologue to, if they may not even be called a part of, that Middle English poetry which drew its new elements from the Normans and their French relationships in literature, both northern and Provençal; which when it seized on the subjects of romance, curiously preferred—and the preference has been carried on through English literature into the poetry of the nineteenth century—the Celtic to the Teutonic traditions as the subject-matter of its verse.

APPENDIX

THE STORM ON LAND
Riddle II

WHO so wary and so wise of the warriors lives,
That he dare declare who doth drive me on my way,
When I start up in my strength! Oft in stormy wrath,
Hugely then I thunder, tear along in gusts,
Fare above the floor of earth, burn the folk-halls down,
Ravage all the rooms! Then the reek ariseth
Gray above the gables! Great on earth the din,
And the slaughter-qualm of men. Then I shake the woodland,
Forests rich in fruit; then I fell the trees;—
I with water over-vaulted—by the wondrous Powers
Sent upon my way, far and wide to drive along!
On my back I carry that which covered once
All the tribes of Earth's indwellers, spirits and all flesh,
In the sand together! Say who shuts me in,
Or what is my name—I who bear this burden!

THE STORM ON SEA
Riddle III

WHILES, my way I take, how men ween it not,
Under seething of the surges, seeking out the earth,
Ocean's deep abyss: all a-stirred the sea is.
Urged the flood is then, whirled the foam on high,
Fiercely wails the whale-mere, wrathful roars aloud;
Beat the sea-streams on the shore, shooting momently on high
Upon the soaring cliffs, with the sand and stones,
With the weed and wave. But I, warring on,
Shrouded with the ocean's mass, stir into the earth
Into vasty sea-grounds! From the water's helm
I may not on journey loose me, ere he let me go

Who my master is.—Say, O man of thought,
Who may draw me (like a sword) from the bosomed depths of ocean,
When the streams again on the sea are still,
And the surges silent that shrouded me before?

THE HURRICANE

Riddle IV

OFTENTIMES my Wielder weighs me firmly down,
Then again he urges my immeasurable breast
Underneath the fruitful fields, forces me to rest.
Drives me down to darkness, me, the doughty warrior,
Pins me down in prison, where upon my back
Sits the Earth, my jailor. No escape have I
From that savage sorrow—but I mightily shake then
Heirships old of heroes! Totter then the hornèd halls,
Village-steads of men; all the walls are rocking
High above the house-wards. . . .
      . . . Calm abideth,
O'er the land, the lift; lullèd is the sea;
Till that I from thraldom outwards thrust my way,
Howsoe'er He leads me on, who had laid of old
At creation's dawning wreathen chains on me,
With their braces, with their bands, that I might not bend me
Out of his great Power who points me out my paths.
Sometimes shall I, from above, make the surges seethe
Stir up the sea-streamings, and to shore crush on
Gray as flint, the flood; foaming fighteth then
'Gainst the wall of rock, the wave! Wan ariseth now
O'er the deep a mountain-down; darkening on its track
Follows on another, with all ocean blended.
Till they (now commingled) near the mark of land and sea
Meet the lofty linches. Loud is then the Sea-wood,
Loud the seamen's shout. But the stony cliffs,
Rising steep, in stillness wait of the sea the onset,
Battle-whirl of billows, when the high upbreak of water
Crashes on the cliffs. In the Keel is dread expecting,
With despairing striving, lest the sea should bear it
Full of living ghosts on to that grim hour (of death);
So that of its steering power it should be bereft;
And of living crew forfoughten, foaming drift away
On the shoulders of the surges. Then is shown to men
Many of the terrors there of Those I must obey—

I upon the storm-path strong! Who makes me be still?
Whiles, I rush along thorough that which rides my back,
Vats of water black: wide asunder do I thrust them
Full of lakes of rain; then again I let them
Glide together. Greatest that is of all sounds,
Of all tumults over towns; and of thunderings the loudest,
When one stormy shower rattles sharp against another,
Sword against a sword. See, the swarthy shapes,
Forward pressing o'er the peoples, sweat their fire forth;
Flaring is the flashing! Onward fare the thunders,
Gloomed, above the multitudes, with a mickle din;
Fighting fling along; and let fall adown
Swarthy sap of showers sounding from their breast,
Waters from their womb. Waging war they go,
Grisly troop on troop; Terror rises up!
Mickle is the misery 'mid the kin of men;
In the burgs is panic when the Phantom pale
Shoots with his sharp weapons, stalking (through the sky).
Then the dullard does not dread him of the deadly spears;
Nathless shall he surely die, if the soothfast Lord
Right against him, through the rain-cloud,
From the upper thunder, let the arrow fly—
Dart that fareth fast! Few are they that 'scape
Whom the spear doth strike of the Spirit of the rain.
I beginning make of this gruesome war
When I rush on high 'mid the roaring shock of clouds,
Through their thundering throng to press, with a triumph great,
O'er the breast of torrents! Bursts out with a roar
The high congregated cloud-band.
      Then my crest again I bow,
Low the lift-helm under, to the land anearer;
And I heap upon my back that I have to bear,
By the might commanded of my mastering Lord.

So do I, a strongful servant, often strive in war!
Sometimes under earth am I; then again I must
Stoop beneath the surges deep; then above the surface sea
Stir to storm its streams. Then I soar on high,
Whirl the wind-drift of the clouds. Far and wide I go,
Swift and strong (for joy). Say what I am called,
Or who lifts me up to life, when I may no longer rest;
Or who it is that stays me, when I'm still again.

SEAFARER

The Old Man—

SOOTH the song that I of myself can sing,
Telling of my travels; how in troublous days,
Hours of hardship oft I've borne!
With a bitter breast-care I have been abiding:
Many seats of sorrow in my ship have known!
Frightful was the whirl of waves, when it was my part
Narrow watch at night to keep, on my vessel's prow
When it rushed the rocks along. By the rigid cold
Fast my feet were pinched, fettered by the frost,
By the chains of cold. Care was sighing then
Hot my heart around; hunger rent to shreds within
Courage in me, me sea-wearied! This the man knows not,
He to whom it happens happiest on earth,
How I, carked with care, on the ice-cold sea,
Overwent the winter on my wander-ways,
All forlorn of happiness, all bereft of loving kinsmen,
Hung about with icicles: flew the hail in showers.
Nothing heard I there save the howling of the sea,
And the ice-chilled billow, whiles the crying of the swan!
All the glee I got me was the gannet's scream,
And the swoughing of the seal, 'stead of mirth of men;
'Stead of the mead-drinking, moaning of the sea-mew.
There the storms smote on the crags, there the swallow of the sea
Answered to them, icy-plumed; and that answer oft the earn—
Wet his wings were—barked aloud.
                      . . . None of all my kinsmen
Could this sorrow-laden soul stir to any joy.
Little then does he believe who life's pleasure owns,
While he tarried in the towns, and but trifling balefulness,—
Proud and insolent with wine—how out-wearied I
Often must outstay on the ocean path!
Sombre grew the shade of night, and it snowed from nor'rard,
Frost the field enchained, fell the hail on earth,
Coldest of all corns.

Young Man—
                      Wherefore now then crash together
Thoughts my soul within that I should myself adventure

The high streamings of the sea, and the sport of the salt waves!
For a passion of the mind every moment pricks me on
All my life to set a-faring ; so that far from hence
I may seek the shore of the strange outlanders.

Old Man—

Yes, so haughty of his heart is no hero on the earth,
Nor so good in all his giving, nor so generous in youth,
Nor so daring in his deeds, nor so dear unto his lord,
That he has not always yearning unto his sea-faring,
To whatever work his Lord may have will to make for him.
For the harp he has no heart, nor for having of the rings,
Nor in woman is his weal ; in the world he's no delight,
Nor in anything whatever save the tossing o'er the waves!
O for ever he has longing who is urged towards the sea.

Young Man—

Trees rebloom with blossoms, burghs are fair again,
Winsome are the wide plains, and the world is gay—
All doth only challenge the impassioned heart
Of his courage to the voyage, whosoever thus bethinks him,
O'er the ocean billows, far away to go.

Old Man—

Every cuckoo calls a warning, with his chant of sorrow!
Sings the summer's watchman, sorrow is he boding,
Bitter in the bosom's hoard. This the brave man wots not of,
Not the warrior rich in welfare—what the wanderer endures,
Who his paths of banishment widest places on the sea.

Young Man—

For behold, my thought hovers now above my heart;
O'er the surging flood of sea now my spirit flies,
O'er the homeland of the whale—hovers then afar
O'er the foldings of the earth! Now again it flies to me
Full of yearning, greedy! Yells that lonely flier ;
Whets upon the Whale-way irresistibly my heart,
O'er the storming of the seas!

THE WANDERER

Prologue

OFT a lonely wanderer wins at last to pity,
Wins the grace of God, though, begloomed with care,
He must o'er the water-ways, for a weary time,
Push the ice-cold ocean, oaring with his hands,
Wade through ways of banishment! For the weird is fully wrought.
Thus there quoth an Earth-stepper—of his troubles taking thought,
Of the fall of friendly kinsmen, of the fearful slaughters.

Oft I must alone, at each breaking of the day,
Here complain my care! Of the Quick there is not one
Unto whom I dare me now declare with openness
All my secret soul. Of a sooth, I know
That for any Earl excellent the habit is
That he closely bind all the casket of his soul,
Hold his hoard-coffer secure—but think in heart his will!
Never will the weary spirit stand the Wyrd against,
Nor the heart of heaviness for its help provide;
Therefore this unhappy heart oft do Honour-seekers
Closely bind and cover in the coffer of their breast.
So it happed that I—oft-unhappy me!
Far from friendly kinsmen, forced away from home—
Had to seal securely all my secret soul,
After that my Gold-friend, in the gone-by years,
Darkness of the earth bedecked! Dreary-hearted, from that time,
Went I, winter-wretched, o'er the woven waves of sea,
Searching, sorrow-smitten, for some Treasure-spender's hall,
Where, or far or near, I might find a man,
Who, amidst the mead-halls, might acquainted be with love,
Or to me the friendless fain would comfort give,
Pleasure me with pleasures. He who proves it, knows,
What a cruel comrade careful sorrow is to him,
Who in life but little store of loved forestanders has!
His the track of exile is, not the twisted gold,
His the frozen bosom, not the earth's fertility!
He the Hall remembers then, heroes, and the treasure-taking,
How of yore his Gold-friend, when he but a youngling was,

Customed him to festal days! Fallen is all that joy!
O too well he wots of this, who must long forego
All the lore-redes of his Lord, of his loved, his trusted friend,
Then when sleep and sorrow, set together at one time,
Often lay their bondage on the lonely wretched man.
And it seemeth him, in spirit, that he seeth his Man-lord,
Clippeth him and kisseth him; on his knees he layeth
Hands and head alike, as when he from hour to hour,
Erewhile, in the older days, did enjoy the gift-stool.
Then the friendless man forthwith doth awaken,
And he sees before him nought but fallow waves,
And sea-birds a-bathing, broadening out their plumes;
And the falling sleet and snow sifted through with hail—
Then the wounds of heart all the heavier are,
Sorely aching for One's-own! Ever new is pain.

For the memory of kinsmen o'er his mind is floating,
With glee-staves he greeteth them, gladly gazes on them—
These companionships of comrades swim away again!
Of the old familiar songs few the spirits bring
Of these floaters in the air. Fresh again is care
For the exile who must urge, often, oh how often,
O'er the welding of the waters his out-wearied heart!
Wherefore I must wonder in this world of ours
Why my soul should not shroud itself in blackness,
When about the life of earls I am wholly wrapt in thought,
How they in one instant gave their household up,
Mighty mooded thanes! So this middle-earth,
Day succeeding day, droops and falls away!

Wherefore no one may be wise till he weareth through
Share of winters in the world-realm. Patient must the wise man be,
Neither too hot-hearted, nor too hasty-worded,
Nor too weak of mind a warrior, nor too wanting in good heed,
Nor o'er-fearful, nor too glad, nor too greedy of possessions,
Never overfond of boasting till he throughly know himself.
Every son of man must wait ere he make a haughty vow
Till, however courage-hearted, he may know with certainty
Whither wills to turn its way the thought within his heart.

A grave man should grasp this thought—how ghostlike it is
When the welfare of this world all a-wasted is—

Just as now, most manifold, o'er this middle-garth,
Walls of burgs are standing by the breezes over-blown,
Covered thick with chill frost, and the courts decayed.
Wears to dust the wine-hall, and its Wielder lies
Dispossessed of pleasure. All the peers are fallen,
Stately by the ramparts! War hath ravished some away,
Led them on the forth-way; one the flying ship has borne
O'er high-heaving ocean—one the hoary wolf
Dragged to shreds when dead! Drear his cheek with tears,
One an earl has hidden deep in earthen hollow.

So the Maker of mankind hath this mid-earth desert made,
Till the ancient Ogres' work idle stood and void
Of its town-indwellers, stripped of all its joys.
Whoso then this Wall-stead wisely has thought over,
And this darkened Life deeply has considered,
Sage of soul within, oft remembers far away
Slaughters cruel and uncounted, and cries out this word,
"Whither went the horse, whither went the man? Whither
    went the Treasure-giver?
What befell the seats of feasting? Whither fled the joys in
    hall?
Ea la! the beaker bright! Ea la! the byrnied warriors!
Ea la! the people's pride! O how perished is that Time!
Veiled beneath night's helm it is, as if it ne'er had been!"

Left behind them, to this hour, by that host of heroes loved,
Stands the Wall, so wondrous high, with worm-images
    adorned!
Strength of ashen spears snatched away the earls,
Swords that for the slaughter hungered, and the <u>Wyrd</u>
    sublime!
See the storms are lashing on the stony ramparts;
Sweeping down, the snow-drift shuts up fast the earth—
Terror of the winter when it cometh wan!
Darkens then the dusk of night, driving from the nor'rard
Heavy drift of hail for the harm of heroes.

All is full of trouble, all this realm of earth!
Doom of <u>weirds</u> is changing all the world below the skies;
Here our fee is fleeting, here the friend is fleeting,
Fleeting here is man, fleeting is the woman,
All the earth's foundation is an idle thing become.

APPENDIX

Epilogue

So quoth the sage in his soul as he sat him apart at the runing.
Brave is the hero who holdeth his troth: nor shall he too hastily ever
Give voice to the woe in his breast, before he can work out its cure,
A chieftain, with courage to act! O well 'tis for him who comfort doth seek
And grace from the Father in Heaven, where the Fastness stands sure for us all.

GNOMIC VERSES

Cotton MS.

1. HE, the King, shall hold the Kingdom. Cities shall afar be seen;
Those that are upon this earth—artful works of giants,
Wondrous work of Wall-stones! Wind in air is swiftest,
Thunder on its path the loudest. Mighty are the powers of Christ!
Wyrd is strongest! Winter coldest,
Most hoar-frosts has Spring, it is cold the longest!
Summer is sun-loveliest; then the sky is hottest!
Autumn above all is glorious; unto men it brings
All the graining of the year God doth send to them.

13 Woe is wonderfully clinging. Onward wend the clouds;
Valiant comrades ever shall their youthful Ætheling
Bolden to the battle and the bracelet-giving!
Courage in the earl, sword-edge on the helm
Bide the battle through! On the cliff the hawk,
Wild, shall won at home. In the wood the wolf,
Wretched one, apart shall dwell; in the holt the boar,
Strong with strength of teeth, abides.

50. Good shall with evil, youth shall with eld,
Life shall with death, light shall with darkness,
Army with army, one foe with another,
Wrong against wrong—strive o'er the land,
Fight out their feud; and the wise man shall ever
Think on the strife of the world.

Exeter MS. (B.)

1. Frost shall freeze; fire melt wood,
Earth shall be growing, ice make a bridge,
The Water-helm bear, and lock wondrously up
The seedlings of earth. One shall unbind
The fetters of frost—God the Almighty.
Winter shall pass, fair weather return;
Summer is sun-hot, the sea is unstill.
The dead depth of ocean for ever is dark.

82. A king shall with cattle, with armlets and beakers,
Purchase his queen; and both, from the first,
With their gifts shall be free. The spirit of battle
Shall grow in the man, but the woman shall thrive,
Beloved, 'mid her folk; shall light-hearted live,
Counsel shall keep, shall large-hearted be!
With horses and treasure, and at giving of mead,
Everywhere, always—she shall earliest greet
The prince of the nobles, before his companions.
To the hand of her lord, the first cup of all
Straightway she shall give; and they both shall take rede,
House-owners, together.

126. Gold is befitting upon a man's sword;
Good victory-gear! Gems on a queen;
A good Scôp for men; for warriors the war-dart,
To hold in the fight the defences of home!
A shield for the striver, a shaft for the thief,
A ring for the bride, a book for the learner,
For holy men Housel, and ills for the heathen.

THE BATTLE OF MALDON[1]

HERE follows a literal translation of the Battle of Maldon. It has been made by Miss Kate Warren.

Then Byrhtnoth bade the men leave their horses, let them go, and turn to warfare, think on strength and good courage. Then Offa's kinsman found that the Earl would bear with no faint-heartedness.

---

[1] This translation only attempts to give the metrical effect of the original in the speeches of the warriors. The whole poem is, of course, in the short alliterative line.

So he let his well-loved hawk fly away from his hand to the wood, and strode to the battle. One might know, from that, that the youth would not fail in the fight when once he had taken his weapons. Eadric, too, would help his lord in the strife. He bore forth the spear to battle; he was bold of thought while he could hold the shield and broadsword in his hands. He made good his boasting when he had to fight before his lord.

Then Byrhtnoth began to put his men in array; he rode about and gave rede, he showed his warriors how they should stand and keep the field, and bade them hold their spears aright, fast in their hands, and fear nothing. When he had well arrayed his troop, then he alighted amid his people, where it most pleased him, where his most faithful hearth-companions [1] were.

Then on the other side of the shore stood the Vikings' herald, who shouted mighty words; boasting, he sent from the bank the message of the sea-farers to the earl :—

"Swift sea-rovers have sent me unto thee,
  Bade me say to thee—that thou must send us quickly
  Rings to ward us from you. And better 'twill be found
  To turn away with tribute the onset of the spear
  Than so dread a warfare to let us wage with you.
  No need there is for slaughter, if ye can but settle that:
  Firm the peace we'll make with you, if ye give the gold.
  If thou so resolvest—thou who here art ruler,—
  That thou wilt (this instant) set thy people free;
  Giving to the rovers whatsoe'er they may decree
  Of treasure for their friendship, taking from us peace :—
  We, then, with the booty, to our boats will turn again,
  And passing o'er the water keep a peace with you."

Then Byrhtnoth spake and raised his shield, waving his slender ashen spear he uttered words, ireful and steadfast, and gave him answer :—

"Wilt thou hear, O sailor, what this people say ?—
  Spears for their tribute will they give to you,
  The venom-tippèd point, and the ancient sword of war,
  Naught shall *that* battle gear bring to you in warfare !
  Herald of the seamen! Answer back again,
  Telling to thy people tidings yet more dreadful :
  That here an Earl of honour standeth with his host,
  Who, fearless, will defend this, our fatherland,

---

[1] *Heorð-werod*, lit. hearth-troop.

Kinsfolk and country, the realm of Æthelred—
Whom I own as lord. Low shall now the heathen
Sink to earth in warfare! Too shameful it meseemeth
That ye with our money should march away to sea
All unfought by us now ye so far hither,
Right to our own land, here within, are come.
Nor shall ye all so easily treasure gather in,
Spear-point and sword-edge shall bring us, first, together,
Grim shall be the game of war ere we give you tribute."

Then he bade the warriors go forward, bearing their shields, until they all stood on the river bank. Neither host could get at the other for the water; after the ebb had come the flowing flood-tide. The waters parted them,[1] and too long it seemed until their spears could meet. There they stood in array about the Panta stream, the East Saxons and the army from the ships, yet could neither harm the other, unless the arrows' flight should fell any one of them.

The flood-tide went out, the seamen stood ready, the crowd of Vikings eager for war. Then the lord of heroes bade a war-hardened warrior hold the bridge. He was named Wulfstan, and was son of Ceola, bold among his kinsmen. With his spear he struck down the first man who most hardily stepped on the bridge. Beside Wulfstan there stood fearless warriors, Ælfere and Maccus, a brave-mooded twain, who would never flee the ford, but steadfastly warded them against the foe as long as they could wield a weapon.

When the Vikings knew that, and surely saw that they had found the bridge-warders bitter, then those hateful strangers began to use their guile and asked that they might have passage, go across the ford with their troops. So the Earl in his disdain gave too much of the land to that hostile folk. Byrhthelm's son called to them across the cold water, and the men listened:—

"Now here is room for you, quickly come ye over,
Warriors unto warfare. God alone foreseeth
Which of us shall win upon the battle-field."

Then the slaughter-wolves went across, west over Panta, the Viking host recked not of the water. Over the shining water they bore their shields, the seamen bore their linden shields to land. Byrhtnoth and his men stood ready against the cruel foe; he bade his men make the war-hedge with their shields, and hold themselves firm against the foe.

[1] *Lucon lagustreamas*, or, perhaps, "the waters enclosed them."

Then drew nigh the fighting, the glory of strife; the time had come for the doomed to fall.

"Then a cry was raised, round the ravens flew,
And the eagle, carrion-greedy; there was shouting on the earth."

Then they let fly from their hands the sharp-filed javelin, the well-ground spear; the bows were busy, the shield caught the spear; bitter was the battle-rush, the warriors fell and the youths lay dead on every side. Wulfmær was wounded, he chose the bed of death; he was Byrhtnoth's kinsman, his sister's son; sorely was he hewn about with the bills. Then was given back payment to the Vikings. I heard that Edward struck down one mightily with his sword, he withheld not the blow, so that the doomed warrior fell at his feet. For that his lord gave thanks to his "bower-thegn"[1] when he found the time for it. So the strong-hearted men stood firm in the battle. They took thought who among them could first reach the life of the doomed, those warriors with weapons. The slain fell on the earth. They stood steadfast; Byrhtnoth urged them on, and bade every hero think on war, would he win glory from the Danes.

Then the Hard-in-war went forward, holding aloft his weapon, his sheltering shield, and strode towards a warrior. The steadfast Earl stepped up to the man—each thought on ill to the other. Then the seaman sent a southern[2] dart, wherewith the Lord of warriors was wounded. He then thrust with his shield, that the shaft burst asunder and the spear broke, so that it sprang back again. The warrior was enraged; with his spear he pierced the proud Viking who had dealt him the wound. Skilful was the hero; he drove his spear through the throat of the man; he guided his hand so that he reached the life of that scathing foe. Then quickly he shot another, which rent the byrnie asunder; the Viking was wounded in the breast through the woven rings, at his heart stood the venomous point. The Earl was the blither; the brave man laughed, gave his Maker thanks for the day's work that the Lord had given him. Then a certain warrior let a dart fly from his hands, from his fingers, so that it pierced the noble thegn of Æthelred. There stood beside him in the battle an unwaxen boy, the son of Wulfstan, the young Wulfmær, a youth in battle who full quickly drew the bloody dart from the man and let that sharp spear fly back again, so that its point drove in and he lay low on the earth who before had sorely struck his lord. Then an armed warrior went towards the Earl, he would seize the hero's bracelets, his armour, rings, and graven sword. So Byrhtnoth drew his bill from its sheath, broad

---

[1] *Burŝene*, attendant, retainer.
[2] *Southern* may perhaps mean *foreign*.

and brown-edged, and struck at his byrnie—too quickly one of the sea-folk hindered him when he maimed the Earl's arm. Then the fallow-hilted sword fell to earth, no more could he hold the sharp blade or wield the weapon. Yet still the hoary warrior spake words, heartened his men, bade his good comrades go forward. He then could stand no longer on his feet, he looked up to heaven :—

"To Thee I offer thanks, O Ruler of the peoples,
For all of the delightfulness I've found upon the earth.
Now, O Lord of mercy, utmost need have I
Grace upon my spirit that Thou grant me here;
So my soul in safety may soar away to Thee,
Into Thine own keeping, O Thou Prince of angels,
Passing hence in peacefulness. Now I pray of Thee
That the harming fiends of hell may not hurt my soul."

Then the heathen wretches hewed him down, and both the men who stood by him, Ælfnoth and Wulfmær, were brought low, when they gave up their life beside their lord. Then there turned from the battle those who would not bide the end. First in flight were the sons of Odda; Godric forsook the fight and left his lord who oft had given him many a steed. He leaped on the horse that had been his lord's, on those war-trappings, as was not right, and with him fled both his brothers Godric and Godwig. They recked nought of the battle but left the fight and sought the wood, fled to a fastness to save their life, and more men with them than was at all seemly had they been mindful of all the good things which he had done for them. Even so had Offa said, earlier in the day on the battlefield,[1] when he had held a meeting, that many there had spoken bravely who afterwards, when need was, would not bear it out.

Then the prince of the people, Æthelred's earl, had fallen; all his comrades saw that their lord lay dead. Then came forth proud thegns, uncowardly men hastened up eagerly, all of them would one of two things, either lose their life or avenge their lord. So the son of Ælfric cheered them forth; a warrior, young in winters, uttered words; bravely he spake, Ælfwine said :—

"Remember now the words which at mead we often spake,
When bold upon the bench we lifted up our boasting,
Warriors in the hall, about the warfare keen.
Now it can be tested who truly brave will be.

[1] This seems to be the most probable meaning of the passage "*on dæg ær asæde, on ðam mæðelstede,*" etc., though it may perhaps refer more indefinitely to a "certain day" some time before that of the battle.

> Here will I my lineage uphold before you all :—
> Among the Mercian kindred I come of noble race,
> Of my father's father, Ealdhelm was the name,
> Wise, an alderman, worldly-wealthy, too.
> Not among my tribesmen ever shall they twit me
> That *I* from this warfare wished to turn away,
> Wished to find my home, while my hero lieth
> Hewn adown in war—worst of all is that to me—
> He was both at once my kinsman and my lord."

Then he went forth, mindful of the feud, so that he struck one of the seamen with his spear that he lay dead on the earth, beaten down with his weapon. Then he urged his fellows and comrades to go forward.

Offa spake, and shook his ashen spear :—

> " Lo ! thou, Ælfwine, hast every one uprousèd,
> All the thegns at need. Now our leader's low,
> Our earl upon the earth, need is for us all
> That every man among us embolden should the other
> Warrior to the war, while he can his weapon
> Have in hand and hold, the hardened battle brand,
> Spear and goodly sword. All of us hath Godric,
> Cowardly son of Offa, utterly bewrayed.
> Many a man believed, as he the horse bestrode,
> (Haughty was the stallion,) him to be our lord ;
> So upon the battle-field the folk were scattered all ;
> Broken was the shield-wall ! Cursed be his deed,
> For that made he here so many a man to flee ! "

Leofsunu spake, upraised his linden-wood, his sheltering shield, and answered again that hero :—

> " Here I vow it truly, that never will I hence
> Flee away a foot's length, but will forward go,
> Avenging in the battle my beloved lord.
> Neither round the Stourmere need the sturdy heroes
> Flout me in their words now my friend has fallen,
> That from here I, lordless, homeward have returned,
> Wending from the warfare ; but weapons shall me slay,
> Spear and iron sword ! "

Full irefully he strode forth, and fought steadfastly, far too proud for flight.

Then Dunnere spake, an aged man,[1] he shook his spear and called over them all, bidding every hero revenge Byrhtnoth :—

"Now he may not linger, nor be mindful of his life,
Who meaneth here his lord to avenge upon this folk."

Then they went forward, recked nothing of life; the Earl's men fought hardily, raging spear-bearers, and besought God that they might avenge their beloved lord and work ruin on their foes. And the hostage helped them, he was of a bold kindred in Northumbria, the son of Ecglaf, and his name was Æscferth. He never flinched in the war play, but often drove the arrow forth; sometimes he shot on a shield, sometimes he wounded a man; ever from time to time he gave a wound to some one, as long as he could wield a weapon. Still in the front stood Edward the Long, alert and eager, and spake boasting words that he would not flee a foot's space of the land or turn backward while his Better[2] lay there dead. He broke the shield-wall and fought the warriors until he had worthily avenged his Treasure-giver on those seamen, ere he lay dead on the field. So also did Etheric, a noble comrade, ready and eager in the fray, very zealously he fought, that brother of Sibyrht, and many another too, who clove the hollow shield and warded them boldly. The shield rim was shattered and the byrnie sang a gruesome song. Then in the battle Offa struck a seaman, so that he fell to earth, and there Gad's kinsman sought the ground. Soon was Offa hewn down in the fight, yet he had fulfilled what he promised his lord when he had boasted before to his Ring-giver that they should both together ride into the burg, unhurt, to their home, or fall in the battle, die of wounds on the slaughter-field. Thegn-like he lay dead near his lord.

Then was there clashing of shields; the seamen strode forth, ireful in war. The spear often drove through the life-house of the doomed. Then Wistan went forth, the son of Thurstan, he fought with those warriors, he was the slayer of three in the throng ere he, the son of Wigeline, lay dead on the field. There was fierce encounter; firm stood the warriors in the strife, the heroes sank down, weary with wounds; the slain fell on the earth. Both the brothers, Oswald and Ealdwold, all the time encouraged the men, besought their dear kinsmen to bear up in time of need and use their weapons strongly. Byrhtwold spake, upraised his shield, shook his spear, he was an aged comrade; full boldly he urged on the heroes :—

"The mind must be the firmer, the heart must be the keener,
The mood must be the bolder, as our might lesseneth.

[1] *Ceorl.* [2] *Betera*—i.e. of course, his lord, Byrhtnoth.

Here our Lord lieth, all to pieces hewn,
Goodly on the ground. Ever may he grieve
Whoso from this war-play thinketh now to wend.
I am old in years, never hence will I,
But here, I, by the side of my well-beloved lord,
By the man so dear, mean in death to lie."

So also Godric, the son of Æthelgar, emboldened them all to the fighting. Often he let the dart forth, the slaughter spear fly among the Vikings, as he went foremost amid his folk. He hewed down and laid them low until he sank in the battle. That was not the Godric who fled from the fight . .

BIBLIOGRAPHY

POETRY

I. The Manuscripts

1. **Beowulf.**
   The MS. is in the Cottonian Library in the British Museum (Codex Vitellius, A. xv.). It is a parchment codex in quarto, and was probably written in the tenth century. Two handwritings may be detected in it; one goes to the middle of l. 1939; the other, a less skilful handwriting, runs on to the end. The MS. was originally kept in Deans Yard, Westminster, and was slightly injured in the fire which, in 1731, destroyed so many MSS. In 1753, having spent some time in the old dormitory at Westminster, it was transferred to the British Museum. Wanley, employed by Hickes, the Anglo-Saxon scholar, to make a catalogue of the old northern books in the kingdom, first drew attention to this MS. in 1705, and called it a *tractatus nobilissimus poetice scriptus*. Grímr. Jónsson Thorkelin, an Icelandic scholar, had two copies made of it in 1786, and published the whole of it for the first time in 1815. Through this edition the poem became known in England, Germany, and Denmark. But Sharon Turner gave the first account of it in 1805. In 1833 (2nd edition, 1835) John M. Kemble issued a complete edition of the text of Beowulf, and in 1837 translated the whole of it into English.
   The Beowulf MS. contains also the poem of *Judith*.

2. **The Exeter Book** (Codex Exoniensis).
   This MS. formed part of the library which Leofric, the first Bishop of Exeter, left to his Cathedral Church in 1071. He catalogued it himself as a *mycel Englise boc be gehwilcum pingum on leodwisan geworht:* "A mickle English book on all kinds of things wrought in verse." It is still kept in Exeter

Cathedral. It has lost the first seven pages, and the eighth has suffered sorely, as well as the last page. The handwriting is clear, and is of the beginning of the eleventh century; it was probably written by a single hand. It was first mentioned in Wanley's Catalogue in 1705. It contains a varied anthology of poems in the following order: 1. The Christ. 2. Guthlac. 3. Azarias. 4. Phœnix. 5. Juliana. 6. Wanderer. 7. Gifts of Men. 8. The Father's Teaching. 9. Seafarer. 10. Spirit of Men. 11. Widsið (The Singer's Wandering). 12. Fates of Men. 13. Gnomic Verses. 14. Wonders of Creation. 15. Rhyme Song. 16. Panther. 17. Whale. 18. Partridge. 19. Address of the Soul to the Body. 20. Deor (The Singer's Consolation). 21. Riddles, 1-60. 22. The Wife's Complaint. 23. The Last Judgment. 24. A Prayer. 25. Descent into Hell. 26. Alms. 27. Pharaoh. 28. Fragments of a Paternoster. 29. Fragment of a Didactic Poem. 30. Another Form of Riddle 31, and Riddle 61. 31. The Husband's Message. 32. The Ruin. 33. Riddles, 62-89.

3. **The Vercelli Book** (Codex Vercellensis).

This is a large MS. volume of Anglo-Saxon homilies, among which are interspersed six poems. It was discovered in 1822, at Vercelli, in North Italy, by a German scholar, Dr. Blum. The handwriting is of the eleventh century, and the poems contained in this MS. are: 1. The Andreas. 2. Fates of the Apostles. 3. Address of the Soul to the Body. 4. Falseness of Men (a fragment). 5. Dream of the Rood. 6. Elene.

The MS. is still at Vercelli, in the Capitular Library, but an excellent photographic reproduction of it has been issued by Professor Wülker.

4. **The Junian MS. of the (so-called) Cædmonian Poems.**

This MS. was bequeathed to the Bodleian by Junius (Francis Du Jon). It was edited by him, and printed, in 1655, at Amsterdam. (For an account of it see p. 135.)

5. **The Fight at Finsburg.**

This fragment was discovered by Hickes, in the seventeenth century, on the cover of a MS. of Homilies in the Lambeth Palace Library. The MS. of the poem has since been lost, and the original only now exists in the copy of it made by Hickes. (See vol. i. pp. 192, 193 of George Hickes's great work on the Northern languages—commonly called his "Thesaurus," but the full title runs, "Linguarum Vett. Septentrionalium Thesaurus Grammatico-Criticus et Archæologicus, Oxford, 1703-1705.")

6. **Waldhere.**
   This fragment is written upon two vellum leaves which were discovered by Professor Werlauff, librarian at the King's Library, Copenhagen. They were published, with a translation, by Prof. George Stephens, in 1860.
7. **The Charms.**
   These exist in MSS. at the British Museum and the Library of Corpus Christi College, Cambridge.
8. **Gnomic Verses.**
   Three sets of these proverbs are found in the Exeter Book, but there is a fourth in the MS. of the Abingdon Chronicle— one of the Cotton MSS. in the British Museum.
   In the same MS. is found the *Menologium*.
9. **The Rune Song** exists only in a copy of the original MS. made by Hickes (vol. i. p. 135 of Hickes's *Thesaurus*).
10. Of the two metrical dialogues of **Salomo and Saturn** there are two MSS., both at Corpus Christi Library, Cambridge.
11. The **Battle of Brunanburh** is found in the Parker MS. of the *Chronicle* (Corpus Christi, Cambridge).
12. The **Battle of Maldon** exists only in a copy of the original MS. made by Thomas Hearne. (See vol. ii. pp. 570-577, "Johannis Glastoniensis Chronica sive Historia de Rebus Glastoniensibus," ed. Th. Hearnius, Oxonii, 1726.)

II. EDITIONS AND TRANSLATIONS

For a *full* bibliography of these, including foreign publications, the student is referred to Wülker's *Grundriss zur Geschichte der Angelsächsischen Litteratur*, and also to the same scholar's edition of Grein's *Bibliothek der Angelsächsischen Poesie* (3 vols. Leipzig, 1883-1897). The original edition, by Grein himself, was issued in 1857-58, but is now out of print.

The complete text of *all* the old English poetry may be found in the above editions of Grein's *Bibliothek*.

A German translation of most of the poems in his *Bibliothek* was issued by Grein in 1857 — "Dichtungen der Angelsachsen" (Göttingen).

Conybeare's "Illustrations of Anglo-Saxon Poetry" appeared in 1826. It contains selections from A.S. Poetry (text and free translation). It is now out of print, but its early date and its scholarship make it worthy of mention.

The (*so-called*) **Cædmonian Poems** were edited and translated by Benjamin Thorpe in 1832, under the title of "Cædmon's Metrical Paraphrase," etc.

The **Exeter Book** was also edited and translated by the same scholar in 1842. These are now out of print, and both text and translation are antiquated, but are still useful for reference.

The poems of the **Vercelli Book** were edited and translated by J. M. Kemble in 1843. This book, too, is somewhat antiquated beside the work of modern scholarship, but of great use for reference.

A new edition of the **Exeter Book** (edited and translated by Israel Gollancz, M.A.) is being issued by the Early English Text Society, of which Part I. has already appeared. (In the list below, reference is made to the poems contained in Part I.)

Some other useful editions and translations of separate poems are named in the following list:—

1. **Beowulf**, edited by Harrison and Sharp. (Founded on Heyne's edition, below; and forming vol. i. of the Library of Anglo-Saxon Poetry. Ginn and Company, Boston, 1888.)
   Beowulf, edited by A. J. Wyatt (Camb. Univ. Press, 1894).
   Two valuable German editions of "Beowulf" are those of M. Heyne (Paderborn, 1879) and A. Holder (Freiburg i. B. und Tübingen, 1884).
   The Early English Text Society has issued an autotype facsimile of the Beowulf MS., with transliteration and notes by Zupitza (London, 1882).
   The Ta'e of Beowulf, done out of the old English tongue by William Morris and A. J. Wyatt (Kelmscott Press, 1895).
   The Deeds of Beowulf, a prose translation by Prof. J. Earle (1892, Clar. Press).
   Beowulf, and the Fight at Finsburg, literally translated by J. M. Garnett (1882, Boston). Other translations of "Beowulf" have been issued by Thorpe, Kemble, T. Arnold, Lumsden-Hall, etc.

2. **The (so-called) Cædmonian Poems.**
   Exodus and Daniel, edited by T. W. Hunt (Boston, 1888; forming vol. ii. of the Library of Anglo-Saxon Poetry).
   The only complete translation of the "Cædmonian Poems" is the ancient one by Thorpe in his edition of "Cædmon's Metrical Paraphrase" (Soc. of Antiquaries, London, 1832).
   That part of the *Genesis* relating to the "Fall of Man" has been translated into verse by W. H. F. Bosanquet: "The Fall of Man or Paradise Lost of Cædmon" (London, 1860).

3. **Judith.**
   Judith, edited, with a free translation, by A. S. Cook (Boston, 1889).
   The full Old English text is also given in Sweet's Anglo-Saxon Reader.
   Judith, literally translated by J. M. Garnett (Boston, 1889).

4. **The Elegies.**
   The Ruin.
   "An ancient Saxon poem of a city in ruins, supposed to be Bath." Text and translation by J. Earle (Bath, 1872).
   In Thorpe's Exeter Book will also be found a translation.

   The Wanderer.
   The text may be found in Sweet's Anglo-Saxon Reader, and in Bright's Anglo-Saxon Reader.
   A Translation on p. 314 of this book.
   Text and translation also in Gollancz's Exeter Book.

   The Seafarer.
   Text in Sweet's Anglo-Saxon Reader (7th edition).
   Translation, p. 312 of this book.
   Of the *Wife's Complaint* and the *Husband's Message,* a translation may be found in Thorpe's Exeter Book.

5. The **Poems of Cynewulf,** or attributed to him.
   The *Riddles.*
   There is no separate text or full translation of these in English. For a German translation see A. Prehn's "Rätsel" (Paderborn, 1883).
   The text of seven of them is given in Sweet's Reader.
   Riddles 2, 3, and 4 will be found translated on pp. 309, 310 of this book, and many others in "Early English Literature" (Stopford A. Brooke, London, 1892).

   Juliana.
   Text and translation in Gollancz's Exeter Book.

   The *Christ.*
   Edited with a modern rendering by I. Gollancz (D. Nutt, London, 1892).
   Text and translation also in Gollancz's Exeter Book.

   The *Phœnix.*
   Text in Bright's Anglo-Saxon Reader.
   Text and translation in Gollancz's Exeter Book.

   Guthlac.
   Text and translation in Gollancz's Exeter Book.

Fates of the Apostles.
    Text and translation in J. M. Kemble's "Poetry of the Vercelli Book."

Elene.
    Elene, edited by J. Zupitza (Berlin, 1877, 1883), a German edition.
    Elene, edited by C. W. Kent (Boston, 1889; forming vol. iii. of the Library of Anglo-Saxon Poetry).
    Elene, translated by J. M. Garnett (Boston, 1889).
    A text and translation appear also in J. M. Kemble's "Poetry of the Vercelli Book" (1856).

Andreas.
    Andreas, edited by W. M. Baskerville (Boston, 1889).
    A text and translation are also to be found in J. M. Kemble's Vercelli Book.
    Grimm's edition of *Andreas and Elene* (Preface and notes in German), though issued in 1840, and now out of print, is still of exceptional value to the student.

Dream of the Rood.
    Text in Sweet's Anglo-Saxon Reader.
    Text and translation in Kemble's Vercelli Book.

5. **Other poems or fragments.**
    Widsið, translated in Guest's "English Rhythms," p. 375.
    Deor, translated in Thorpe's Exeter Book.
    Finsburg, literal translation in Garnett's "Beowulf."
    Waldhere, edited and translated by Prof. George Stephens, "Two Leaves of King Waldere's Lay."
    The Battle of Brunanburh, edited by C. L. Crow (Boston, 1897; forming vol. iv. of the Library of Anglo-Saxon Poetry).
    Text also in Bright's Reader.
    Tennyson's translation will be found on p. 256 of this book.
    A literal translation by J. Garnett (Boston, 1889).
    The Battle of Maldon, edited by C. L. Crow (Boston, 1897; forming vol. iv. of the Library of Anglo-Saxon Poetry).
    Text also in Sweet's Reader and in Bright's Reader.
    Translation on pp. 264 and 318 of this book.
    Translation (and suggestive article) by Lumsden in Macmillan's Magazine, March 1887.
    Translation by E. Hickey in "Verse Tales" (Liverpool, 1889).
    A literal translation by J. Garnett (Boston, 1889).

The *Charms.*
    Text of two of these in Sweet's Reader.

Full text and translation in Cockayne's "Leechdoms" (3 vols. Lond. 1864-66, Rolls Series).
Translation also of several of these in "Early English Literature" (Stopford A. Brooke, 1892).

The *Rune Song*.
Text and translation in French, by L. Botkine (Havre, 1879). Grimm's work, " Ueber Deutsche Runen" (1821), contains a German translation.

Cædmon's *Hymn* and Bæda's *Death Song*, together with the text of other fragments, will be found in Sweet's "Oldest English Texts"—an invaluable book, "intended to include all the extant Old English texts up to about 900 that are preserved in contemporary MSS., with the exception of the *Chronicle* and the *Works of Alfred.*"

PROSE

I. THE MANUSCRIPTS

The Manuscripts in which the old English prose is handed down to us are numerous, and many of them still remain unedited. It is only necessary to mention those of importance.

1. **Ælfred's translations,** etc. :—

    The *Cura Pastoralis*. Three MSS., dating from the end of the ninth or beginning of the tenth century; one in the Bodleian, two in the British Museum.

    Bæda's *Historia Ecclesiastica*. Five MSS., two at Oxford, two at Cambridge, one in the British Museum.

    Orosius' *History of the World*. Two MSS., one at Helmingham Hall, Suffolk, in the possession of the Tollemache family; one in the British Museum.

    Boethius' *De Consolatione Philosophiae*. Two MSS., one at the Bodleian, one in the British Museum.

    The so-called *Metra* are in Anglo-Saxon verse in the MS. of this work in the British Museum. In the later MS. at Oxford they are in prose.

    The *Soliloquies of Augustine* only exist in the MS. which contains the poems of Beowulf.

    The *Laws of Ælfred*. Four MSS., two at Cambridge, one at the British Museum, and the fourth, the Textus Roffensis.

    The *Dialogues of Gregory*, a translation made at Ælfred's instance by Bishop Werfrith of Worcester, is in the three MSS. at Oxford, Cambridge, and the British Museum.

The other works attributed to Ælfred are of slight importance, and the places of their MSS. need not be detailed.

2. Of **Ælfric's** works, and of the few **Homilies** now allotted to Archbishop *Wulfstan*, we have a great number of MSS. in Oxford, Cambridge, and London, but of the earlier *Blickling Homilies* only one MS. exists. The *Homilies* in the *Vercelli Book*, twenty-two in number, are followed by a prose *Life of S. Guðlac*, and we possess another Anglo-Saxon *Life of Guðlac* in a MS. in the Cottonian Library, which is an adaptation of the Latin life of the saint by Felix of Croyland. We need not record the MSS. of the large number of short works produced in the eleventh century (see Chap. XVII. of this book).

3. Of the **Old English Chronicle** seven MSS. exist. The first (MS. *A*) was written at Winchester, and continuing to the year 1001 was preserved in the Library of the Monastery of Christ's Church, Canterbury; thence falling into the hands of Archbishop Parker in the sixteenth century, it was finally transferred to Corpus Christi College, Cambridge. This is the Parker MS.

MS. *B* is in the British Museum, and was produced in the Monastery of S. Augustine at Canterbury.

MS. *C*, an Abingdon Chronicle, is in the Museum.

MS. *D*, written at Worcester, is also in the Museum.

MS. *E* was kept at Peterborough. It is in the Bodleian, and is known as the Laud MS.

MS. *F* was probably kept at Canterbury, and was written partly in English, partly in Latin, and some French words intrude into it. It is now in the British Museum.

MS. *G*, probably a Canterbury Chronicle, apparently a copy of MS. *A*. It is in the Museum.

The *Chronicle* (MS. *G*) was first printed by Wheloc in 1643, as an appendix to Ælfred's Bæda.

II. Editions and Translations

For a *full* bibliography see, as before, Wülker's *Grundriss*.

1. Works by **Ælfred**, or attributed to him.

A *complete translation* of these (without the Old English text) will be found in the Jubilee Edition of Ælfred's Works, 1852-53.

In addition see the following :—

Cura Pastoralis.
 Edited by Henry Sweet, with a translation (Early Eng. Text Soc., 1871).
 A translation of Ælfred's Preface to this will be found on p. 221 of this book.

Bæda's Ecclesiastical History.
 Text and translation by T. Miller (Early Eng. Text Soc. 1890-98). Translation of Bæda's Latin text by J. A. Giles, in Bohn's Antiquarian Library.

Orosius' History.
 Text with Latin original, edited by H. Sweet (Early Eng. Text Soc.).
 Extracts from Orosius (text only), H. Sweet (Clar. Press, 1893).
 Text and translation also in Bohn's Antiquarian Library.

Boethius.
 Text and translation by J. S. Cardale (London, 1829; translation by S. Fox, in Bohn's Series).
 A new edition of the Old English text is promised shortly by the Clar. Press.

Soliloquies of Augustine.
 Text by Wülker, in Paul and Braune's "Beiträge zur Geschichte der Deutschen Sprache und Literatur," vol. iv.
 Another and earlier text will be found in Cockayne's Shrine.

The *Laws of Ælfred.*
 "Extracts from the Anglo-Saxon Laws," ed. by A. Cook (New York, 1880).

The *Dialogues of Gregory.*
 Ælfred's Preface to this work, text and translation, may be found in Prof. Earle's "Anglo-Saxon Literature."
 A new edition of the Dialogues is to be issued shortly.

2. **Works of Ælfric.**
 Homilies of the Anglo-Saxon Church, ed., with translation, by B. Thorpe (2 vols. London, 1844-46).
 Lives of the Saints, ed. by W. W. Skeat (London, 1881).
 Selections from the *Homilies*, H. Sweet (Clar. Press, 1896).

3. **Homilies of Wulfstan.**
 Edited by Prof. Napier (Berlin, 1883), forming vol. iv. of *Sammlung englischer Denkmäler in kritischen Ausgaben.*

4. **Blickling Homilies.**
 Edited by R. Morris, with translation (Early Eng. Text Soc., 1874-80).

One of the Blickling Homilies may be found in Bright's Reader.

5. **Old English Chronicle.**
Two of the Saxon Chronicles parallel, revised text, edited by Plummer, on the basis of J. Earle's edition, 1892.
This contains the complete texts of MSS. *A* and *E*, with extracts from the others.
The complete text of all the MSS., with a translation (by B. Thorpe), will be found in the Rolls Series (*Chronicles of Great Britain and Ireland*), Longmans, 1861.

INDEX

Acca, Bishop of Hexham, encouraged learning, 115
Adamnan, his account of Arculf's voyage, 114 and *note*
Address of a Father to a Son, didactic poem, 206
Ælfred the Great, the father of English prose, 212; his early life and reign, 212-214; his wars, 214, 216; his work in education, law, literature, 217-241, 269-271; *Proverbs of Ælfred*, 307
Ælfric, Abbot, his life and literary work, 251, 279-288; his *Homilies* often copied, 303
Ælfric Bata, his edition of Ælfric's *Colloquium*, 281
Æthelberht, Archbishop, his work and scholarship, 121, 122
Æthelwold, Bishop of Winchester, takes part in monastic revival, 276; his literary work, 278
Aidan, preached and taught in Northumbria, 21, 23, 113
Alcuin, his work in education and literature, 122, 123
Aldfrith, King of Northumbria, encouraged literature, 22, 114
Alexander, Romance of, in Old English, 292
Andreas, poem of, sea-passages in, 94, 95; war-spirit in, 102, 103; is it by Cynewulf? 187-189; described, 189-197
Aneurin, a Cymric poet, 29, 30, 32
Angles, tribe of the, 36; their home on the continent, 36, 37; their coming to Britain, 84, 85
Apollonius of Tyre, Old English version of, 292
Armorica (Brittany), emigration of Britons to, 26
Arthur, King, his story not native to Brittany, 27, 28; its appearance in English literature, 34, 35
Asser, his friendship with King Ælfred, 218; his *Life* of the King, 237
Augustine, St., his preaching of Christianity in England, 107
Azarias, the *Prayer of*, 134; natural description in, 103; part of it found in the *Daniel*, 149

Bæda, his life and literary work, 115-120; his *Ecclesiastical History*, 117-119; translated by Ælfred, 223, 224; his *Letter* to Ecgberht, 119; his verse-making, 23; his English verses, 120
Benedict Biscop, the founder of Latin learning in Northumbria, 113, 114
Beowulf (1) the hero: how far historical, 58, 59, 60; his character, 61-64
Beowulf (2) the poem: allusions to heathen sagas or poems in, 53-57; historic lays in, 59; mythical and folk-lore elements in, 59, 65-67, 68, 69; the poem described, 68-80; its date, 81; its form narrative rather than epic, 81-83
Bevis of Hampton, 306
Bible, translation of the, by Ælfric, 282, 283
Blickling Homilies, the, 75, 278, 279
Boadicea, written of in English poetry, 13
Boethius, his *Consolation of Philosophy*, translated by Ælfred, 228, 229-234; his *Metra*, translated by whom? 234, 235
Boniface, St., 110
Book of Martyrs, compiled by wish of Ælfred (?), 237
Britain, early races in, 1-8; early condition of, 9-11; bearing of this on literature, 11, 12; Roman occupa-

tion of, 13 ; its influence on literature, 14, 16-20
Brunanburh, poem of the *Battle of*, 255, 256 ; Tennyson's translation, 256-260
Brythons, a Celtic people, settle in Britain, 6, 7; driven out by the English, 8; their settlements, 8; their influence on English literature, 25-34. See also *Gildas, Nennius, Cymry*
Byrchtfercth, the scholar, his literary work, 286, 287
Byrhtnoth, poem on *Death of*. See *Maldon*

Cædmon, his name, 127; life at Whitby, 127, 128 ; Bæda's account of his vision, 128-131 ; his hymn, 129 and *note ;* character of his work, 131-133 ; poems of the *School of Cædmon*, 134-151 ; Junian MS. of these, 135, 136. See also *Genesis, Exoduš, Daniel*
Canones Ælfrici, pastoral letter of Ælfric, 283
Celts, the ; their early migrations to Europe, 5, 6 ; their love of wild nature, 11, 12 ; their influence on Old English literature, 96, 292-299
Ceolfrid, successor of Benedict Biscop, his encouragement of learning, 114 and *note*
Charms, Old English, 42-46
Christ, Cynewulf's poem of the, 167-175
Christ and Satan, the collection of poems known as, 248
Christianity, influence on English literature of British, 14-16 ; Irish Christianity in England, 16, 21, 23, 113 ; influence of Christianity on English poetry, 86, 87, 98-105 ; 149-151
Chronicle, the *Old English*, Ælfred's work on, 224, 225, 227, *note ;* poems and fragments of poems in the, 253, 261 ; Ælfred's work carried on later in, 271, 272 ; *Winchester Annals* in, 301 ; *Worcester Annals* in, 292, 301·303 ; *Peterborough Annals* in, 301. See also the Bibliography, pp. 333, 335
Cnut, King, his encouragement of literature in England, 290, 291
Columba, St., founded Iona, 21 ; wrote lyrics and encouraged learning, 21, 22 ; *Life* of, 114 and *note*

Crafts of Men. See *Gifts of Men*
Cuthbert, Bæda's *Life* of St., 117
Cymry, the (Welsh), 28, 29 ; their poetry, records of English war, 29-32 ; their relations with the English, 33, 34
Cynewulf, the poet, his love of nature, 96, 97 ; his *Riddles*, 159-162 ; who and what was he ? 160-162 ; where did he live ? 163-165 ; his signed poems, 163-179

Dallan Forgaill, Irish poet, 20
Daniel, Bishop of Winchester, 108
Daniel, poem of, described, 148, 149
Danish influence on English literature, 297, 298
Deor, Complaint of, Old English heathen poem, 42, 48
Descent into Hell, fragment of poem of, 186, 187
Discourse of the Soul to the Body. See *Soul*
Dream of the Rood, war spirit in, 101 ; relates conversion of Cynewulf (?), 165 ; poem described, 197-202
Dunstan, his early life and education, 272, 273 ; biographies of, 272, *note ;* his love of learning and art, 274, 275 ; his connection with the court, 275 ; his school at Glastonbury, 275 ; his share in the monastic revival, 275, 276

Eadgar, King, ballads concerning, 261, 262 ; his encouragement of English monasticism, 276, 277, and of literature and education, 277, 278
Eadmund, King, song of his *Overcoming of the Five Towns*, 261
Ealdhelm, his education, 108 ; his life and literary work, 23, 108-110
Ecclesiastical History of the English people. See *Bæda*
Ecgberht, Archbishop of York, Bæda's *Letter* to, 117 ; encourages art and learning, 121
Elegies in Old English poetry, 152-159
Elene, description of battle in Cynewulf's poem of, 90 ; the poem described, 176-179
English Literature, the mingling of elements in, 293-299
Exeter Book. See Bibliography, pp. 326, 327

INDEX

Exodus, description of battle in poem of the, 89; the poem described, 143-146

Fallen Angels, poem of the, 248, 249
Fates of the Apostles, Cynewulf's poem of the, 163, 165, 166, 175
Felix of Crowland. See *Guthlac, St.*
Finsburg, the *Battle of*, Old English fragment on, 51-53

Genesis (A), nature in poem of, 103, 104; the poem described, 136-142
Genesis (B), the Later Genesis; the poem described, 242, 243
Gifts of Men, poem of the, 207
Gildas, the historian, 25; his *Epistola*, 25, 26
Glossaries of eleventh century, Latin and English, 289, 290
Gnomic Verses, the, 207, 208, 317-318
Grammar and *Glossary*, Ælfric's, 280
Gregory the Great, his *Cura Pastoralis*, translated by Ælfred, 219-223; his *Dialogues*, translated by Ælfred, 237
Goidels, the, a Celtic tribe, 6, 7; their influence on English literature, 20-25
Guthlac, poem of *St.*, 183-186; prose *Life* of, 112, 184, 279
Guy of Warwick, 306

Hadubrand and Hildebrand, Lay of, 81
Handbook, King Ælfred's, 218, 219
Harrowing of Hell, war spirit in, 101, 102; poem described, 249, 250
Hatton Gospels, the, 303
Havelok, the saga of, 306
Heathen poetry, Old English, 41-57
Heliand, poem of the, 242
Hereward, lays concerning, 305; Latin history of, 305
Homiliæ Catholicæ, Ælfric's, 280
Horn, the saga of, 306
Husband's Message, poem of the, 153, 154, 155, 156

Ine, King of Wessex. See *Laws*
Iona, monastery and school at, 21, 22
Irish poetry, early, its influence on English literature, 20. See also *Celts*

John of Beverley, his life and school, 115
Judith, description of battle in poem of, 89; the poem described, 146-148
Juliana, Cynewulf's poem of, 166, 167, 169

Jutes, the tribe of the, 26; their home in Europe, 37, 38; conquest of Kent, 84

Kent, the cradle of English learning, 107

Last Judgment, poem of the, 252
Latin prose in Old English literature, 106-125
Law-Book, compiled by Ælfred, 219
Laws, of Æthelberht of Kent, 107, 219; of Ine of Wessex, 109, 110, 219; of Offa, 219
Leech Books, Old English, 278, 289, 303
Leofric Missal, the, 290
Lindisfarne Gospels, the, 289
Llywarch Hen, Cymric poet, 29, 30, 31
Lost Soul to its Body, the. See *Soul*
Lullus, Archbishop of Mainz, 110

Maldon, poem of the *Battle of*, 255, 256, 263-268, 318-325
Malmesbury, school at, 108, 109
Menologium, the, an Old English calendar, 251
Mercia, learning and literature in, 111, 112, 124
Merddin, Cymric poet, 29

Natural description in Old English poetry, 90-97, 103-105
Nature myths in Old English poetry, 41
Nennius, the historian, his *Historia Britonum*, 27, 28
Neolithic tribes in Britain, 2; the Picts of history, 7
Northumbria, literature in, 112-125; Danes destroy learning in, 124, 125

Offa, King of Mercia, 112, 219
Ohthere relates his voyage to Ælfred, 226, 227
Orosius, his *History of the World* translated by Ælfred, 225, 226
Ossian, Celtic spirit in Macpherson's, 24
Oswald, King of Northumbria, companion of Aidan, 21
Oswin, King of Deira, follower of Aidan, 21
Oswiu, King of Northumbria, encourages Irish Christianity in England, 21, 22

Paleolithic tribes in Britain, 2
Panther, fragment of poem on the, 204
Paris Psalter, the, 236 and *note*

INDEX

Partridge, fragment of poem on the, 204
Passiones Sanctorum, Ælfric's, 281, 282
Paternoster, twelfth-century poem on the, 307
Phœnix, nature in poem of the, 104, 105; the poem described, 180-183
Physiologus, the English, 203, 204
Poema Morale, 307
Pre-Celtic peoples in Britain, 1-5

Rhyme Song, the, 209, 254
Riddles, Old English: on weapons of war, 87-89; on birds and animals, 91, 92; on the sea, 93-95; on the Sun and Moon, 96; their value and authorship discussed, 159-162; Riddles on the Storm and Hurricane (translated in full), 309-311
Ritual of Durham, the, 289
Romans, the, their occupation of Britain and its influence on English literature, 13-20
Ruined Burg, poem of the, 85, 86
Rune Song, the, 209
Runes in poems of Cynewulf, 168, 175
Rushworth Gospels, the, 290
Ruthwell Cross, the, 132, 133

Salomo and Saturn, poems of, 210, 211; prose dialogue of, 289
Saxons, tribe of the, their home in Europe, 36, 37, 38; a general name for English tribes, 39; their conquests in Britain, 84
Scôp, the, or Old English poet, 40. See *Widsith*, *Deor*
Seafarer, poem of the, 152, 153, 154, 155, 157, 312-313
Sigmund the Wælsing, the oldest form of his story in *Beowulf*, 54, 55
Skallagrimsson, Egill, in England, 254
Soliloquia, the, of St. Augustine, translated by Ælfred, 235, 236
Song of the Three Children, poem of, 134, 149

Soul to the Body, Discourse of the, 206, 207

Taliessin, Cymric poet, 29, 30, 31, 32
Tatwine, Archbishop, his *Ænigmata*, 108
Theodore of Tarsus, his school at Canterbury, 107; the work of his successors, 108

Vercelli Book, Homilies in the, 279. For full description of the *Book* see Bibliography, p. 327
Vision of the Rood. See *Dream of the Rood*

Wada, Middle English poem of, 305
Waldhere, fragment of poem of, 50
Waltheof, saga of, 306
Wanderer, poem of the, 153, 154, 155, 157, 158, 314-317
War in Old English poetry, 87-90; how affected by Christianity, 100-103
Weirds of Men, poem on the, 208
Weland, English saga of, 305
Wessex, literary life of, before Ælfred's time, 107-111
Whale, fragment of poem on the, 204, 205
Whitby (Streoneshalh), an educational centre, 22; synod of, 22. See *Cædmon*
Widsith, poem of, 42, 46-48
Wife's Complaint, poem of the, 91, 92, 153, 154, 155, 156, 157
Wilfrid, leader of Latin Christianity in Northumbria, 113; his biography, 114
Willibald, his travels as missionary, 110
Winfrid. See *Boniface*
Winwæd, verses on battle at the, 111
Wulfstan, voyage of, written down by Ælfred, 224
Wulfstan, Archbishop, his *Homilies*, 251, 285, 286
Wulfstan, monk of Winchester, literary work of, 291

York, School of, 120, 125

THE END

Printed by R. & R. Clark, Limited, *Edinburgh*

www.ingramcontent.com/pod-product-compliance
Lightning Source LLC
Chambersburg PA
CBHW032356230426
43672CB00007B/716